AF340670

THE 5 DISCIPLINES OF INCLUSIVE ORGANIZATIONS

THE 5 DISCIPLINES OF INCLUSIVE ORGANIZATIONS

How Diverse and Equitable Enterprises Will **Transform** the World

ANDRÉS T. TAPIA & FAYRUZ KIRTZMAN

Foreword by TALITA RAMOS ERICKSON, Chief Diversity and Inclusion Officer, Barilla Group

BK

Berrett–Koehler Publishers, Inc.

Berrett-Koehler Publishers, Inc.
1333 Broadway, Suite 1000
Oakland, CA 94612-1921
Tel: (510) 817-2277
Fax: (510) 817-2278
www.bkconnection.com

ORDERING INFORMATION

Quantity sales. Special discounts are available on quantity purchases by corporations, associations, and others. For details, contact the "Special Sales Department" at the Berrett-Koehler address above.

Individual sales. Berrett-Koehler publications are available through most bookstores. They can also be ordered directly from Berrett-Koehler: Tel: (800) 929-2929; Fax: (802) 864-7626; www.bkconnection.com.

Orders for college textbook / course adoption use. Please contact Berrett-Koehler: Tel: (800) 929-2929; Fax: (802) 864-7626.

Distributed to the U.S. trade and internationally by Penguin Random House Publisher Services.

Berrett-Koehler and the BK logo are registered trademarks of Berrett-Koehler Publishers, Inc.

Printed in Canada

Berrett-Koehler books are printed on long-lasting acid-free paper. When it is available, we choose paper that has been manufactured by environmentally responsible processes. These may include using trees grown in sustainable forests, incorporating recycled paper, minimizing chlorine in bleaching, or recycling the energy produced at the paper mill.

Library of Congress Cataloging-in-Publication Data

Names: Tapia, Andrés, 1960- author. | Kirtzman, Fayruz, author.
Title: The 5 disciplines of inclusive organizations : how diverse and
    equitable enterprises will transform the world / Andrés T. Tapia and
    Fayruz Kirtzman.
Other titles: Five disciplines of inclusive organizations
Description: First edition. | Oakland, CA : Berrett-Koehler Publishers,
    Inc., [2023] | Series: The 5 inclusive disciplines series | Includes
    bibliographical references and index.
Identifiers: LCCN 2022049273 (print) | LCCN 2022049274 (ebook) | ISBN
    9781523003839 (hardcover ; alk. paper) | ISBN 9781523003846 (pdf) | ISBN
    9781523003853 (epub) | ISBN 9781523003860 (audio)
Subjects: LCSH: Diversity in the workplace. | Multiculturalism. |
    Marginality, Social. | Intersectionality (Sociology) | Organizational
    change. | Social justice. | Environmental justice.
Classification: LCC HF5549.5 .T375 2023 (print) | LCC HF5549.5 (ebook) |
    DDC 658.3008—dc23/eng/20230206
LC record available at https://lccn.loc.gov/2022049273
LC ebook record available at https://lccn.loc.gov/2022049274

First Edition

30 29 28 27 26 25 24 23   10 9 8 7 6 5 4 3 2 1

Book production and design: Seventeenth Street Studios
Cover design: Daniel Tesser
Figure 4 reproduced with kind permission of Unilever IP Holdings B.V.
All other figures courtesy of Korn Ferry.

To my clients—you've taught me so much by what you know, what you need, and what you dream.

—Andrés

To my father-in-law, Marvin Friedman, who, while he was with us, saw the writer in me long before I did.

—Fayruz

CONTENTS

Foreword   ix

Preface: How This Trilogy Came About   xiii

Introduction: Diverse and Equitable Enterprises Will
Transform the World   1

PART 1: THE FIVE DISCIPLINES OF INCLUSIVE ORGANIZATIONS   17

1. Discipline 1: Manage the Risk   21

2. Discipline 2: Explode the Awareness   37

3. Discipline 3: Maximize the Talent Systems   53

4. Discipline 4: Master the Logistics   75

5. Discipline 5: See the Marketplace   91

6. How Do We Know It Works? Measuring Success
of the Five Disciplines   107

PART 2: THE FOUR VITAL TASKS   111

7. Vital Task 1: Diversify Leadership   117

8. Vital Task 2: Eradicate Polarization   133

9. Vital Task 3: Achieve Justice   149

10. Vital Task 4: Save the Planet   169

Conclusion: The Irrevocable Responsibility to Use
Power for Good   189

Contents

Appendix A: How to Create Your Own Best-in-Class
DE&I Scorecard — 201

Appendix B: How DE&I Enables Environmental,
Social, and Governance (ESG) — 217

Appendix C: Research Methodology of a Korn Ferry
Root Cause DE&I Diagnostic — 221

Appendix D: Summary: The Five Disciplines of Inclusive
Organizations — 225

Notes — 229

Bibliography — 243

Acknowledgments — 245

Index — 249

About the Authors — 257

About Korn Ferry — 261

FOREWORD

I N 2021, BARILLA UNVEILED ITS NEW PURPOSE: "The joy of food for a better life." This purpose is an evolution of the public promise that our business would be "Good for you, good for the planet." On the one hand, this intentional declaration was simply a manifestation of what had already been inherent in our family-owned company's 140-year history. From our origins, we have prided ourselves on high-quality ingredients, foods with healthy nutritional value, and a family-based culture both in how we saw the role of pasta in bringing families together around the table as well as in our seeking to create a community for our employees.

Though we focused our efforts on meaningful, accelerated, and large-scale positive impact on people and the planet, we did not realize at the time that diversity, equity, and inclusion (DEI), as well as ESG (measuring our impact on the environment, society, and governance), would be key enablers to delivering on this agenda.

By this time, Barilla had grown to nearly nine thousand employees working in a dozen different countries with products in more than one hundred countries. But from a diversity and inclusion perspective, being an Italian-owned and headquartered company created unexpected challenges. Our culinary brand is and will always remain Italian, but our talent brand needed to become global—inclusive of the various countries we were operating in, and their unique demographics. While still seeking to retain our employee value proposition of a family-like culture, we needed to allow for the different cultures in which we were operating to express themselves more fully, and in fact to be additive to our being an Italian-based company. This was a DEI issue.

In parallel, the reality of the impact of climate change on food production, and of food production on the climate, went to the heart of what we produced and how we produced it. Given our size, where we sourced ingredients and what it took to go from raw materials to finished product had a measurable impact on resources and on emissions, which we needed to fully own. This was an ESG issue.

Further, the ambition to be good for people, good for the planet was going to require the best talent from all talent pools, working inclusively to deliver the innovation and efficiencies necessary to follow through on our promise. This was a combined DEI and ESG issue.

To help the company tackle some of these challenges, I was named Barilla Group's first-ever Chief Diversity Officer in 2013.

We created internal and external D&I boards to provide our CEO and Barilla's board of directors with strategic advice, operational road maps, external benchmarks, and inspiration. Along this journey, we asked Korn Ferry to help us in those areas they were expert in. This is where my relationship with Andrés, Fayruz, and their colleagues began. For several years we did intensive work together, and we remain partners as different needs come up.

After reading *The 5 Disciplines of Inclusive Organizations*, I realized that this book is a codification of their already well-established philosophical, strategic, and operational approach. I experienced much of what is between these pages in how we collectively and collegially went about the work that ended up bringing about so much change at Barilla. Today, we are more diverse, more inclusive, and more equitable than when we first started the journey. And while the scope of what we did together did not explicitly focus on our parallel efforts around ESG and sustainability, it is clear to me how our DEI enhancements have been catalysts for our breakthroughs in sustainability.

THE PERSONAL ENABLES THE ORGANIZATIONAL

As a lawyer, I have always been personally devoted to addressing issues of ethics, equity, and justice. However, it was not until I became formally responsible for DEI that I started to be more intentional about my development in the field. As I reflected on my own journey to become a more inclusive leader, I recalled one of the first things I learned from Andrés.

One of my initial steps was to take an intercultural assessment. At that time, Andrés explained that our ability to identify, value, and engage with people different from us is developed based on how rich our experiences around diversity were at three different inflection points in our lives: growing up, moving on by yourself (for example, going to college), and then joining a workplace. While people can consciously or unconsciously remain in fairly homogeneous bubbles in the first two, in the workplace, people now more than ever cannot choose to abstain from dealing with differences. In places with a history of segregation or marginalization, the workplace may be the only environment where people are exposed to others who look, behave, believe, eat, or love in a different way.

I am thankful for Andrés and Fayruz for gifting us *The 5 Disciplines of Inclusive Organizations.* In this book, they skillfully lay out a framework for how organizations can comprehensively tackle the many layers and elements of DEI depending on their stage of DEI maturity. I particularly appreciate that they provide digestible to-do lists to address both the inward- and outward-facing aspects of integrating DEI into talent, operational, and marketplace practices.

In my experience, it is quite common to drop all of DEI into the S of ESG strategies. However, Andrés and Fayruz make the case for a broader, interconnected, and more meaningful guiding purpose for DEI efforts, which cuts across all elements of ESG. They meticulously outline the connections between DEI and ESG under an umbrella of "inclusive sustainability." They show how the five DEI disciplines provide a road map for leaders to not only make their organizations more inclusive but also perform four vital tasks that will transform our world: diversify leadership, eradicate polarization, achieve justice, and save the planet.

As a DEI practitioner, I find inclusive sustainability is a helpful mental model to engage with other internal allies to move ahead with a comprehensive ESG agenda. The recognition that governance includes broad stakeholder management and that the impact of environmental issues is not evenly distributed across demographic groups leads to a refreshing and useful people-centric view of ESG.

I have often been called overly idealistic, even naive, throughout my life for believing that human beings are generally good and that absent distorted incentives they will choose to act in a way that does not harm others. Over the past twenty-plus years of my career, I have observed some supporting evidence for my beliefs in the evolution of the "talent case" for ESG efforts. I still believe most people do not want to work to perpetuate something evil, and organizations all over the world now spend significant time and money to articulate how their businesses are good for people and the planet. Having an inspirational purpose has become a key tool for attracting and retaining top talent.

Which brings me back to my belief that workplaces are ripe with opportunities for positive impact for people, society, and the planet. In the workplace, hearts and minds can be changed if organizations are committed to, and intentional about, driving inclusion behaviorally and systemically.

This is why I so value the authors' strong case for urgent action in this valuable manifesto. Obviously, the call for urgency can be directed at leadership, but I took it as a call to action for organizations to engage all the individuals in its spheres of control and influence. One lesson that I personally learned from the COVID-19 pandemic, and which was reinforced by findings in a 2022 Edelman Trust Barometer report, is that employees' understanding of risk and urgency is increasingly becoming a function of how their employers discuss issues in the workplace.

Organizations must—and have one of the most compelling platforms to—engage people to spread the sense of urgency much needed today.

The clock is ticking. We cannot fight for another 130 years, per data extrapolation, to have fair representation of women in power, for example, nor can we wait another decade to avoid the point of no return on climate change.

The collective result of people in organizations, moving from oblivion to awareness, from apathy to action, could be the tipping point in a path toward a more equitable and sustainable future for humanity, toward transforming our broken world.

In your hands, your organization has a survive-and-thrive guide to do just that.

Talita Ramos Erickson

Talita Ramos Erickson is the Chief Transformation Officer for the Barilla Group and previously served as the group's first Chief D&I Officer.

How This Trilogy Came About

WRITERS ARE ALWAYS WRITING OR THINKING ABOUT writing. As soon as one piece of writing, such as a blog, an article, or a book, is done, the question invariably resurfaces: "What's next?!"

And so as I (Andrés) was basking in the twinkles of Christmas tree lights a year after the publication of *The 5 Disciplines of Inclusive Leaders: Unleashing the Power of All of Us*, which I coauthored with my Korn Ferry colleague Alina Polonskaia, that perennial question announced itself once again.

I picked up the book and flipped to the Inclusive Leader model that we had fully unpacked through exposition, research, proof of concept, stories, and application suggestions . . . at least we thought we had fully unpacked it.

As I looked at the model that by then had been etched in my mind's eye, my attention went to the outermost of the three concentric circles. Placed deliberately in its margins were the labels "Leading Self," "Leading Teams," and "Leading Organization," as you can see in figure 1. It had been our final structural insight into the model. We had mapped the leader's ever-widening concentric circles of impact—self, team, and organization—against the five disciplines: Leading Self was mapped to the discipline of Builds Interpersonal Trust; Leading Teams to the disciplines of Integrates Diverse Perspectives and Optimizes Talent; and Leading Organization to the disciplines of Applies an Adaptive Mindset and Achieves Transformation.

Hmm . . .

Figure 1. The Inclusive Leader model.

The 5 Disciplines of Inclusive Leaders was the book about leading self. What if we now had *The 5 Disciplines of Inclusive Teams*—the book about leading teams? And *The 5 Disciplines of Inclusive Organizations*—the book about leading organizations?

Right there at the foot of the Christmas tree, the idea of a Five Inclusive Disciplines trilogy was born.

After the holidays, I gathered various thought leaders at Korn Ferry to test out the concepts. For Inclusive Organizations, I went right to my good friend and colleague Fayruz Kirtzman. Fayruz and I have collaborated on nearly fifty diversity, equity, and inclusion organizational root cause diagnostics. Along the way we also cowrote various white papers. We pulled out the Korn Ferry DE&I Maturity Model we had conceptualized and designed over the past couple of years with my first coauthor, Alina, and our colleague Gustavo Gisbert. Turns out there are five dimensions of maturity for inclusive organizations, and from there it was easy to develop the five actionable disciplines that inclusive organizations must practice.

From a diversity perspective, Fayruz and I have very different personal backgrounds and very different thinking and working styles. It's what generates a good amount of innovation when we engage with each other. But we also have key commonalities, such as being purpose driven, a compatible philosophy on the role of DE&I in the world, and a similar vision for how best to achieve organizational transformation. With our diversity as an asset, and our philosophical compatibility as a foundation, I asked Fayruz if she would be my coauthor for this book.

For the next book, I have already created an Inclusive Teams research and development team. Since we have not done as much work on inclusive teams as we have with organizations, our starting point was further back in terms of research. That said, we are not starting with a blank slate. Korn Ferry has been doing team effectiveness work for decades. Emerging as a leader out of this R&D team was Michel Buffet from Korn Ferry's Top Team Effectiveness practice. Michel is a certified coach in the Inclusive Leader model and had already begun to partner with me on bringing these concepts into teamwork in an integrated way. Michel and I are also very different in terms of identity, background, and thinking and execution styles. Yet here again we were compatible in key foundational ways. So another ask, another yes. Book 3 of the trilogy, written by the two of us, is scheduled to be released in 2024.

By the way, I recognize that from a logical sequence perspective, Inclusive Teams should have been book 2. But one needs to go with what is already done, and Fayruz and I had seven years' worth of research already captured in those fifty-plus organizational DE&I assessments and root cause analyses. So, welcome to book 2!

INTRODUCTION

Diverse and Equitable Enterprises Will Transform the World

If you can see the invisible, you can achieve the impossible.

Shiv Khera,
Indian author and activist

DETROIT ENERGY (DTE), A 118-YEAR-OLD COMPANY IN an old-school industrial sector, is the surprising new face of a clean, sustainable, diverse, and inclusive future.

By declaring a commitment to being carbon neutral by 2050, DTE is completely overhauling how it generates energy and how it will prepare its employees for a whole new way of keeping Michigan powered up.

DTE embarked on its sustainability journey more than a decade ago, when senior management realized that achieving their environmental goals required prioritizing diversity, equity, and inclusion (DE&I) in their sustainability strategy. Jerry Norcia, DTE's president and CEO, explains, "To achieve our company's ambitious goals, we need to build a diverse and inclusive culture where everyone contributes to the innovation and generation of clean, reliable, affordable energy and drives equity to ensure prosperous economies and thriving communities."

These bold and unexpected words took the role of DE&I to a whole new level. It made it clear that organizational diversity, equity, and inclusion are not simply an end in themselves, they are a means to achieving comprehensive sustainability for customers, communities, and the earth—all while still satisfying shareholders focused on profitability.

This balance across varied stakeholders is something conventional capitalist wisdom has said cannot be achieved. But DTE is among a growing chorus of for-profit companies saying, "Not true." Recent research also shows that organizations benefit economically when they pull social and environmental responsibility into their strategic focus.[1] For too long, companies' ledger sheets have not accounted for their hidden costs to the environment, society, and peoples' well-being, all of which have combined to create structural inequities in our societies and organizations and have damaged our planet.

For this reason, companies such as Apple, AstraZeneca, IKEA, Google, Microsoft, and Unilever are making their own bold commitments to causes well beyond their companies' economic prosperity. In fact, they are beginning to define prosperity much more broadly. Societies, governments, and vanguard companies are now seeing that their profit and loss ledger must also include the costs of harm to the environment due to pollution, of harm to low-income communities due to gentrification, and of harm to small towns due to relocating factory jobs offshore. The true costs of doing business could even be greater once we factor in the cost of social unrest that arises from the creation of these structural inequities.

This acceptance of responsibility for the full cost of providing goods and services is a prerequisite for motivating the capitalist system to solve the existential threats that imperil societies and all inhabitants of planet Earth. And this paradigm shift requires a different type of organization.

One that embraces a broader set of responsibilities for its actions and that seeks to harness its economic, talent, and technological power for the broader good while still thriving economically.

One that evaluates its people as valuable assets with very human needs for fair remuneration, for protection through thoughtful benefits, for feeling valued for who they are, and for the resources necessary to do their best work.

One that believes in the richness that diversity—in all its forms—brings to their culture, their innovation, and their business results.

One that understands that business today can't just be about profits.

One that we call an inclusive organization.

Of course, there are the skeptics who say that business should just be about goods, services, and profit, that all this extra seems like a distraction, a bunch of soft stuff. But here's the reality: The world is in grave pain right now and will be for the coming generations. The effects of the COVID-19 pandemic will be with us for years. There have been years lost at critical junctures in education, in careers, in marriages, in intellectual and emotional development. Millions of families of color, working hard to climb out of poverty, have fallen back a generation. Millions of highly talented women have left the workforce to care for their children due to preschools and schools being shut down, and they may never return. Millions of people have not returned to the workforce due to long COVID and other COVID-related medical issues; immune-compromised grocery cashiers, for example, may not want to risk doing their jobs anymore. Political polarization is rending the fabric of neighborhoods, cities, and nations. Polar caps are melting, seas are rising, coastal cities are threatened, wildfires are raging, and rivers are evaporating.

Meanwhile, the perennial issues of equitable representation, access, opportunity, and pay for marginalized groups in every country in the world remain with us. While we have seen some progress—albeit uneven—we are still falling short of the values and ideals of fair and just societies and workplaces.

When we are brought in to help our clients become truly inclusive organizations, we seek to help them become more diverse, equitable, and inclusive both for their own sake, because it's the right thing to do, and to become talent attractors and optimizers of the full spectrum of diverse talent pools. We help them go beyond the borders of the organization by leveraging their diversity, equity, and inclusion to have impact outside their boundaries—because it's the right *and* profitable thing to do. This includes making the most of their DE&I to help them sell goods and services that benefit consumers and to operate in a manner that betters society and the environment.

None of this is soft stuff.

Companies can't just sit out the DE&I and environmental, social, and governance (ESG) trends. They're in the crossfire. Consumers and employees expect them to weigh in on social and racial justice issues, they expect them to care for the environment, they expect them to treat their employees fairly, and they expect them to use their powers for good. Otherwise they will go work somewhere else or buy from someone else.

Research by various management consulting firms reveals that in 2020, 86% of people wanted to see a more equitable and sustainable world after the pandemic, and three-fourths wanted their own lives to change, too.[2] Moreover, 35% of employees said they would reconsider their current job if their company is not doing enough to address social justice externally, and 80% of consumers said companies need to recognize their role in systemic racial inequality, regardless of whether those companies' products and services have anything directly to do with social justice.

When employees quit a company, the cost of employee turnover is high—some estimates put that cost at 100% to 150% of an employee's salary for technical positions and up to 213% of an employee's salary for C-suite positions.[3] This is a hard-core chunk off the bottom line for any organization. Conversely, consumers making decisions based on social considerations rather than just on price and quality take a chunk off the top line.

The Great Resignation of 2021 and 2022 is expected to have long-term consequences for how employees view their employers and the very nature

WHAT CONSUMERS AND EMPLOYEES WANT TODAY

1. 86% of people want to see a more suitable and sustainable world after the pandemic. Almost three-quarters want their own lives to change, too.

2. 80% of consumers say companies need to recognize their role in systemic racial inequality.

3. 35% of employees are reconsidering their current job because their company is not doing enough to address social justice issues externally.

Sources: The Business Imperative for Social Justice Today, Porter Novelli Purpose Tracker, June 2020, https://www.porternovelli.com/wp-content/uploads/2020/06/PN-Purpose-Tracker_Business-Imperative-for-Social-Justice-Today.pdf; "2020 Edelman Trust Barometer 2020," Edelman, January 19, 2020, https://www.edelman.com/trust/2020-trust-barometer; Accenture's 2018 Global Consumer Pulse Research Survey of nearly 21,000 adults in twenty-eight countries, conducted by the World Economic Forum and Ipsos, quoted in Accenture, "Majority of Consumers Buying From Companies That Take a Stand on Issues They Care About and Ditching Those That Don't, Accenture Study Finds," Newsroom, December 5, 2018, https://newsroom.accenture.com/news/majority-of-consumers-buying-from-companies-that-take-a-stand-on-issues-they-care-about-and-ditching-those-that-dont-accenture-study-finds.htm.

of work.[4] This revolutionary mind shift can feel daunting for organizational leaders. Yet we believe that an inclusive organization is able to take better care of its people as well as the planet and society (and therefore to address the higher expectations people have of organizations) while still generating profits.[5] More diverse and inclusive organizations are more likely to capture

THE BUSINESS CASE FOR DIVERSITY, EQUITY, AND INCLUSION

Done well, diversity and inclusion maximize the performance of individuals, teams, and organizations in the workplace. Here's how diverse and inclusive organizations outperform their peers.

- They are 70% more likely to capture new markets.

- They are 36% more likely to outperform on profitability.

- 87% of the time, diverse and inclusive teams make better decisions.

- They are 76% more likely to see ideas become productized.

- Their innovation revenue is 19% higher.

- 87% of the most admired companies see a positive impact of diversity and inclusion on their business performance.

Sources: Sylvia Ann Hewlett, Melinda Marshall, and Laura Sherbin, with Tara Gonsalves, *Innovation, Diversity, and Market Growth* (Center for Talent Innovation, 2013); Erik Larson, "Infographic: Diversity + Inclusion = Better Decision Making At Work," Cloverpop, September 19, 2017, https://www .cloverpop.com/blog/infographic-diversity-inclusion-better-decision-making -at-work; Sundiatu Dixon-Fyle, Kevin Dolan, Dame Vivian Hunt, and Sara Prince, "Diversity Wins: How Inclusion Matters," McKinsey & Company, May 19, 2020, https://www.mckinsey.com/featured-insights/diversity-and -inclusion/diversity-wins-how-inclusion-matters; Rocío Lorenzo, Nicole Voigt, Miki Tsusaka, Matt Krentz, and Katie Abouzahr, "How Diverse Leadership Teams Boost Innovation," Boston Consulting Group, January 23, 2018, https://www.bcg.com/en-us/publications/2018/how-diverse-leadership -teams-boost-innovation; "Korn Ferry Partners with Fortune for the 21st Year on World's Most Admired Companies List," Korn Ferry, January 30, 2019; "Inclusive Mobility: How Mobilizing a Diverse Workforce Can Drive Business Results," Deloitte, https://www2.deloitte.com/us/en/pages/tax/articles /inclusive-mobility-diverse-workforce-drive-business-performance.html.

new markets, to outperform on profitability, to see ideas turned into products, and to see higher revenue based on innovation.

"Simply put, diverse teams achieve stronger results," Molly Brennan, founding partner of Koya Partners told *HRO Today* magazine. Multiple studies show that "diverse teams are more creative, come up with better solutions, and have stronger financial performance. Diversity [and inclusion] also plays a critical role in employee engagement and organizational culture, particularly when it comes to recruiting the next generation of leaders."[6]

Which brings us to why we wrote this book, the second in a three-part series about the five disciplines of inclusive leaders, inclusive teams, and inclusive organizations. The research that led us to this work began at Korn Ferry, where we have been developing comprehensive DE&I strategies for clients worldwide.

We have led dozens of DE&I diagnostics rooted in quantitative and qualitative analyses in organizations of all sizes, in industries, and on every continent. These diagnostics are necessary to explain the enduring lack of proportional representation in an organization's positions of influence and leadership, the chronic pay gap between underrepresented groups and White males, the patterns of lower engagement scores and higher attrition rates for these same underrepresented groups, the vigilance that women must still practice to ward off unwanted sexual advances in the workplace, and the millions of LGBTQ+ employees who still choose to remain closeted because they do not feel safe to come out at work.

It is these diagnostics that spawned the concepts and practices presented in this book and that are an integral part of Korn Ferry's DE&I work with companies.

Our work and our passion is helping clients discover exactly why they fall short of their bold DE&I aspirations. It is shaping transformational, strategic, and operational road maps that yield major, measurable results. Together we have more than four decades of experience helping organizations become more diverse, equitable, and inclusive.

Andrés is a trained journalist and writer, who through a series of circumstances and choices entered the corporate world as an organizational development professional and then climbed the ranks to become Hewitt Associates' (now Aon Hewitt) first-ever Chief Diversity Officer. In that role, he was charged with building a global DE&I center of expertise. He worked with the executive team to see DE&I as more than an internal talent optimization and cultural enhancement play but also as an enabler of innovative solutions and business growth. This led to Hewitt launching a DE&I consulting practice within its talent solutions portfolio, the first ever within a major managing consulting firm. After nearly eight years, he became president of the DE&I think tank Diversity Best Practices and is now a Senior Partner at Korn Ferry, where he leads Korn Ferry's DE&I research and development (R&D) efforts as Global DE&I and ESG strategist. One of the innovations stemming from his work has been the Inclusive Leader model, assessment, and coaching solution, which he wrote about in the first book of this trilogy, *The 5 Disciplines of Inclusive Leaders*. The present book on inclusive organizations will be followed by one on inclusive teams, set for publication in 2024.

Korn Ferry is also the place where Andrés met Fayruz.

Fayruz is a linguist by training. She began her career at a global translation and communications agency, where she rose to Director of Language and Culture, in charge of all linguistic and cultural analysis as well as brand name and corporate identity analysis in more than one hundred languages. At the agency, she was passionate about culturally competent marketing and collaborated in the development of global marketing and advertising strategies to target specific markets. Fueled by the desire to apply cultural competencies to the workplace beyond the written word, she joined Korn Ferry through a series of acquisitions, after which she emerged as a thought leader in her field and is now a Senior Partner and the Global DE&I Diagnostic Leader at the firm.

One of the innovations coming from her work as she led the practice has been the Korn Ferry DE&I Maturity Model, which is used to assess the current state of an organization's DE&I maturity and forms the basis for charting an organization's strategic DE&I progress.

For a decade, we have worked together closely on more than fifty DE&I client engagements, countless white papers, and the development of differentiated commercial solutions. We are experts at launching and nurturing employee and business resource groups (ERGs and BRGs). We have facilitated DE&I training for thousands around the world. We have designed and managed mentoring and sponsoring programs. We have chartered and activated hundreds of diversity councils.

But these are just the basics that set the stage; they are not what brings about DE&I transformation. Over that decade of working together, along with interdisciplinary teams combining DE&I, ESG, and other talent system experts, we have helped clients in all industries, of all sizes, and on all continents discover the root causes of why they are falling short of their bold DE&I aspirations. We have worked together to help them shape transformational strategic and operational road maps that have yielded major, measurable results. Along the way we have enabled hundreds of consultants to deliver on this type of work.

What we know for sure: programs focused on behavior change alone simply will not work.

When organizations ignore structural inclusion, they fall far short of creating inclusive environments. We define structural inclusion as the organizational systems and processes in place to prevent and mitigate unconscious bias. Organizations are like living organisms. Their very sizes, cultures, and brands have a power of their own that is greater than the sum of the parts of their leaders and teams. To address the big issues of DE&I within, as well as the critical environmental, social, and governance issues outside an organization, the organization itself must be a systematic, process-oriented engineer of change. That's what this book is about: how to make your organization a systematic, process-oriented engineer of change for the full range of your stakeholders.

To address this approach, we derived the five disciplines for inclusive organizations—the foundation for this book—from the DE&I Maturity Model.

A DIFFERENTIATED DE&I MATURITY MODEL

DE&I Maturity Models are attractive because they offer a simple yet comprehensive snapshot of an organization's current state and can help in developing a strategic road map toward their desired one.

While most maturity models are presented linearly, our experience with transformational change has shown us that the linear approach does not adequately support a multipronged DE&I change strategy. In this context, linearity no longer makes sense; an organization needs to mature across various dimensions, but not necessarily sequentially.

These realizations led us to our current Korn Ferry DE&I Maturity Model (figure 2), in which five dimensions—Risk Management, Awareness, Talent Integration, Operation Integration, and Market Integration—are organized as wedges of a circumplex. Within each

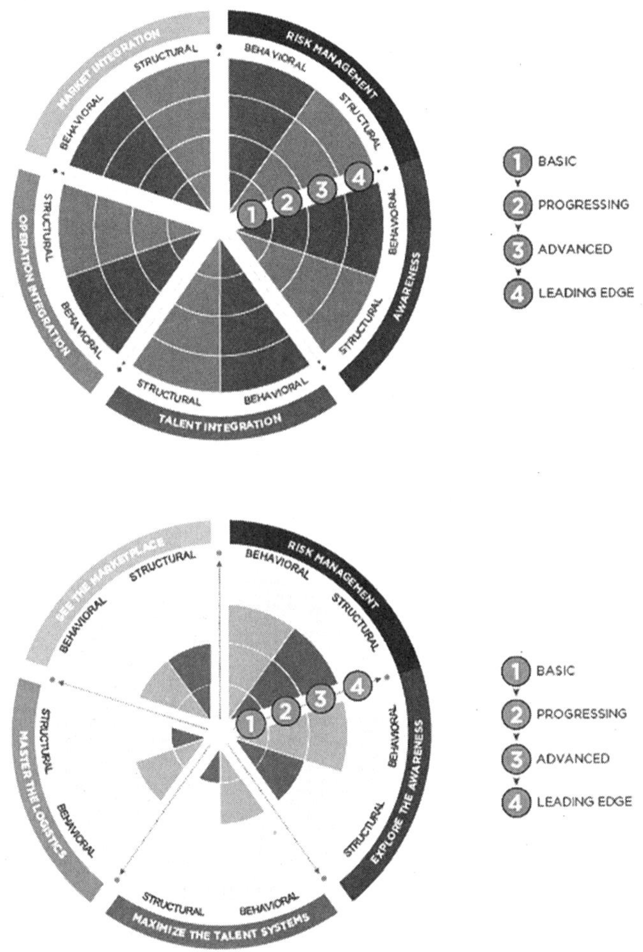

Figure 2. The Korn Ferry DE&I Maturity Model and sample scoring.

dimension, diagnostic findings and scores plot whether an organization is performing at a Basic, Progressing, Advanced, or Leading Edge level in terms of behavioral and structural inclusion. Behavioral inclusion is the conduct of individuals as they undergo a journey of self-discovery and become more alert to the biases that hamper their decision-making, while structural inclusion is the equity and transparency of the systems and processes in place to prevent and mitigate unconscious bias.

While conversations about behavioral inclusion are often more intuitive and more grounded in our DE&I conversations, structural inclusion forms the foundation of all inclusion work. Without inclusive practices, systems, and processes providing the springboard for actions, inclusive behaviors will never have a multiplier effect. Simply put, it is structural inclusion that makes behavioral inclusion stick.

LEVELS OF MATURITY

Moving away from a sequential maturity model as one moves from dimension to dimension does not mean sequence is gone. It still lives on *within* each of the dimensions, as our DE&I diagnostic findings and scores will plot whether an organization is performing at a Basic, Progressing, Advanced, or Leading Edge level within each dimension. Here's what each level of maturity means.

BASIC

Across dimensions, when organizations are at the Basic level of maturity, their approach to DE&I tends to be reactive. They may define diversity along one or two visible aspects of diversity, such as race, gender, or age, and leaders usually have very limited involvement in driving DE&I forward.

PROGRESSING

Here, the focus tends to be purpose driven, with leaders assuming some responsibility for DE&I. The definition of diversity expands to include both visible and invisible dimensions of diversity, such as neurodiversity. At this stage, an organization may have a dedicated staff and budget for DE&I.

ADVANCED

Organizations at this stage pay attention to the intersections of different identities when thinking about diversity. Their leaders exhibit inclusive leadership skills and are held accountable for creating a diverse, equitable, and inclusive environment. They often have DE&I resources and budgets distributed throughout other functional areas, such as human resources (HR), information technology, and operations, as well as across business units and geographic regions.

LEADING EDGE

These organizations take a sustainable approach to DE&I in which leaders are expected to lead holistically and inclusively, be key DE&I change agents, and hold the organization accountable. In addition to their internal resources, they often have external DE&I advisory boards that guide them on leading-edge practices.

WHO'S RESPONSIBLE FOR WHAT?

By structuring the DE&I Maturity Model in a circumplex, each dimension can be assigned a distinct owner, a distinct business case, and a particular objective (see table 1). This underscores the notion that organizations can be at various stages of DE&I maturity across the five dimensions.

The more we worked with clients using this maturity model, the more our understanding evolved. We realized that these five dimensions of DE&I maturity were in fact the five disciplines that inclusive organizations need to achieve DE&I transformation. So we turned the *what* of the five DE&I dimensions into the *how* of inclusive organizations, which we'll discuss next.

We have found that these five disciplines—Manage the Risk, Explode the Awareness, Maximize the Talent Systems, Master the Logistics, and

Table 1 Organizational Function Responsibility for the Five Diversity, Equity, and Inclusion Dimensions.

DIMENSION	WHO IS RESPONSIBLE	BUSINESS CASE
Risk management	Risk management/legal function	Risk mitigation
Awareness	Diversity, equity, and inclusion function	Employer of choice
Talent integration	Human resources function	Enhanced talent pipeline
Operations integration	Business functions focused on internal efficiencies, such as finance, procurement, or quality assurance	Enhanced bottom line
Market integration	Business functions focused on customer and community, such as marketing, sales, research and development, or corporate social responsibility	Enhanced top line

See the Marketplace (figure 3)—encompass the structures, mindsets, behaviors, and accountabilities required to drive increasing DE&I maturity across organizations. It is the practice of these disciplines that positively affects an organization's talent, culture, products, and services, and the societies in which they operate, so the maturity model itself becomes a tool to determine an organization's readiness to grow in its maturity and for leaders of inclusive organizations to stay the course in a methodical and disciplined way.

We believe this maturity model and accompanying five inclusive organization disciplines approach align much more closely with reality than the traditional linear model. Just as human beings possess different levels of physical, emotional, intellectual, and spiritual maturity at a given age, so too do organizations possess different levels of behavioral and structural inclusion within different dimensions of their organizational health and ability to optimize their own diversity and inclusion.

The quantitative tools include a talent flow analysis, pay equity and performance ratings audits, as well as an organization-wide survey. The

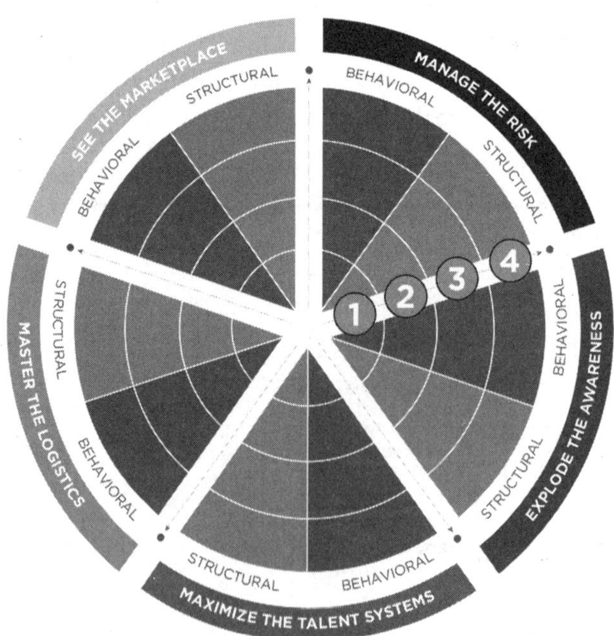

Figure 3: The 5 Disciplines of Inclusive Organizations, based on the Korn Ferry DE&I Maturity Model 2022.

qualitative tools include executive interviews, focus groups, and brand audits. We also audit the talent processes for bias and then help client organizations design inclusive talent processes.

When done together, these diagnostics allow organizations to discover the root causes of why they are not advancing on DE&I as desired and to focus on targets based on data rather than on hunches.

It is these organizational root cause diagnostics (each a research project in itself!) from which we derived the many illustrative examples and stories we tell in this book, as well as the recommendations for action. To supplement and add to this research, we also analyzed our collection of diagnostics data as a whole to see what the macro trends across all of them were.

HOW THIS BOOK IS ORGANIZED

In part 1 we dedicate a chapter to each of the five disciplines of inclusive organizations. We describe what that discipline entails at each of the four stages of maturity, both behaviorally and structurally.

Because we know that structural inclusion is the foundation for a truly inclusive organization, we start with the more complex structural inclusion discussion for each discipline. We then explore the behavioral inclusion that will be required to engage with the structural inclusion put in place to bring about DE&I transformation.

Along the way, we provide case studies of organizations at various stages of maturity, which have attempted—and sometimes failed—to apply each discipline. These are written by a collection of colleagues who put into practice the five disciplines of inclusive organizations, or by journalists reporting on different industries. We present statistics that reflect the current DE&I landscape and the perspectives of leaders, managers, employees, customers, community organizations, and researchers doing the work to create more inclusive organizations.

In part 2 we shift from the tactical how-to of becoming an inclusive organization to the aspirational—our vision for a world of inclusive organizations that are spreading equity and inclusion beyond their own walls and making a measurable impact on the problems that plague our society.

We will explore the symbiotic relationship between DE&I and the rapidly ascending concepts behind the environmental, social, and governance movement that aims to hold companies accountable for the impact of their actions—and inactions—on climate change, people, and communities. By (rightly) blurring the lines between business and society, ESG is the way forward for measuring and acting on what is mutually good for profits, people, and the planet.

And DE&I lies at the heart of it.

Much more than a prime directive to "hire more diversity," DE&I—through the development of inclusive organizations—is how we transform the world. This evolution is already shaping the next generation of DE&I work, as we will show. The reality is that more diverse, inclusive, and equitable organizations are essential for achieving ESG's ambitious sustainability goals.

We also introduce the four vital tasks that inclusive organizations must tackle, leveraging their DE&I prowess, to achieve equity and inclusion in their greater societies and in the world at large:

1. Diversify leadership

2. Eradicate polarization

3. Achieve justice

4. Save the planet

We highlight companies committed to these vital tasks, companies that are harnessing their power, stock market presence, and iconic branding to partner with governments, nongovernmental organizations, and all sorts of good people. Companies that are working hard to realize the promise of diversity, equity, and inclusion for all beings. That said, we fully recognize that no organization, whether for-profit or not, has a "perfect score" on the vital tasks we believe inclusive organizations must address. In many cases, the most exemplary organizations are the ones seeking to reverse the harm they themselves have imposed on societies and the planet.

But we didn't write this book to dwell on the sins of the past.

There is a place for that, but it's not here. Instead, given the hole we are in on so many issues that are affecting us, and given that our collective survival depends on each of us bringing our best *right now* to save the day, we need as many organizations as possible, with their scalable prowess, to be in the good fight.

There are plenty that are, and these are the ones we have chosen to showcase, even though they may not be 100% virtuous in all their actions and domains. We accept that reality, and we hope you can too. The fact remains that organizations moving toward greater inclusion on any front are the ones that will transform our world, and to do so, they require intent and discipline.

Five disciplines, in fact. So let's now turn our attention to fully exploring each one.

THE FIVE DISCIPLINES OF INCLUSIVE ORGANIZATIONS

THE FIVE DISCIPLINES OF INCLUSIVE ORGANIZATIONS

Get ready for a connect-the-dots journey to becoming an inclusive organization, discipline by discipline. In each of the discipline chapters, you will learn how organizations can progress from Basic to Leading Edge and you will encounter real-life examples of the Good, the Bad, and the Ugly.

Before we dive in, here's a quick overview of what each discipline entails.

Discipline 1: Manage the Risk. The extent to which an organization effectively manages DE&I-related risk.

Discipline 2: Explode the Awareness. The extent to which an organization's leaders and employees are aware of and committed to the value of DE&I.

Discipline 3: Maximize the Talent Systems. The extent to which an organization has integrated diversity, equity, and inclusion into its talent systems, and to which leaders and managers display inclusive behaviors in all aspects of talent management.

Discipline 4: Master the Logistics. The bottom-line impact of integrating DE&I into the organization's operations in ways that lead to improved efficiencies.

Discipline 5: See the Marketplace. The top-line impact of integrating DE&I into marketplace efforts through expanding to markets of new consumers, enhanced customer service, and effective partnerships with communities.

The stage is set. Let the curtain rise.

1

Discipline 1: Manage the Risk

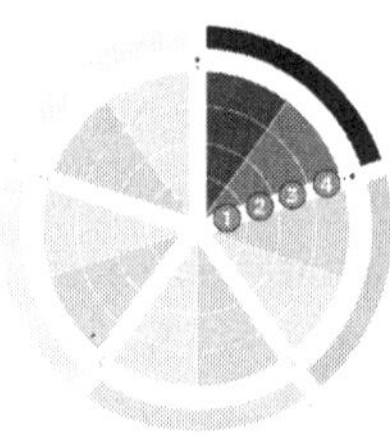

Maturity measure: the extent to which an organization effectively manages DE&I-related risk.

"Practicas algun deporte de riesgo?"—"Si, a veces doy mi opinion." (Do you practice any risk sports?—Yes, I sometimes give my opinion.)

Mafalda,
Argentine comic strip character

OVER THE PAST TWENTY YEARS, THE POWERHOUSE United States Women's National Soccer Team has won five World Cup titles as well as four Olympic gold medals. In contrast, their male counterparts have never won a World Cup nor have they even come close to winning an Olympic medal—more often than not they have not even qualified for the event.

However, you would never know how much more successful the women's team has been compared to the men's team based on their World Cup remuneration and earnings. For reaching Round 16 in 2014, the US men's team received $5.375 million, whereas one year later, the women's team received a mere $1.725 million for *winning the whole tournament.*

So the women's team sued. And won. Their six-year-long litigation ended on February 22, 2022, the eve of Equal Pay Day, with $24 million in back pay, plus a pledge that pay for both national teams going forward would be equalized.

This is a classic example of an organization failing to manage DE&I-related risk—in this case, the risk of a gender-related wage gap.

Much is at stake when the DE&I-related risk is not managed. US Soccer paid dearly in the form of millions in litigation fees, lost sponsors, lost fans, and a bruised reputation. And their superstar women—Wambach, Solo, Scurry, Rapinoe, Morgan, Lloyd, Lilly, Hamm, Foudy, Chastain, and on—were left feeling excluded throughout their careers, even as they brought joy and pride to millions of fans.

US Soccer joins a long list of the most iconic corporations in the Fortune 500 that failed at managing DE&I-related risk. Consider the 1999 class action lawsuit filed by Black employees against Coca-Cola in the United States. The charge was systemic discrimination resulting in lower pay, fewer promotions, and poor performance evaluations. There were claims of "glass ceiling" and "glass wall" policies that kept African Americans away from the top jobs. In the end, Coca-Cola agreed to a $192 million settlement, at the time the largest settlement in a corporate racial discrimination case. Abercrombie & Fitch, McDonald's, Nextel, Nike, Novartis, Texaco, and Walmart are just a few of the other big names that were made to pay settlements to the tune of hundreds of millions of dollars related to employee discrimination on a number of fronts.[1]

In 2021 alone, there were at least 1,607 workplace class action suits in the United States, totaling a record $3.62 billion in damages.[2] This is a far cry from having it under control.

Why does this keep happening? Throughout civilization's history, empires, nations, and colonies have in one way or another perpetuated exclusion through enslavement, segregation, and prohibitions against certain groups of people. Conversely, there is also an arc as old as time of sociopolitical forces driving toward equality, justice, and fairness, leading to laws that freed those enslaved, that gave the right to vote to women, and that sought to protect those in the minority from discriminatory labor practices.

While this measurable progress means that some of the most egregious injustices, such as legal slavery, are a thing of the past in most countries, discrimination in opportunity, promotions, firings, and pay is not. Neither are hostile and violent acts, such as hate crimes based on race, sexual orientation, or disability, or sexual harassment and assault. The thousands of global, national, and local laws protecting the most vulnerable employees from these acts show how much societies have progressed. At the same time, they have increased the risk for companies, since they are now rightfully accountable for what happens within their walls—to their employees and because of their employees. And so they keep being sued.

But managing the risk is not just about staying out of trouble by avoiding litigation, as important as that is. That's just the starting point. Truly mature inclusive organizations think beyond just the punitive aspect of risk management. Inclusive organizations know that managing the risk is key to staying competitive as an employer and as a provider of goods and services.

Managing the risk to stay competitive can take many forms. Beyond litigation avoidance, there are other risks to consider—the risk of losing existing customers, the risk of not gaining new customers and stifling growth, the risk of high attrition among highly skilled employees, or the risk of not attracting that highly skilled workforce in the first place.

The adage "There's no such thing as bad publicity" is false. Turns out, bad press—such as branding a company as noninclusive or not on the forefront of social justice—is indeed bad. For example, the sociopolitical convulsions following the May 2020 George Floyd murder in the United States and its reverberations across the world have had a profound impact on consumers and on their relationship with retailers. Eighty percent now say companies need to recognize their role in systemic racial inequality.[3]

Such sentiments affect buying decisions. They lead to boycotts of certain products and companies. The megaphone of social media amplifies these voices exponentially, and the repercussions are instant. That's some risk to manage!

Moreover, these sentiments affect employees. A lot has been said about this being a great time for employees to reorient themselves. The market has seen people leave their jobs in greater numbers, with organizations clamoring for talent, and paying a premium for it. This is in part due to employees wanting to work for employers that care—for them as individuals, for society, and for the environment. And if they feel that the company doesn't, those employees will go elsewhere. Given the runaway costs of hiring and upskilling new employees, poor employee morale is yet another high-stakes risk to manage.

To manage the risk legally and from a talent management and branding perspective, inclusive organizations must focus on both the structures in place (policies, systems, and safeguards) and the behavior being exhibited (mindsets, skill sets, and relationships) as they evolve on a scale from (1) Basic to (2) Progressing to (3) Advanced, and finally, to (4) Leading Edge.

MANAGE THE RISK—STRUCTURALLY

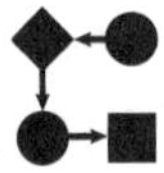

BASIC

From a structural perspective, an organization that is at a Basic level of Manage the Risk is usually focused on compliance and litigation avoidance by having solid antidiscrimination policies in place. The responsibility for inclusion may even lie with the legal team, with a mandate to "not get in trouble." For organizations that—in the United States—do business with the federal government, affirmative action goals will be in place and initial efforts might be under way to track representation data accordingly. Representation of underrepresented groups in these companies is often very low or concentrated in lower-level jobs.

PROGRESSING

As an organization moves to the next stage, Progressing, we find that either the CEO or the board—or both—have started to pay more attention to DE&I. They may have faced some outside pressure from investors or the media and are now aware they must "do something," although more often than not they are not sure what that is. It is at this stage that organizations may conduct adverse impact analyses of their employment practices to make sure they don't run afoul of any equal employment opportunity (EEO) laws.

Adverse impact analyses are meant to root out discriminatory practices that are unintentionally built into the system. They look at employment practices that are seemingly fair and neutral as written but are biased against one or more demographic groups in actual practice. Such bias can happen in any phase of the talent management processes—recruiting, hiring, developing, or promoting people. Some examples are educational requirements, fitness tests, or fixed hours for certain jobs. Why should applicants have to prove they can lift sixty pounds—a requirement that may exclude a higher percentage of women than men as well as people with disabilities—for a warehouse job when workers have access to robots and exoskeleton suits to do the heavy lifting? How does a grade point average prove competence for a job? Or is a college degree even necessary for, say, a programming job? Does the job truly require eight continuous hours to be done well—a requirement that can exclude many who juggle caregiver responsibilities outside work during the day—or can it be broken up into different, dispersed time segments?

ADVANCED

In the Advanced stage, what was once a simple compliance exercise starts being considered through a broader risk management lens. The organization really starts to consider the reputational risk of either doing the wrong thing or—on the flip side—*not* doing the right thing. This is where leadership becomes more forward looking and considers how it wants to be known in the market as well as among its own employees.

An example of this is the Brazilian office of financial technology company Serasa Experian. More than twenty-five years ago, the Brazilian government instituted one of the world's first quota requirements for employing people with disabilities (2% to 5% of the workforce, depending on the company's size). Serasa Experian decided to blow past that minimum. It was convinced it would find a much richer pool of talent than people assumed was there and that this would become a competitive advantage for the company.

They were right. When you walk onto Serasa Experian's campus in São Paulo today, you will find dozens of people in wheelchairs, who are sight and hearing impaired, and who are neurodiverse, having autism or Down syndrome. They are in professional roles such as sales, legal, research and development, human resources, and communications. Their most accurate proofreader is someone who cannot see. Turnover among Serasa Experian's employees with disabilities is lower than the organizational average. This is how leveraging the discipline of Manage the Risk shows up as a competitive advantage with respect to talent attraction.

LEADING EDGE

In our experience, very few organizations have achieved Leading Edge maturity in any discipline. But as any journey must have an aspirational goal, we include Leading Edge *here as the stage companies must strive toward. It is attained when DE&I is fully integrated in the larger risk management discussion.*

The reputational risks of not doing the right thing must be considered from a talent perspective. But at this stage it goes way beyond that. What about the risks of *not* expanding into new, underrepresented markets? Of not developing products with marginalized groups in mind? Of not having diverse perspectives at the table to spur innovation and growth? At this level of maturity, these risks must be actively monitored, assessed, and mitigated by leadership, by HR, and by the DE&I function.

A company at the Leading Edge level of maturity in risk management is also bold about holding even its highest-revenue-producing, rainmaking leaders accountable for violating nondiscrimination policies, ignoring antiharassment rules, or creating a hostile work environment. While many organizations toe a very close line here between wanting to do the right thing and not wanting to lose a moneymaker, Leading Edge organizations are clear: there are consequences for these behaviors, regardless of who you are.

MANAGE THE RISK—BEHAVIORALLY

BASIC

In an organization that is at the Basic level of managing DE&I-related behavioral risks, leaders get caught off guard when major incidents occur. This is because they have only a rudimentary understanding of the DE&I risks for the business and culture of their organization. The organization may have basic compliance training in place and therefore leaders and managers—and in fact all employees—may be focused only on what this training is telling them. Often it will be "Oh, now I cannot say or do this anymore," accompanied with an eye roll.

Clearly, this is not going to set an organization up for success around DE&I risk management—or even to avoid illegal discriminatory practices. In our DE&I consulting work, we have come across plenty of examples of companies at this level falling short and paying the price. Take the manager who automatically offered an advancement opportunity to the man on his team. He assumed the equally qualified woman on his team did not want to take on additional responsibility and travel, because she had young children. No thought was given to the discriminatory nature of this assumption; on the contrary, the manager "meant well." Or the manager whose performance feedback to one of his Black employees included descriptions like "a chip on the shoulder," "aggressive," and "lacking motivation"—supposedly unaware that these are damaging stereotypes. How quickly trouble can find you when Manage the Risk is not lived behaviorally.

PROGRESSING

As an organization moves from Basic to Progressing, you will see a greater focus on creating a respectful workplace for all employees. This is the stage of "good intentions" and of greater awareness of what might be disrespectful or even discriminatory behavior. People managers are more aware of what the rules and policies around equitable and inclusive people management means and are applying policies and rules with more consistency. Employees have been educated on what fair treatment looks like, and they feel empowered to stand up if they witness a violation. You may see someone take aside a peer after a meeting and point out that calling a colleague a "girl" during the meeting diminished her contributions and could be considered a microaggression, or pointing out the inappropriateness of using the culturally charged phrase "open up the kimono" to convey transparency, of all things.

ADVANCED

In the Advanced stage, behavior shifts from the Golden Rule (treating others like you want to be treated) to the Platinum Rule (treating others like *they* want to be treated). In an organization at the Advanced level, employees feel empowered to speak up with their ideas as well as their concerns, without fear of negative consequences if these ideas are opposed

NOT IN THIS HOUSE

In a virtual town hall meeting, the CEO of a large international beverage company was explaining his vision for a more inclusive organization. He gave all the right business stats and also laid out his personal values and how they guided this new path. It was 2020, at the height of the social upheaval following George Floyd's murder. The town hall was attended by all employees, including those from manufacturing settings, which traditionally can be less discreet in displaying biases. The virtual team meeting had the comment feature turned on and the comments were pouring in. Many were anonymous and painful, denouncing the CEO as "caving to liberal pressure" and voicing their discontent at having to work with "those people" they'd rather not interact with.

At one point, the CEO stopped in his prepared talking points, paused, and then said, "I am seeing the comments that are coming in, and frankly, I am shocked and ashamed that this is the climate in our organization. Hear me say this clearly: we will embark on this inclusion journey, and we will create a climate where all employees have a place to belong and advance, and if you cannot abide by these values, this company is not the place for you."

This CEO knew that allowing exclusionary and downright discriminatory attitudes and behaviors to fester posed a risk he was not willing to take. He was not willing to see the engagement scores from an underrepresented group plummet or watch this group exit the organization in larger numbers. And so he drew a line in the sand. This is what advanced risk management behavior looks like.

---

to the ones suggested by the leader. You may witness brainstorming meetings where people from different backgrounds bounce ideas back and forth. You may witness leaders very vocally supporting DE&I. There is psychological safety, and the culture is one of trust and encouragement.

LEADING EDGE

In this aspirational stage, organizations at the Leading Edge of risk management will have a workforce that fully understands the risks and impact associated with harassment, bullying, and discrimination, and behaves accordingly. If negative behaviors occur, managers and leaders know how to counteract them, and they do so with no qualms.

Earlier, we talked about the importance of having a process in place that holds leaders accountable for behaving inclusively. Yet it is one thing to have a zero-tolerance policy in place for bad behavior; it is quite another for leaders to behave in a manner that honors that policy.

In one Fortune 500 company, we know of a leader who was placed on the succession path to the CEO role. He began to observe firsthand the abusive behaviors of the company's leading salesperson. He witnessed this leader publicly berating, belittling, and ridiculing members of his team and creating a climate of fear and intimidation. He was alarmed by the behavior and by the fact that no one spoke up or called him out.

So he decided to do what others would not. He pulled this sales leader aside, pointed out his infractions, and gave him a chance to rectify his ways. When the salesperson did not and the abusive behaviors continued, this leader went to the CEO to discuss how to best address the issue. Here, he hit a brick wall. The CEO made it clear the offender was a top revenue producer and he refused to call him out on his abusive ways. The CEO advised his successor to let it go.

He didn't.

Instead, he gave the offender another warning and then, on the third infraction, let him go. *This* is Leading Edge behavior. No one had taken his stance seriously, least of all the offender. A career-limiting move is what they saw when he fired the rainmaker. But the leader stood firm. To him, it was the right thing to do, as well as the best way to manage the risk of having an abusive employee in a prominent role.

Epilogue: he ended up becoming the CEO.

ANATOMY OF A DEBACLE: RACIAL FAUX PAS AT AN ADVERTISING AGENCY

Many years ago, Fayruz, in her role as a DE&I consultant, got called into a meeting with a leading global advertising agency. The information she received when they set up this meeting was cryptic. They wanted to get some advice about how to handle a certain situation. As she was sitting in the lobby of a fancy metropolitan high-rise, waiting for the head of human resources and the head of diversity and inclusion to call her in, the receptionist came over to her, looking over her shoulder.

"I know why you are here," she whispered.

"Excuse me?" Fayruz was taken aback.

"I know why you are here. If they had just run that ad by me, I could've told them it would backfire."

Aha. Now Fayruz had a bit more information as to why she was there. Once she had a chance to meet with the head of HR and the larger team, she unearthed what had happened. An ad was created for a product; the ad was supposed to run outside the United States. The layout and photo had caused an outcry for its depiction of Black men in a subjugated role. There was a lot of hand-wringing and questions about how this could happen.

Many mistakes were made here. The ad was not run by members of the Black community because—sadly but unsurprisingly—there were no Black creatives on the team. Nor did the agency think to engage Black employees from other parts of the firm. Part of the reason was that this ad was supposed to run in the Asia-Pacific region, so who in the US would see it anyway? On the client side, no one caught it either.

The ad agency's client was now furious—they were getting backlash and calls for boycotts and had to do a lot of damage control. There were calls for the CEO to resign. Leaders at the agency were stunned and taken aback. Clearly, managing inclusion risk hadn't been high on their list. And now both the higher-ups at the agency and the client were in full panic mode.

This was not a mistake by one single person or even by one team. The whole structure of creating impactful ads was flawed by a lack of diversity and inclusion, and there were failures at every decision point. There was the creative director who came up with the concept and who had no idea that it would be offensive to the Black community. Then there was the rest of the creative team, who thought this was a great idea and expanded upon it with various iterations of the concept. There were photographers, copy editors, and senior leaders who all signed off on this ad, both the concept and the final product. And the same happened on the client side. At no point was the system set up to catch this snafu. Why not?

Because nowhere in the chain of command at the agency—or with the client—did a Black person, or someone with cultural insights into Black culture, actually look at the concept. The creative team did not have a single Black team member, nor did any of the other people who touched the project. In addition—and perhaps even more telling—even though the teams were homogeneous, no one thought to run the ad concept by anyone from the community to ensure it was culturally appropriate or at least not outright offensive.

There was neither diversity nor a structural process to mitigate the risk of not being inclusive. It was a casebook system breakdown.

It was one thing to have low representation of underrepresented groups at certain levels or in particular areas, such as the creative team. It was quite another not to even *think* about creating inclusive—or at least inoffensive—ads. Clearly, this client was at the very Basic level on their journey of structural DE&I-related risk management.

With Fayruz's help, the ad agency set to work with a multiprong approach. It tackled its blind spots from many perspectives, both behaviorally and structurally.

Behaviorally, leaders, managers, and creatives were urged and motivated to think and operate in a more intentionally inclusive way by simply being more attuned to who was and was not in the room where ideas were being developed and tested. If they identified a lack of diversity, they were empowered to take steps in the moment to do something about it.

Structurally, there was a focus on increasing the diversity of employees at all levels, from both a recruiting and a development point of view. The agency launched an initiative to systematically seek input on ads before they were released, looking to existing employees with a diverse set of backgrounds, regardless of where they sat in the agency. The receptionist who spoke to Fayruz before her first meeting, for instance, was now one of many tagged for input. By embedding this approach into its culture and structure, and integrating DE&I into the larger risk management discussion, the organization moved from Basic to Progressing in its risk management maturity.

As an Advanced step on the behavioral inclusion side, there was an effort by the creatives in the agency to partner with their corporate clients and utilize their diversity to test ideas and ads. The structural inclusion step, for example, established protocols to tap into clients' existing employee resource groups, which represented many identity groups.

And this is how the agency was slowly able to move forward in Manage the Risk and to become more inclusive.

TRIP UPS

No matter how research-based, field-tested, or elegant a methodology is, addressing DE&I in an organization is complex, messy, and full of dilemmas. The most common Manage the Risk trip ups we have observed during our client work are overindexing on one group, ridiculing compliance as irrelevant, and letting the lawyers rule.

TRIP UP 1: OVERINDEXING ON ONE GROUP

We've seen it both in organizations and in society at large: calls for broad diversity are answered with progress for just one group.

Globally, a focus on diversity often has been synonymous with a focus on gender equity. In many countries, gender is the one category that is tracked, and so it has become a placeholder for all categories. Take the EU Gender Equality Index, which shows countries such as Sweden and France at the top of the list. Does this mean that these countries—and their companies—have solved the diversity and inclusion challenge? Hardly.

In 2022, a female candidate, Marine Le Pen, ran for president of France and came close to winning, with 41% of the population's vote. Her popularity stemmed from her hard anti-immigration agenda, indicating that there is still a good amount of diversity, equity, and inclusion work to be done and that gender can't be the only thing we focus on.

Even when focusing just on women, the progress in countries with a good amount of racial diversity has largely been made by White women at the expense of women of color. For example, according to a McKinsey study, women hold 19% of C-suite positions while women of color hold a mere 4%.[4] We also worked with a tech organization that claimed to do well around racial equity, only to find that their population of people of color consisted of 80% expatriates from just one country and were predominately positioned in the lower ranks.

The focus on diversity and inclusion cannot be solved by overindexing on one group only. A few years ago, the hashtag #OscarsSoWhite dominated the conversation after a ceremony that awarded twenty acting nominations to White actors for the first of two consecutive years. After a few years of fits and starts to do better, the 2022 Oscars were indeed more diverse—both in nominees as well as in performers. The full production team was all-Black, the opening act was Black celebrities, two of the three female hosts were Black. Progress, right?

Yes, but only on one front. As the night wore on, the number of Black performers became unmistakably lopsided compared to representatives from other minority racial and ethnic groups. A similar dynamic has taken place in the workplace, where Asians, Latinos, and Indigenous people have been largely invisible in efforts that have overindexed on addressing Black talent, especially given the added scrutiny after the George Floyd murder and the wave of Black Lives Matter protests around the world. Despite the undeniable urgency to rectify past wrongs for this group, true inclusion means inclusion of all traditionally underrepresented groups.

TRIP UP 2: RIDICULING COMPLIANCE AS IRRELEVANT

As we alluded earlier in the chapter, many organizations want to move their DE&I conversations as far away from the legal arena as possible, even though that's where it all began. We hear it all the time: "We are long beyond focusing on compliance," or "Equating DE&I with compliance brings us back to the 1980s," or even "Isn't this focus on compliance just about establishing the numbers?"

Yes, and . . .

We understand that inclusive organizations strive to be so much more than adhering to the local antidiscrimination laws. This is why we highlight the five disciplines in the first place. But compliance is not going away. We still have not rid our society and organizations of practices and behaviors that disadvantage and drive away underrepresented talent. And while having diversity goals for underrepresented talent may be a crude instrument for advancing DE&I, it remains necessary.

We still see thousands of class action suits being filed and won every year. We still see organizations being fined billions of dollars. In addition, have we really accomplished what these antidiscrimination laws set out to fix? Does your organization have equitable representation in its leadership ranks? Few do, so ridiculing compliance as irrelevant is misguided.

Talking about compliance may not be as sexy as talking about innovation, but compliance still plays a vital role in DE&I efforts and ignoring it will surely come around to bite and set you back.

TRIP UP 3: LETTING THE LAWYERS RULE

One of the risks that stands in the way of managing the risk progress is, ironically, the lawyers themselves. In many organizations, the lawyers are very involved in managing DE&I information and data. Their involvement often consists of keeping their foot on the brake. Cutting survey data by demographic groups? Too risky. Conducting listening circles to learn about different experiences? Too risky. Looking at advancement and promotions by race and gender? Too risky. Who knows what dark organizational secrets such information will reveal.

We see many diversity leaders in their organizations with their hands tied by highly risk-adverse lawyers for whom the whole topic of diversity is a land mine to be avoided. In an era of high premiums put on DE&I commitments and demands for greater transparency, this is counterproductive.

There's a place for diversity leaders to push back on the lawyers who understandably are trying to manage the risk. One key way is to acknowledge the importance of managing risk. Ask them, "So, how risky is it, really?" Not everything is equally risky, and this should become a risk management conversation. Is it a low-risk endeavor? Medium-risk? High-risk? Insist that the legal department truly quantify the risk.

Part of the conversation should also involve a discussion of the risk of *not* doing something. What is riskier, to not share representation data with the public when it's obvious to all there is not much diversity at the top (so what are you trying to hide?) or being transparent with your numbers and humbly acknowledging you have a way to go?

Another way to push back is to remember that the legal department is there to advise the business leaders who sponsor DE&I efforts; they are not the decision-makers. If you are feeling stuck, lean on your business sponsor to weigh in, since they have the ultimate decision-making power.

Keeping in mind that this is not a linear model, we will nevertheless say "Next" as we move on to Discipline 2: Explode the Awareness.

SODEXO: FROM RISK MANAGEMENT MELTDOWN TO EXEMPLAR COMPANY

Stephanie Collins

It took an $80 million lawsuit over racial inequities in the early 2000s for Sodexo to take diversity seriously. But from that point to today, Sodexo—a major food facilities business based in France and operating in more than seventy countries—has become one of the most admired companies in diversity, equity, and inclusion, and for good reason.

Rohini Anand, the former Senior Vice President of Corporate Responsibility and Global Chief Diversity, who presided over this transformation, describes diversity and inclusion at Sodexo as being "a true business imperative and part of our company's DNA."

Michel Landel, Sodexo's CEO during Anand's tenure, illustrated this point when he said, "Greater diversity and inclusiveness are part of a cultural transformation that requires time and humility. It needs a set of clear, measurable, and attainable long-term objectives for management. Teams must be held accountable and accountability cascaded throughout the organization. We all know that without targets, nothing gets measured and nothing changes."

What sparked the DE&I transformation at Sodexo was thousands of Black employees being pushed aside for promotion by less qualified White peers. Along with payments to previous employees, Sodexo's $80 million settlement also required the establishment of new policies to improve DE&I through updated trainings, promotion paths, incentives, and metrics. Regarding the settlement, Sodexo's CEO Richard Macedonia said, "We are pleased this case has been resolved. . . . We are a stronger and better organization as a result of this process." Macedonia is now one of DE&I's biggest supporters in the company, according to Anand.

In addition to a renewed focus on racial equity, Sodexo expanded its DE&I emphasis to include gender equity. To achieve a better gender balance, the company asked questions and listened to employees, leveraged female voices, and created measurable targets.

Sodexo started by asking female employees what they needed to be successful. In India, for example, many families live together, and after work, the female employees return home to cook and clean. If they return late, they may be chastised by their family members. When asked how Sodexo could support them, these employees

(continued)

SODEXO: FROM RISK MANAGEMENT MELTDOWN TO EXEMPLAR COMPANY

(continued)

suggested a recognition program so their families could see the importance of their work, which transformed how they were seen at home. Now, other family members take on more cleaning and cooking and no longer scold the employees for returning late, aiding both the employees and the business. This illustrates the importance of listening to diverse employees' needs and going to employees for creative, inclusive solutions.

Sodexo has continued the work for gender balance by committing to have women represent 40% of leadership roles by 2025 (the company was at 32% as of 2018). Additionally, the company established an international employee business resource group for women, dedicated to women's professional development and growth. The resource group includes both men and women, effectively tapping into an ally network. Supporting underrepresented groups through allies is one of the themes that makes Sodexo's DE&I work successful. For instance, the CEO and general counsel, who were hesitant about DE&I's impact, now are some of its biggest champions, after attending an African American Leadership Forum and other employee business resource group meetings.

At Sodexo, DE&I benefits its employees as well as its business. A recent Sodexo study found there were positive business results for management teams with an equal gender balance. These teams had increased employee engagement, brand awareness, client retention, professional growth, revenue, and gross profit. In 2015, the DE&I team leveraged its business case, resulting in a profit of more than $1.2 billion through its work of supporting more diverse candidate slates and an inclusive client experience.

Sources: Erin Texeira, "US: Sodexho Settles Large Racial Bias Case," CorpWatch, April 27, 2005, https://www.corpwatch.org/article/us-sodexho -settles-large-racial-bias-case; "Sodexo Recognized as a Top Company for Diversity by DiversityInc for 10 Consecutive Years," Cision, May 3, 2018, https://www.prnewswire.com/news-releases/sodexo-recognized-as-a-top -company-for-diversity-by-diversityinc-for-10-consecutive-years-300641999 .html; Shané Schutte, "Sodexo: How Diversity Commitments Have Become Part of Its Culture," RealBusiness, May 26, 2016, https://realbusiness. co.uk/sodexo-how-diversity-commitments-have-become-part-of-its-culture; Wharton School, "Sodexo's Story of Managing Diversity in the Global Context: Leading Diversity@Wharton," YouTube video, 1:01:46, December 4, 2019, https://www.youtube.com/watch?v=EZz8DLqK2°M7yh77.

2

Discipline 2: Explode the Awareness

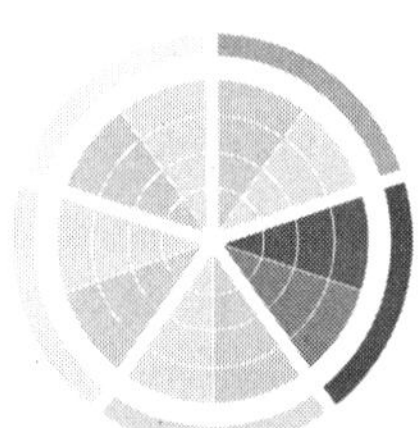

Maturity measure: the extent to which an organization's leaders and employees are aware of and committed to the value of DE&I.

Why be a star when you can make a constellation?

Naomi Murakawa, tweet on Mariame
Kaba's *We Do This 'til We Free Us*

A KILLING, A WHISTLEBLOWER, A CLASS ACTION SUIT. It often takes a cataclysmic event to open our eyes to the injustices all around us. And when it happens, an explosion of awareness shakes society, organizations, and individuals to the core.

In 1994, the bombing of a Jewish cultural center in Buenos Aires that killed eighty-five people exploded the awareness of antisemitism everywhere. In 1998, Matthew Shepard's senseless beating and subsequent death in Wyoming exploded the awareness of homophobia in every corner of US society. The US government's so-called Muslim ban of 2016 exploded the awareness of anti-Muslim hate in the country. In the past few years, George Floyd's murder by a policeman exploded the awareness of systemic racial injustice against those of African descent around the world. Meanwhile, blame for the COVID-19 pandemic and attacks on people of Asian descent on the street exploded the awareness of anti-Asian hate on multiple continents. And the exposure of rape and sexual harassment by powerful players in politics, entertainment, and so many other industries exploded the awareness of the exploitation of women in the workplace around the world. Most recently, during the writing of this book, the death of a young woman, Mahsa Amini, at the hands of Iran's *Gasht-e-Ershad* ("guidance patrols") exploded the awareness that vast numbers of Iranians are enraged about how controlled women are.

These tragedies of hurting people specifically because of some aspect of their identity have been part of humanity's history. From the time of the cavepeople through today, humans have hurt those unlike themselves, in the worst possible ways.

This is the societal background against which we try to do diversity, equity, and inclusion work. While corporations, with their nondiscrimination policies, vigilance against racism and sexual harassment, and philosophy of meritocracy, seek to create safe havens for those who are different within their organizational boundaries, these boundaries are more porous than we would like to admit. People hurting people because of some aspect of their identity has, sadly, always been part of humanity's history. And while it may seem too intense and ubiquitous for corporations to take on, the hard truth is that we don't have a choice—our employees, our consumers, and our communities are being profoundly affected, and they are looking to organizations to use their power to do something.

Spiritual leaders, psychologists, philosophers, addiction counselors, and leadership development experts all concur on where all transformation work must begin: in self-awareness. This brings us to the second discipline of inclusive organizations: the ability and commitment to Explode the Awareness. Until organizations acknowledge that there are inequities within their culture, meaningful change will not happen.

Awareness begins with two key questions: What? and Why?

1. *What* is not working well in the organization? Is it representation in leadership, people feeling like they don't belong, for instance, or higher turnover for underrepresented talent?

2. *Why* is this happening? Is the cause unconscious bias, outright discrimination, stereotyping?

These questions are not easy to ask, and few commit to sticking around to hear the answers.

Self-awareness begins with the realization that there is inequity in the environment and that inequitable results for different groups are evidence that the organization is not living up to its values. Values-driven organizations treat these deficiencies as seriously as they treat financial projection shortfalls.

However, organizations don't have to be deeply values-driven to approach this discipline. When the *what* that is not working well is high turnover and low engagement resulting in low productivity and increased recruitment costs, leaders and managers have a clear business case to mitigate the impact of inequity.

Unfortunately, leaders often have a limited understanding of the intersection of various issues inside and outside the organization that cause the inequities that harm the bottom line. Most aspire to show awareness but do not actually grasp it. They wrongly assume that a democracy or an organization that espouses equal opportunity actually is meritocratic. Awareness requires a willingness to question whether meritocracy is truly happening, and if it isn't, to determine what is preventing it. It requires a basic awareness that some groups experience particular headwinds due to their identities. Just asking the question about whether meritocracy is being achieved and being open to the answer is the start of awareness.

Next comes the question of why they exist, and here we must first go to the outside. Is there equity in society for Blacks, Latinos, Asians, Indigenous people, immigrants, or refugees; for those who are gay, lesbian, or transgender; for those who have disabilities? Using the metrics of education level,[1] income,[2] police treatment,[3] housing opportunities,[4] and incarceration rates,[5] the answers are no, no, no, no, and no. This raises the question of why this is the case. Inclusive organizations exercising the Explode the Awareness discipline begin to invite voices from the outside to help educate them on the answers.

Although organizations and their leaders can't fix all of society's ills, as part of this discipline, they must explode their awareness of how the equity gaps on the inside mirror the ones on the outside. It's not about equal housing opportunity in corporations, but it is about development and advancement opportunities. It's not about higher incarceration rates; it's about higher incidences of disciplinary actions or involuntary turnover. It's not about access to capital via the bank; it's about access to the internal networks of influencers and decision-makers.

Why is this happening in our organizations? Why have we not been aware of this? As organizations mature in this discipline, they begin to acquire greater knowledge to answer these questions via external speakers, celebrating heritage month events, and sponsoring the creation of employee resource groups. All these actions raise the awareness of the sociological realities that are contributing to the inequities both outside and, most relevant to the leaders, inside the organization.

This explosion of the awareness will, in a good way, shake the foundations of the organization as those in power realize—through their collective unconscious biases—that they have been perpetuating the inequitable processes that course through our broader societies.

EXPLODE THE AWARENESS—STRUCTURALLY

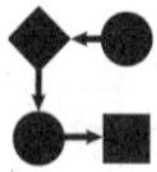

BASIC

At the Basic level, an organization will create initiatives to raise awareness of what DE&I is. It may publish and communicate its unique definition of diversity, equity, and inclusion. Often, that definition is limited to a few dimensions of diversity: race/ethnicity, gender, maybe LGBTQ+ status, or age.

Organizations might focus on celebrating diversity, or diversity days. Statements are put out on International Women's Day or Black History Month, and cultural events may be sponsored, offering up a variety of ethnic foods, from fajitas to sauerkraut, with bands playing salsa or jazz. Sometimes an organization will start establishing early-stage employee resource groups, more likely to be identity-based affinity groups, or encourage employees to join industry-wide identity-based networks such as Women in Tech in the United Kingdom, which is dedicated to women looking to kick-start their career or progress in the technology industry.[6]

PROGRESSING

As organizations move from Basic to Progressing, they will be bolder about their commitment to DE&I. The organization may have a diversity statement on its website, maybe even a full diversity page listing its commitments and accomplishments to date. From a DE&I governance perspective, organizations may establish a DE&I council that sets the overarching DE&I strategy.

Affinity Groups may develop into well-established employee resource groups (ERGs) that offer support for the recruiting and retention of members. ERGs may be called upon to create or broaden corporate visibility and communication efforts. Here is where such groups may add executive sponsors, who often are executives different from the group's identity, to help explode the awareness for both the sponsor and the group. Organizations foster ERGs with names such as COPA (Creating Our Path) for Latino employees at Brown-Forman, Hola Pride (a cross-section of Latino and LGBTQ+ employees), Connected, WOVEN, Greyglers (older Googlers), and UberABLE (Uber employees with disabilities). They act as beacons to continually surface DE&I issues that arise and to not let the organization off the hook.

ADVANCED

In the Advanced stage, organizations speak of diversity in its broadest form, encompassing the full range of human differences and similarities. The DE&I council is fully operational and expanding to other locations. It seeks to have members from the C-suite, who not only can advise on the strategy but also have the leverage to drive initiatives down the organization. Large organizations may establish regional councils that will balance corporate DE&I strategy with regional needs. It is at this stage that the council(s) and/or DE&I team may set diversity and inclusion goals for the organization, attach metrics to those goals, and enlist their executive sponsors in pushing accountability for adhering to these goals.

ERGs broaden from the initial groups focused on gender and race/ethnicity identities to other shared identities and causes. There may now be ERGs for parents, for caregivers, for health and wellness, for immigrants, and for many others. These ERGs are now a strong voice for underrepresented groups and equally strong partners to the various business units and functions. In other words, their goals and initiatives are aligned with the overall business strategy. ERGs are consulted on recruiting efforts, engagement gaps, and ways in which the organization can nurture an environment where those from underrepresented groups can feel a greater sense of belonging, acceptance, and respect.

At this stage, the organization will also start engaging with the community and seeing itself as part of a larger ecosystem. It may institute paid service days when employees can volunteer with an organization of their choosing once a month or once a quarter. Leaders may poll the organization and choose to financially support a few nonprofits that are important to their employees.

LEADING EDGE

In a truly Leading Edge organization, the integration of DE&I as a core value of the organization is complete. The CEO, the C-suite, and the board all have recognized the importance of DE&I to their business and make it a priority in all business decisions. DE&I is woven into the fabric of the organization, and it is understood that leading an inclusive organization is good leadership and good business. A focus on DE&I, goals, metrics, accountability, and progress is a standard part of the organization's annual report—not an afterthought but rather a strategic pillar.

Diversity is defined broadly and is viewed through the lenses of multidimensionality and intersectionality. The organization sees its employees not only as Black, White, Asian, women, men, gay, or straight but also as individuals who might be a Boomer African American General Manager with Adult Kids or an Immigrant Woman Muslim Engineer or an Extroverted Person with a Disability.

ERGs have evolved to business resource groups (BRGs), with charters and missions aligned to the overall business strategy. All efforts must have a business impact, and their focal areas are talent, customer engagement, and social capital, each of these equipped with robust metrics, processes, and outcomes. They, too, take into consideration the multidimensionality of their members' and customers' identities. At this stage, Explode the Awareness also means staying in touch with employees. Asking them for input. Hearing them. Engagement and pulse surveys are conducted, and the results are cut by demographic groups to truly understand whether efforts have had an impact.

As a result, Leading Edge organizations see their employee engagement scores rise and the equity gaps among demographic groups narrow. Employees strongly believe their organization is serious about DE&I and about its investment in them. Leading Edge organizations get recognized for their efforts internally by increased engagement scores, externally through awards and public write-ups, and, more to the point, by customer loyalty, which is always good for business.

EXPLODE THE AWARENESS—BEHAVIORALLY

BASIC

When it comes to behaviors that explode the awareness, most organizations start out not knowing what they don't know. Usually, an entity such as human resources or the DE&I function initiates the awareness building. They understand the importance for the organization, and they believe in congruence between an organization's stated values and its behaviors, so they start leading the charge in trying to bring that awareness to the rest of the organization. Another starting point may be more grassroots—a leader may create a book group on topics related to diversity and inclusion, sparked by recent societal events. The message to the organization is not necessarily about the business benefits, but it's also not about risk management. It is really about the desire to do the right thing. To be respectful of others. To be a good person.

At this stage, leaders are usually not involved in leading DE&I—they leave "doing the right thing" to their HR teams and hope that by providing and funding DE&I training or unconscious bias training, they will have fulfilled their duty.

PROGRESSING

As an organization moves from Basic to Progressing, we see more action and teeth behind that desire to do the right thing. For example, unconscious bias training focuses more on skill building. What are the expected inclusive behaviors and how can we teach them? What must we do differently and how? Leaders at this stage are enlisted to play their part, though initiatives are still mostly run by HR and the DE&I functions. Some leaders may sponsor an identity-based employee resource group, or attend or even speak at internal and external DE&I events. The business benefit of a diverse, inclusive, and equitable workplace has crystallized for them, and they are willing to spread the word.

Many organizations revise their values, not necessarily just by adding diversity, inclusion, or equity to the list but also by adding the expected behaviors they want to see. Employees, too, start to take an interest in hearing their leaders talk about the subject more. Leaders and managers may convene focus groups or listening circles with a variety of employees from different backgrounds to learn about their experiences inside and outside work.

Within three years, one of our clients, an insurance company, evolved from the Basic stage of not even being able to define the business case for DE&I to the Progressing stage of maturity. When it first put together its DEI council, most members did not even know what the term meant or why they had been appointed to the council. Now, three years later, their organizational leaders have gone through Inclusive Leader assessment and coaching, their people managers have taken Managing Inclusion training, and frontline employees have gone through Conscious Inclusion training. Behaviorally, all of this awareness maturity has led to a flurry of events celebrating various forms of diversity. It is noteworthy that training participants rated the impact of their learning very high—generally above a 7.5 out of 10 for learning to lead others inclusively and the ability to support others in doing their best work. Similar high scores were recorded when participants rated their ability to improve business results based on their learning.

ADVANCED

During the Advanced phase, the focus shifts from a DE&I passion to do the right thing to DE&I competency as a business imperative. Leaders are now quite aware of the importance of inclusive leadership and of their role in it. They see it as a critical skill and are willing to learn the how. Many organizations support those leaders by offering inclusive leadership assessments followed by coaching and development.

Rather than focusing on unconscious bias training, there is a shift toward conscious inclusion education. Employees learn to spot potential biases in themselves and others and how to turn the behavior around. They are able and willing to point out nonexclusive behaviors in a constructive manner and to move from bystander to upstander. They embrace the concept of allyship.

In the aftermath of the racial reckoning in 2020, DE&I consultancies small and large consistently reported a tripling in revenues as awareness exploded around the world—more in some regions than in others. Some organizations in the Advanced stage who enlisted this type of consulting help have maintained their commitment and investment since then. They have pressed forward toward learning more sophisticated inclusion skills and have instituted higher levels of accountability.

LEADING EDGE

An organization at the Leading Edge stage of Explode the Awareness has inclusion and equity built into all leadership and employee actions. The CEO and business leaders are fierce in their advocacy for DE&I at all levels. You hear leaders weave the importance of inclusive workplaces into their communications even when they are not specifically discussing DE&I. Business leaders attend internal and external DE&I events, host and speak at inclusion summits, and release personal thoughts on a variety of inclusion topics. Leaders are now authentically modeling inclusion and are seen as "walking the talk," and their employees take note.

Between 2020 and 2022, Korn Ferry assessed and coached more than 2,500 leaders globally on their inclusive leadership. We saw leaders take proactive steps to increase the chances of hearing voices that are often not heard, whether it was due to being voices of the minority or because of personality traits such as introversion. Those leaders sent out agendas prior to their meetings asking participants to come prepared to share their ideas and noting that they wanted to hear from everyone.

The inclusion angle here? It allowed introverts and those who may feel that there is risk in speaking up, due to their minority status, to think through an issue before sharing ideas publicly. It also shows that every person's ideas are valued, not just the ideas of those with more conventional views or who are considered to have more status. From a sexism perspective, we saw managers intervene when a man talked over a woman and to instead ask the woman to continue.

Fayruz encountered a CEO who stated that he wanted his organization, a media-tech company, to become more outcome driven, as opposed to expecting twelve-hour days with "butts in seats." He wanted his employees to have balance in their lives and to attend to their personal lives, rather than boasting about long hours behind the screen or in meetings, and he told a story about his own learning journey and what it meant to become aware of his own behaviors.

On a business trip to Hong Kong, he found himself with a half day of free time and decided to use it to do a little sightseeing. While visiting the Chi Lin Nunnery, he snapped a selfie of himself and sent it home to his family. He wanted to post the picture to his company intranet site with greetings from Hong Kong, but then he paused. Would it look like he was enjoying himself during company time? Would he come across as a slacker?

Then he remembered: that was exactly what he was asking his employees to do, in his effort to be more inclusive. He wanted his employees to have balance, and here was his chance to model it. He posted the picture and received much affirming feedback. It was a learning experience for him on how to model an inclusive life.

CASE STUDY: EXPLODE THE AWARENESS AT HEARST

Hearst is a leading global diversified media, information, and services company that encompasses more than 360 businesses with twenty-four thousand employees around the world. Among its holdings are major cable television networks, local television stations, newspapers, magazines, digital services businesses, medical information and services businesses, and transportation assets.

Hearst has long had a commitment to diversity, equity, and respect for all of its employees. The company had built an informal culture designed to make everyone feel welcome. But not all Hearst employees knew how they could play a role in reflecting the organization's commitment to diversity and inclusion. HR leaders decided they needed help building a formal diversity, equity, and inclusion education program and embedding more inclusive behaviors in the workforce. Korn Ferry started partnering with a dedicated Hearst working group during the summer of 2020, with the goal of having a program in place by year's end. This program, which started with a two-hour session for thirty-five senior executives, has grown rapidly. By the end of 2021, the company had trained more than fifteen thousand employees, created a certified Change Agent model, and established even loftier goals for 2022.

Hearst built this inclusion journey in two phases. The first phase used the concept of Conscious Inclusion, a model designed to increase awareness of biases in the workplace, help people behave in more intentionally inclusive ways, and foster a more inclusive and diverse culture. After training executives, Hearst rolled out four-hour leadership sessions to each division. By the end of the first quarter, more than eight hundred leaders had completed the sessions. The organization had moved from Basic to Progressing and the momentum snowballed from there. In just sixty days, Hearst rolled out Conscious Inclusion eLearning and trained fifteen thousand employees. To reinforce the program and its takeaways and to move to the Advanced stage of Explode the Awareness, the company created a special branding campaign, offered giveaways, including merchandise, and even created a deck of cards with the Conscious Inclusion principles.

In phase 2 of the learning journey, leaders rolled out an expanded version of the training to interested Hearst employees, using a train-the-trainer model. Hearst instituted a Change Agent program that allows both leaders and individual contributors to participate in a six-month deep dive on an inclusion topic. Attendees focus on building a safe environment where everyone feels comfortable sharing their own experiences. They learn how to include others and to make sure that everyone has a voice.

After completing the program, participants graduate and become certified change agents. At the end of the first year of the program, more than one thousand people had become certified change agents. One remarked, "I learned how my actions and behaviors have an impact on others and that conscious inclusion benefits everyone. In my role, I'll be able to apply it by actively seeking out the feedback and opinions of others, including those who may think differently from me, to broaden perspectives and get diversity of thought."

Another attendee said, "Diversity is multifaceted and extends beyond the surface. It's not just about race, gender, and age. To be inclusive and equitable, I must understand who people are, allow them to be authentic, meet their individual needs, learn from them, and make sure they are engaged by management."

According to Hearst's Heather Ragone, Vice President, Development of Talent and Learning, what's most remarkable is that this training isn't a one-and-done. "We're building knowledge over time that will have a cumulative effect on behavior and culture change. We've never offered a program that encouraged participation across the entire company and that created opportunities for individual change."

TRIP UPS

Of course, maturing through the different levels is not a seamless process. There are plenty of bumps along the way. Some of the trip ups we have seen our clients encounter in seeking to Explode the Awareness include going for the easy fix, backlash, and getting stuck in the performative aspect of awareness.

TRIP UP 1: GOING FOR THE EASY FIX

No one ever says they're just going for the easy fix, but there are a few best practices that are so visible and compelling—and, when done right, so effective—that you can be deceived into believing that it's all that's needed. They include employee resource groups, mandated diverse slates, and DE&I training. All have been proved to be significantly powerful practices, but they often are implemented in ineffective ways.

Let's take training. We have seen several clients follow this script in their quick-fix approaches: roll out stand-alone diversity training for everyone, on the assumption that once the organization has been trained on the value of diversity, leaders will be fully enabled to lead more inclusively, managers will have gotten rid of their potential biases, and employees will suddenly all work more productively together.

But even the best of training can only go so far if it's a one-and-done scenario. We have all been there. We participated in an amazing training experience, the facilitator was engaging, the material eye-opening, and we emerged energized and hopeful. If the training is well designed, this type of approach often will create quite a positive buzz. But the next morning we get back to our desks, and within hours our day-to-day catches up with us. A week later we barely remember the experience, let alone practice any of the takeaways.

Training is necessary to provide initial awareness, but it's not enough to explode the awareness. To truly explode that awareness, one must consider the larger picture. It helps to understand an organization's maturity level, what might be getting in the way of employees, and what specific headwinds burden specific groups. That way, an organization can deploy the right training content, aligned to the larger business strategy.

It can never be a one-and-done moment. It's a learning journey that requires addressing both behavioral and structural inclusion. It takes multiple touchpoints, via multiple modalities, activating multiple senses, coupled with varied learning modes—in-person, virtual in-person, large group, small group, eLearning, self-paced—plus tools to practice the learning, such as discussion guides and tool kits. These learning journeys should be designed with the audience in mind, meaning that learning journeys for executives will look different from those for middle managers or for individual contributors. And all learning must be reinforced by new behavior expectations, for which managers, employees, and leaders are held accountable in the performance management system.

When done right, training is a useful tool to accelerate the explosion of awareness. When it is deployed as a check-the-box exercise, however, it will fail to ignite the spark and instead may breed cynicism among employees about the organization's sincerity. For a strategic initiative to be successful, it must be just that—strategic—and not a quick fix.

TRIP UP 2: BACKLASH

Each time there is an explosion of awareness, it triggers backlash that seeks to bury the unearthed truths. The backlash may snuff out the newly raised awareness, or an elevated consciousness may rise from the debris.

Not so long ago, many in the United States believed the nation to be in a postracial era—they had just elected their first Black president, so all was equitable and well. But was it? A decade later, we saw blowback so hard it almost brought racial equity to its knees. It began with an openly xenophobic president who called rallying neo-Nazis "very fine people" and continued with an executive order banning all diversity training in government agencies, nonprofits, and other institutions with federal contracts in order to "combat offensive and anti-American race and sex stereotyping." Meanwhile, incidents of police unjustly killing Black Americans continued on, even in the face of greater public exposure. The misperception that the country was unified was fleeting.

Organizations, too, see backlash when they focus on DE&I. Grumbles that someone only got a promotion because they are a minority, or laments that "now White guys will never have a chance for advancement," have always been there. In the Trump era, they have become louder and less hidden.

Along with the society at large, organizations need to brace themselves for the backlash and stay the course if their focus on inclusion is to be authentic. It will require patience, tenacity, and the belief that inclusive organizations don't have winners and losers on the basis of who they are. Everyone wins in an inclusive organization by being able to bring their whole self to work, by being seen and heard, by having a chance to develop, advance, and do their best work.

TRIP UP 3: GETTING STUCK IN THE PERFORMATIVE ASPECT OF AWARENESS

Movies honoring Black heroes during Black History Month, book readings by Asian American authors during AAPI Heritage Month, tamales and empanadas during Hispanic Heritage Month—it seems that there is always a heritage month to celebrate with dinners, awards, and speeches. Many organizations start their DE&I awareness journeys through these types of cultural events, which are intended to bring us closer to other cultures, foods, dress, and customs.

It's a wonderful idea, really, but in and of itself, quite limiting. Of course, it's important to learn about other cultures, but workplace awareness needs to go further. It needs to include spreading awareness that the playing field is not level for everyone, that some people have to prove themselves harder and for longer before they are considered for advancement, that unconscious (and sometimes conscious) bias exists and that it presents headwinds for underrepresented groups. When we Explode the Awareness, we want to make sure it's *actionable* awareness, awareness that includes next steps that aim to eradicate any diversity-related barriers.

Here's another example. In the spirit of inclusion and honoring the Indigenous people of Canada, British Columbia Golf asked a manufacturer to create a medal with an Indigenous design. According to CEO Kris

Jonasson, the executive steering committee really liked the design and proudly shared the result of its proactive move with the president of the organization, Greg Moody, who is Indigenous. When Moody saw it, he asked, "Who is the artist?" No one knew, but once they asked the manufacturer, it became clear that it had not been someone Indigenous.

We have addressed the classics of DE&I transformation through the inclusive organization disciplines of Manage the Risk and Explode the Awareness. It's now time to get to the heart of the matter: the underrepresented talent.

3

Discipline 3: Maximize the Talent Systems

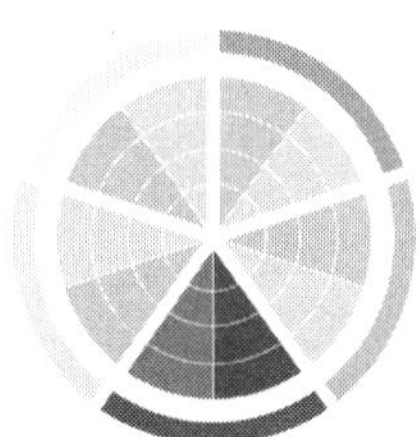

Maturity measure: the extent to which an organization has integrated DE&I into the talent management life cycle.

Develop talent for tomorrow, rather than just hire for yesterday.

Pearl Zhu, author

THE CEO-STUDDED EVENT AT A HILTON BALLROOM brimmed with hundreds of corporate leaders and DE&I practitioners celebrating the best companies for diversity, equity, and inclusion. Amid the glamour of velvet curtains, elaborate floral arrangements, and oversize screens displaying a rotation of corporate brand names, attendees buzzed with anticipation of who this year's winners would be.

By the end of the evening, the CEO of one of the award-winning companies was basking in the recognition. "When it comes to diversity, equity, and inclusion, we get the business case, we get the need for unconscious bias training, we get that we must demand diverse slates of candidates," the CEO declared confidently. Yet, unexpectedly, this was followed with a sigh and a confession: "But for god's sake, after all the time and resources we have devoted to it, we have very little to show for it."

As the stories of the showcased companies were unveiled that evening, the best practices were well known and inspiring: memorable training, connected mentoring, effective sponsorship, business-aligned employee resource groups, over-the-top DE&I summits, and inward-looking C-suite cultural immersions.

These varied award-winning companies had intriguing and energizing design twists to the tried and true, filling participants' heads with big dreams and great expectations of what they might do for their own companies in the coming year.

But would these efforts, in the end, truly make a difference in transforming their organizations into being more diverse, equitable, and inclusive?

The answer for many companies, unfortunately, has been no.

Once we remove all the chest-puffing activity of high-end DE&I programming, what do companies have to show for it?

Have their leaders been more vocal about the business case for DE&I? Yes, they have. Of the companies that participated in Korn Ferry's global DE&I survey, 40% increased their DE&I efforts incrementally while 43% increased it significantly.

Have they actually attracted more diversity? Yes, again. Among the companies that participated in the survey, 43% have seen an increase in attracting and hiring more diverse talent, with North American companies seeing the greatest increase, at 46%.

Have they generated more employee engagement about a more inclusive organization? Mostly. More employees say their companies are committed to DE&I and are excited about that. The survey showed that 30% of companies increased their employee engagement survey scores, with Asia-Pacific companies taking the lead with a 39% increase.[1] However, in the United States, Latinos have lower engagement scores, with 81% believing their "unique perspectives are not valued enough."[2]

And here's where things really run off the rails. People of color remain woefully underrepresented from midlevel to the top. Only 34% of companies in Korn Ferry's global DE&I survey saw an increase of Black talent advancing to senior leadership, even though 45% of companies globally said their DE&I efforts were focused on Black talent or talent of African origins (this rate is even higher in North American companies, at 79%).[3]

Women have made some progress, but only up to a point. While more women took on leadership positions—an increase of 3% among senior vice presidents and of 5% among C-suite executives from 2016 to 2021— they still represent only 29% of senior vice presidents and 24% of C-suite executives.[4] In addition, these numbers obscure the fact that even these modest gains are predominantly made by White women; women of color still lag woefully behind in leadership positions.

People with disabilities continue to have the highest unemployment rate of any demographic group—a 19.1% employment rate in 2021 compared to a 63.7% employment rate among people without disabilities.[5]

In seventy-one countries in 2022, LGBTQ+ people still must remain fully closeted due to various forms of sexual or gender identity and expression being outlawed.[6] Even in countries that supposedly have equal rights for the nonheterosexuals, many are afraid to be out at work.

As we dug deep into our diagnostic and root cause research for our clients, we consistently surfaced performance ratings that were inequitable for people of color as well as for women in many places. No surprise, then, that promotions also were inequitable. And no surprise again, so was turnover. These results matched a research study by Coqual, conducted in October 2021, that found that more than 1 in 5 Black men and more than 1 in 6 Latinos say they were evaluated on different criteria than were their peers. In addition, time-to-promotion was longer for Black men, Latinos, professionals with disabilities, and veterans.[7]

After George Floyd's murder, a lot of conversation emerged about the structural racism and inequities that make it close to impossible for Black Americans, and to an extent other people of color, to live the so-called American Dream. Inequities in education, housing, banking, and yes, policing, while in no way new, became common discussion topics in households, local governments, and municipalities all across the United States. Many thought that there is no way to achieve equity and fairness for African Americans in this current system that was designed for the White man. The solution many clamored for was a dismantling of the current system and a rebuilding of a new, more inclusive one. This is what the calls to defund the police were about. It wasn't aiming to eliminate the police; it was aiming to rethink details and to envision alternatives, such as diverting funds to mental health professionals and social services. In essence, it was a call to reimagine the system.

As we go through this section and describe the different stages of maturity, let's keep in mind that since talent systems are so large, complex, and multiple, not all talent systems will be equally mature at the same time. A company can be more advanced in one talent system than in another. For example, many organizations focus on the recruiting systems first, applying an inclusive lens there, before they think of doing the same for career path, development, or promotion processes.

As we saw earlier, the discipline of Manage the Risk is foundational for the work of DE&I. We have to obey laws and guard against the most serious offenses. And when we looked at Explode the Awareness, we saw that this discipline is about the inspiration of DE&I versus the kick in the butt of compliance. While risk management creates guardrails, awareness puts wind in our sails. But neither fear of litigation nor inspiration is enough to bring the transformational change in that still most vexing DE&I issue: equitably advancing unrepresented talent to the pinnacle of their abilities.

Just like the larger society, organizations have to look at their structures and determine whether they have the systems in place to allow all employees to develop and advance. And as is the case in the larger society, if the answer is no, there now is call to dismantle and disrupt those old systems and start anew.

Here, we must turn to the very machinery that manages how people are hired, onboarded, evaluated, coached, developed, promoted, and identified for bigger and better things. We must Maximize the Talent Systems. If these systems are not fully harnessed to address DE&I, results will fall short. Sometimes, talent processes are established for a particular—and understandable—reason, and their limitations and potential for exclusion only become clear years, sometimes decades later. For example, the desire of many organizations to hire the best and the brightest has, for a long time, limited recruitment to where these "best and brightest" were deemed to be found—in the Ivy League universities. The realization that this practice leaves a lot of "best and brightest" from a diverse pool of candidates by the wayside is relatively recent. The very unconscious biases we all have as individuals, over generations, have been codified systematically into policies, procedures, and criteria checklists by teams of individuals full of unconscious biases. And in this era of proliferating artificial intelligence, this codification of biases is being embedded into algorithms that can cause even greater far-reaching damage.

While talent integration cries out for structural inclusion, it also fully requires behavioral inclusion; otherwise, it all falls apart. The inclusive structures that are designed to remove unintended biases must be used by managers and leaders in their roles as talent optimizers.

Take, for example, self-driving cars, or autonomous vehicles as they are called. There will be an estimated 33 million of them on the road by 2040, and while there is general debate about their safety, one fact has already been established: the algorithms that guide them are biased. In 2021, a report of the Law Commission of England and Wales and the Scottish Law Commission found that autonomous vehicles may "struggle to recognize dark-skinned faces in the dark." In addition, the algorithm may not recognize the movements of a wheelchair, thus putting wheelchair users in danger.[8] These cars clearly are designed for the "Reference Man," which we will discuss, and not for those who deviate from this persona.

Another example is Amazon's now abandoned hiring tool, which used artificial intelligence to choose the most desirable job candidates from a pool of résumés. A great idea in theory—until it became obvious that the tool was sexist. Its ratings were not in fact gender neutral but reflected the biases of the past. The algorithm was programmed to seek candidates based on résumés of those who had been successful in the previous ten years. And who got filtered into the viable sourcing pool in a tech industry not traditionally known for its gender diversity? It was not women. Furthermore, while the tool was clearly programmed to select men, it was not just any man. In fact, it was a very specific man.

MEET THE REFERENCE MAN

This person, or rather this concept, has influenced your life in more ways than you can possibly imagine. First introduced in 1975, the Reference Man concept was initially devised to simplify calculations of radiation exposure, although it went on to be used consistently in research models for nutrition, pharmacology, population, and toxicology. Intended to personify all of humanity, the Reference Man was in fact defined in very specific terms: he was a twenty-five- to thirty-year-old male, weighing 154 pounds (70 kilos), standing 5 feet 6 inches (1.7 meters) tall, Caucasian, with a Western European or North American lifestyle.[9]

The world has been built for the Reference Man. From voice recognition devices to health-monitoring apps to crash-test dummies—if you don't fit the specifications of the Reference Man, many products and services may not work for you. For instance, the "standard" N95 mask doesn't actually protect smaller women because the masks are too loose-fitting.

The same is true for talent systems, which is why it's vital to challenge the Reference Man through this third discipline of Maximize the Talent Systems. Even as managers emerge from unconscious bias training with a heightened awareness of the ways in which they have excluded others through microaggressions, their new, more equitable thinking can get hijacked by unconsciously biased talent systems. Like a car with a badly aligned axle, these talent systems subtly keep pulling them away from the lane of equity and toward the lane that reinforces disparities in how people are evaluated, selected, and rewarded. But there is an antidote.

COUNTERING THE REFERENCE MAN VIA INCLUSIVE DESIGN FOR TALENT SYSTEMS

Rather than design for the Reference Man and then scrambling to retrofit a product—or a process—to fit more people, why not apply inclusive design principles to create inclusive processes from the onset? Inclusive design principles have been applied to everyday products and services to make them more accessible for users with physical abilities. Those same design principles can also be applied within organizations to create talent systems that are inclusive of all human differences. There are four core principles of inclusive design for talent systems.

1. **Define equality.** The concept of equality differs from organization to organization, so inclusive design journeys should begin with an explicit, self-reflective exploration and declaration of what kind of equality the organization stands for and how it manifests itself in talent management practices and processes.

2. **Unearth inequities.** From there, unearth the inequities that stand in the way of equality. Discover the "faults in the default." This can be achieved by examining the data and by exploring the experiences of different talent groups.

3. **Learn from diversity.** The only way to break away from the Reference Man and ensure that inequities are not perpetuated is to modify or create systems using input from all users—from the mainstream to the overlooked. Creators of talent processes must be curious about people's vast differences and consider the needs, wants, and aspirations of even the most excluded user.

4. **Solve for one, benefit all.** Science and experience are showing us—and features such as closed captioning prove—that if we can make something work for the exception, then we will end up with a better design for all. Similar successes can be achieved in talent system designs if we specifically address the needs of overlooked users—those whose experiences, mindsets, and visibility are in the minority.

The disciplines of Manage the Risk and Explode the Awareness prepare organizations to fully challenge their systems and how they may be reinforcing iniquities. To Maximize the Talent Systems, then, the entire enterprise housing the talent systems must be questioned and audited, and where there is systemic inequity being reinforced, it must be dismantled and redesigned.

MAXIMIZE THE TALENT SYSTEMS—STRUCTURALLY

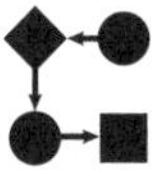

BASIC

The structural component of this discipline is arguably the most important and least visible. Organizations at the Basic level see a focus on DE&I as a stand-alone initiative. There is no integration of DE&I into HR and talent processes. HR operates separately from the DE&I function. It may endorse and fund their initiatives, but HR professionals are not enabled or encouraged to apply an inclusive lens when looking at the design of talent management processes.

WHAT IF THE REFERENCE MAN WERE AN ASIAN AMERICAN WOMAN?

Karen Huang

The Reference Man's world is frequently a poor fit for me, an Asian American woman. In a world designed for him, I not only must expend thought, energy, and money that could be put to better use, but I also don't receive the same opportunities as he.

If Asian American women were to be the new Reference Man, normality, attractiveness, desirability, and prestige would look different. Hooded mono eyelids, dark brown eyes, and black hair would be the standards of attractiveness. People closer to five feet tall would be the ones perceived as better educated and better employed, not the taller people, as is currently the case. People wouldn't subject themselves to costly and painful leg-lengthening or eyelid surgery, since people with our features would be presumed to have power, authority, and leadership.

A new Reference Man would set the stage for a different type of workplace. We wouldn't need to choose between sitting lower than everyone else so our feet touch the floor versus sitting eye level with others at the cost of uncomfortable dangling legs. We wouldn't need to pile on sweaters to keep from shivering, and Zoom cameras would be automatically calibrated to our skin tone.

In addition, talent systems would build partnerships with many Asian American associations and organizations, networks of East Asians could lead to talent pipelines full of East Asians, and leadership perceptions might focus more on competence than on expressed confidence. Leadership would be defined by gracious assertiveness, humility, and deference to expertise rather than voluble candor. Product testing, focus groups, market research, and artificial intelligence learning would focus on populations of Asian American women. Workplace teams and decision-making groups would always include at least one Asian American woman, and discussions would be structured so that all participants listened patiently, didn't interrupt, and had equal opportunities to provide input, which would then receive equitable consideration.

Until the traditional Reference Man is changed, perceptions of leadership will continue to be associated with his features: white skin color, squared face, pronounced eyebrows, and strong jawline. And having Reference Man features will continue to be associated with

(continued)

higher salaries because people perceive leadership in people with those physical features.

When managers decide who will best handle a leadership opportunity, or whom to promote into leadership, they often lean toward the Reference Man partly because he "looks and acts the part," independent of his actual abilities.

By broadening the Reference Man to a diverse range of new Reference People, we will be more likely to wonder, "Who is she and why shouldn't she be in charge?"

Sources: Ariana Eunjung Cha, "Roots of Napoleon Complex May Be Justified: Study Finds Short Men Get Short End of Stick in Life," *Washington Post*, March 9, 2016, https://www.washingtonpost.com/news/to-your-health/wp/2016/03/08/study-being-a-short-man-or-overweight-woman-linked-to-lower-life-chances; Tom Brada, "Leg-Lengthening: The People Having Surgery to Be a Bit Taller," BBC News, December 5, 2020, https://www.bbc.com/news/world-55146906; "How Multiethnic Networking Could Propel More East Asians into US C-Suites," MIT Sloan School of Management, March 28, 2022, https://mitsloan.mit.edu/ideas-made-to-matter/how-multiethnic-networking-could-propel-more-east-asians-us-c-suites; Tomas Chamorro-Premuzic, "Why Do So Many Incompetent Men Become Leaders?," *Harvard Business Review*, August 22, 2013, https://hbr.org/2013/08/why-do-so-many-incompetent-men; "The Look of Leadership," Association for Psychological Science, December 15, 2015, https://www.psychologicalscience.org/blog/the-look-of-leadership.html; Daniel E. Re and Nicholas O. Rule, "The Face of Leadership: How CEOs' Facial Appearance Predicts Business Success," *The Inquisitive Mind* 7, no. 34 (2017), https://www.in-mind.org/article/the-face-of-leadership-how-ceos-facial-appearance-predicts-business-success.

Many organizations focus on the recruiting systems first, applying an inclusive approach there before they think of doing the same for career pathing, development, and promotion processes.

Some basic inclusive recruiting initiatives include recruiting from a broader range of schools to include those with more diverse student bodies; no longer recruiting via current employee referrals, since employees tend to recommend people like themselves; and requiring a diverse slate for lower-level positions. However, some organizations don't actually set these diverse recruits up for success once they are in the door. This is why many see high attrition numbers and a revolving door phenomenon. Once they are hired, a never-ending chorus of "That's not how we do things here" grinds down these entrants, because they don't get the same attention, advice, and assistance as recruits from the traditional schools or backgrounds, who have established support systems in place.

PROGRESSING

As organizations progress on their journey, the realization settles in that more of their talent processes will need to be reviewed for inclusion. Many organizations at this stage embark on a full inclusive talent management audit, and the findings are often overwhelming. The realization that most if not all processes were set up to favor the traditional employee, the Reference Man, often leaves organizations paralyzed about what to do next. HR departments are rarely funded to overhaul all processes; there are not enough resources in place to take on such a large undertaking.

And so, small tweaks are made, such as requiring a diverse interview panel in addition to a diverse candidate pool, or the creation of behavioral-based interview guides to counteract similarity bias in the decision-making. But the larger, more complicated-seeming changes fall by the wayside. Creating a competency-based performance management system that informs promotions at all levels with accountability woven in? Too much change for the organization to swallow. Establishing a succession planning process? Too much of an uphill battle when it comes to securing executive support. So, while at the Progressing stage HR and DE&I functions may *know* that their talent processes need revamping to become more inclusive, they often have neither the funding, the resources, nor the executive support to accomplish this.

ADVANCED

At the Advanced stage, DE&I initiatives become better resourced and true change starts to happen. Inclusion becomes a lens through which all talent management processes are viewed. With more funding, clear career paths are laid out for all levels and jobs, development is available to all to help them move along these paths, and feedback loops are built into everyone's performance management to facilitate continuous improvement.

The organization starts to put in place DE&I metrics that measure the success of its talent processes. It may conduct a talent flow analysis, which tracks talent movements from hiring to promotions to exits by demographic group and across levels to truly understand the drivers of lower representation for certain groups. While the talent management audit looks at the processes and systems, this talent flow analysis shows the direct outcome in numbers. The organization may also dig into the varying employee perceptions of certain processes to understand the *why* behind the talent flow data.

This is the stage when organizations begin orienting themselves outward. They start and deepen partnerships with professional organizations that provide pools of underrepresented talent as well as peer networking and career development, such as the National Black MBA Association, the Association of Hispanic Professionals, and women's career networking and professional associations. They also join LinkedIn groups and post new jobs on a variety of job boards frequented by underrepresented groups, such as iHispano, Recruit Disability, or the Black Career Network, all with the goal to cast a wider net and truly attract the best and the brightest. We have seen large employers develop and launch "recruiting machines" at career fairs, landing dozens, if not hundreds, of new hires from underrepresented groups.

LEADING EDGE

An organization that moves to the aspirational Leading Edge stage will be a place where HR and DE&I are fully integrated and work in true partnership with the full support of the CEO and the leadership team. The DE&I strategy is no longer separate from the talent strategy but instead is fully integrated. Here, any recruiting strategy or succession management program is inclusive by design. Robust talent analytics are applied to inform these strategies, which include not just who gets promoted to what levels but also how long it takes the various groups to get there. Time-to-promotion is as much a retention issue as promotion itself. The most impactful part at this stage is that leaders at all levels are held accountable for applying these inclusive processes and that this accountability is reflected in their own performance rating as well as possibly in their compensation.

Here's an example. When the CEO of a large global insurance company wanted to make the recruiting process more inclusive, he started with the usual steps: a diverse candidate slate, a diverse interview panel, and behavioral-based interview questions. Once the interview panel had interviewed a candidate, they would email in their thoughts and decisions. Oddly, despite the steps taken, more traditional candidates still made the final cut and were selected. So the CEO made a small but meaningful change to the process. Instead of allowing interview panel members to email in their decisions, he mandated that the panel come together one last time and that each member should state out loud their vote and the reasons for it. It quickly became clear that despite the perceived rigor in the process, the last step had still been fraught with bias. For instance, comments like someone being a "better fit" abounded.

Why is this alarming? "Fit" has traditionally been based on who has been in an organization before, reinforcing the norm instead of opening the door for those who have not been there before.

Once the final meetings became part of the process and some of the comments around "fit" were said aloud and heard, the inherent biases became more obvious even to the individuals voicing them. Once they realized what was happening, these "decision meetings" were baked into the process and the organization began seeing a large uptick in the hiring of members from underrepresented groups.

MAXIMIZE THE TALENT SYSTEMS—BEHAVIORALLY

BASIC

At a Basic level of behavioral inclusion, the HR and DE&I departments of an organization begin to address the most obvious—yet still quite common—gaps.

For example, they catch, address, and course correct problematic manager behaviors. Problematic behaviors might include giving feedback with stereotypical tropes, such as commenting on the "emotional" nature of one female's direct report or opining that members of certain racial or ethnic groups are "undisciplined." Often when we surface this as an issue to watch for, we are met with skepticism by companies at this stage of maturity. We share with them data, such as from a Textio research report on language biases in the workplace, which shows that the quality of feedback women, Black employees, Latino employees, and older employees get is far inferior to that received by men and White employees.[10] The former groups tend to receive much more personality-based feedback, which is not actionable. Women, for example, are described as "opinionated" seven times more often than men, and as "abrasive" eleven times

ARE RÉSUMÉS NEEDED ANYMORE?

It's already well known that White, male, Anglo-Saxon, and Protestant names are 50% more likely to get a call back from recruiters than someone considered "foreign" or female due to their name. This is despite having identical skills and professional experiences.

So a Basic structural inclusion response is to use blind résumés, where a person's name or anything that can identify them by gender or ethnicity is removed. This is intended to ensure that decisions to move a candidate forward are based solely on skills and capabilities.

But an emerging Leading Edge move is to do away with résumés altogether. This is because women candidates and those from ethnic backgrounds may not have the experiences that are traditionally required. You can take out the name, but there's still something that the recruiter is always looking for—a particular degree (even though women are more likely to earn degrees than men) or five years' experience doing, for example, data analysis. And because of how women or ethnic minorities may be tracked in school and worked into dead-end jobs, they never get it, and they never will. So the résumé chronology may still be a barrier. Even as traditional candidates tend to be given a leg up in accessing educational and professional opportunities and collecting necessary experiences, underrepresented groups' résumés do not go far, despite a comparable skill level.

So, if no résumés, then what? Some companies have moved to evaluating candidates' skills rather than experience as an initial determiner. There's a tech organization, for instance, that asks clients what skills they require and then creates a skills test. They put the job on the website, but when people "apply," they don't send their résumé. Instead, they are assigned a number and take the skills test. The top scorers on the test are then asked to submit their résumé and the client receives the test results, demonstrating the candidates' skills, before showing the résumés. This method allows recruiters to focus on applicants' skills and abilities rather than getting bogged down by education and experience or falling into the bias of selecting candidates with certain demographic characteristics. Further, using a skills assessment provides recruiters with a broader and more diverse candidate pool.

(continued)

ARE RÉSUMÉS NEEDED ANYMORE?

(continued)

Will the Leading Edge practice become pervasive? We doubt it, since résumés are so entrenched in the talent acquisition processes. Further, the process is not always effective, as a study of hiring managers showed that they feel they can still tell applicants' gender based on other cues, returning to the problem of bias. But given how résumés have served to exclude so many, the companies willing to experiment with this innovation may truly be on to an approach that could break the back of résumé evaluation inequities.

> *Sources:* Peter Cappelli, "Your Approach to Hiring Is All Wrong," *Harvard Business Review,* May–June 2019, https://hbr.org/2019/05/your-approach-to-hiring-is-all-wrong; Stefanie K. Johnson and Jessica F. Kirk, "Research: To Reduce Gender Bias, Anonymize Job Applications," *Harvard Business Review,* March 5, 2020, https://hbr.org/2020/03/research-to-reduce-gender-bias-anonymize-job-applications; "How One Company Increased Diversity in Its IT Function," Korn Ferry, https://www.kornferry.com/insights/featured-topics/diversity-equity-inclusion/how-company-increased-diversity-in-it-function; Meraiah Foley and Sue Williamson, "Does Anonymising Job Applications Reduce Gender Bias? Understanding Managers' Perspectives," *Gender in Management* 33, no. 8: 623–635.

---

more often than men. By contrast, men are three times more likely to be described as "confident" and almost four times more likely to be described as "ambitious." To be at the Basic level, organizations must call this out and prevent any further propagation of this kind of bias.

Another typical instance of basic inclusionary behavior is a dawning realization that the recruiting team is not sourcing enough diversity in their talent pools because they keep going to the same not very diverse sourcing pools to which they have always gone. They also begin to change their recruiting materials and employee value proposition to make their company attractive to different groups of professionals and to workers who have different priorities for what they are looking for in an employer.

PROGRESSING

As the organization progresses in this discipline, HR and DE&I functions start working together to enable their leaders to make more inclusive talent decisions. They educate leaders on how to create a succession management plan for themselves and others. They enlist leaders in sponsoring development plans for underrepresented groups and introducing inclusive feedback discussions. On their part, leaders are becoming more adept at managing their teams inclusively, with the goal of ensuring that each employee experiences the environment for development and advancement equitably. Examples of how they do this include spending more time with employees and being curious about the lived experiences that have provided them with unique ways of seeing the world and added value to the work they do.

ADVANCED

At the Advanced stage of Maximize the Talent Systems, not just HR and DE&I but also their senior leaders work hard to enable their middle managers to make equitable talent decisions and to lead their teams more inclusively, specifically with regard to development, advancement, and promotions. They do this by being more cross-culturally insightful about unique organizational barriers their talent may face because of unconscious or conscious biases all around them, and then taking action to remove those barriers. They do so by standing up for employees when they are being treated unfairly or by guiding them on how to navigate a talent system with which they are unfamiliar. In fact, at this stage middle managers are not just enabled to make more inclusive talent decisions but are expected to do so and are held accountable for creating a diverse pipeline for the next level up.

LEADING EDGE

Organizations that are truly Leading Edge in this area exhibit inclusive behaviors throughout the entire talent management life cycle. Hiring managers hold one another accountable for their decisions and intervene when they believe biased decisions are being made. Team managers regularly sit down with each of their employees to determine their passions and goals and to ensure that they have opportunities to move in their desired directions. Others will make sure their ready-now employees have exposure to their next-level leaders—with "ready-now" being judged by performance and potential, not by fit. In addition, in Leading Edge organizations, leaders, managers, and employees display inclusion skills and leverage their diversity to accelerate team performance and improve decision-making, all the while developing all their talent to be able to contribute to the best of their abilities.

TRIP UPS

In our work helping to assess organizations' DE&I stage, we have discovered that Maximize the Talent Systems plays an outsize role in whether an organization can legitimately move forward on its DE&I journey. Some of the trip ups that get in the way of success in this area include focusing on representation and not on the pipeline, assuming the root cause of a DE&I gap is a DE&I issue, and forgetting about accountability.

TRIP UP 1: FOCUSING ON REPRESENTATION AND NOT ON THE PIPELINE

The number one lack-of-diversity fix that nearly all parties go after is to seek to recruit underrepresented talent. There's a logic to this, given that the absence of diversity is obvious to all and pressure is likely coming from all sides to fix the problem fast and in a very visible way.

But this solution has not worked out at all. One highly visible failure is the National Football League's Rooney Rule, which has been emulated by many corporations, since it seemed to make so much sense. This rule mandates that football teams look at a diverse slate of candidates outside the organization before hiring for any coaching or front office positions.[11] But for all its popularity, at the time of the 2022 Superbowl, nearly twenty years after adoption of the rule, there were only *three* non-White head coaches in the NFL, among thirty-two teams.[12] What?

Diverse slates are simply not enough when exclusionary interviewing protocols and biased hiring processes keep kicking underrepresented talent out of the running. Structural interventions need to be in place to avoid pro forma interviews with candidates that managers never intended to hire in the first place. These include diverse interview panels and setting goals for progress in actual hiring.

Another important consideration is the number of diverse candidates being interviewed. Research conducted by *Harvard Business Review* revealed that where the finalist pool consisted of only one woman or one person of color, the hiring body tended to select the status quo (male or White) candidate. If, however, the finalist pool had at least two women or two people of color, the chances for a woman to be hired increased almost eighty times. For a person of color, the chances increased 193 times.[13] It's a good reminder that adding one token candidate from an underrepresented group won't impact representation in a meaningful way.

But even without these structural talent recruitment issues, hiring for diversity is still no more than a temporary solution to the ongoing representation problem. Diverse talent—whether brought in early in their careers or at the top of their game—leave organizations at a higher rate than talent from the majority groups due in large part to dissatisfaction with their opportunities for advancement.

Where the diversity issue is going to be resolved is in developing a sustainable pipeline of underrepresented talent that allows for advancement to leadership. If an organization can put more effort into developing and advancing the talent pool already inside the organization by removing all the inequitable internal barriers, then they don't have to worry so much about hiring for diversity.

TRIP UP 2: ASSUMING THE ROOT CAUSE OF A DE&I GAP IS A DE&I ISSUE

We worked with a technology consulting firm that wanted to get to the root cause of its high attrition among midlevel female consultants. The organization was sure it was the sixty-plus-hour workweeks and the constant travel that caused the retention issue. They wondered how they could offer their women employees the work–life balance they thought they required. They wanted to find the sweet spot between engaging and retaining them on the one hand and still providing meaningful advancement opportunities for them on the other—without losing a beat in meeting their clients' needs.

However, it turned out that the lack of work–life balance was not the main retention issue among women (although we learned that both men and women craved more flexibility). First, the issue was less about balance and more about flexibility. By nature of who the organization was as a top-notch consultancy, both the women and the men it attracted were hard-charging individuals who came because of, and not despite, the intensity of the work. Second, the need for flexibility was not just a women's issue. Nearly as many men clamored for it as well.

A comprehensive diagnostic revealed that the true root cause of the exodus was something more basic: poor people managers. In the company, professionals who excelled technically were rewarded with promotions that included managerial responsibilities—responsibilities they neither wanted nor were trained for. Talent development systems

THE ENCORE LEGACY TRACK: DISRUPTING ASSUMPTIONS ABOUT THE OLDER WORKER

Andrés Tapia and Annamarya Scaccia

Entry level. Middle management. Senior leadership. Retirement.

The traditional career life cycle suggests that after you reach your peak, it's all downhill from there. You're left counting down the days until you can hand in your keys, collect your things, and enjoy a carefree retirement. Midweek brunches, park time with the grand-kids, random trips across the world.

But the assumptions behind that trajectory face profound challenges as people live much longer, which defies the notion of vitality after a certain age. After all, in 1950, people's life expectancy was six-ty-seven, just two years above the official retirement age at the time. Today, life expectancy in developed economies is 78.6 years, accord-ing to data from the US Centers for Disease Control and Prevention. This means at least ten more years of expenses, lattes, and vacations.

There is more work and intellectual capacity left in a greater number of people in their sixties, but they also have to make sure they don't outlive their money.

For this reason, an increasing number of older professionals have started to reenter the workforce, while others have chosen to stay in their positions past the traditional notice of "retirement age." In fact, the number of older workers reached a record high in 2020, with 10.6 million people sixty-five and older in the workforce, according to federal labor statistics. This trend is expected to increase from 2020 to 2030, with an estimated 96.5% increase in the number of people seventy-five years and older in the US workforce.

This runs counter to the way the traditional career path has been framed. The underlying—and prevailing—assumption is that vitality slumps after a professional's peak. This is one of the reasons companies are struggling with highly successful older leaders who

(continued)

are having a hard time letting go, because of a need to survive and thrive. This can create a bottleneck in their pipeline, leaving midlevel millennial and Gen Z talent with no place to go other than holding on to their job. From a diversity perspective, this also exacerbates the chronic lack of diversity in senior ranks, because the greater numbers of women; racial, ethnic, and out LGBTQ+ people; and people with disabilities sit within these younger generations.

To solve this dilemma of wanting to continue to value and retain older workers while also creating new opportunities for the next generation, what if we rethought the traditional career path life cycle? In this case, what if we create a whole new career management framework before retirement?

Let's call this pre-retirement career phase a "legacy track." It would create a career development path that more directly values and leverages the contributions of older workers while also opening up leadership roles to high-potential talent coming up behind them.

Although organizations would need to tailor the legacy track to their needs, the phase would have some standard elements across companies and industries. For example, legacy track employees would no longer work in a line management capacity but would provide coaching, support, and guidance to appointed successors. They would have fewer day-to-day, operational responsibilities but instead would be assigned to special projects or to new market sectors, playing a role in mentoring, sponsoring, and developing entry-level and midlevel employees.

These ideas quickly raise the implication of lower compensation, which is fair. But what if there were a trade-off? Although base pay might stay the same, there may be less short-term and long-term bonus opportunities and much more paid free time. Those in the legacy track might work reduced hours, say nine months out of a year, or a pattern of three months on, three months off.

Of course, many may resist. For example, those already at the top of the house may be too entrenched and too conditioned to traditional power structure mentalities and may not have the ability to adapt. Given their current positions, these individuals may not be able to change their mindsets so readily. Care would need to be taken to align candidates for this track with a clear understanding of and expectation for the role, to ensure that the

(continued)

THE ENCORE LEGACY TRACK: DISRUPTING ASSUMPTIONS ABOUT THE OLDER WORKER

(continued)

opportunity is seen as practical and beneficial for the incumbent, the manager, the successors, and the organization.

Companies, then, would need to start their legacy track programs now, at the midcareer stage, when executives still climbing the corporate ladder may be more prepared, in terms of mindset, to welcome, down the road, a pre-retirement legacy role focused on influence and guidance. This may then help more rapidly shift corporate cultures to embrace this role rather than seeing it as a compromise that relegates older workers to out-to-pasture roles.

Writer Diane Eastabrook reports that furniture maker Herman Miller has a FlexRetirement Program, which lets workers over sixty, with at least five years' experience, phase into retirement over a six-month to two-year period. She writes, "The employees work reduced hours with reduced compensation. Herman Miller then uses the cost savings to invest in new employees or technology. 'We let [the FlexRetirement workers] figure out what their hours ought to be and when their end date is going to be,' says Kim Chaumillon, Herman Miller's vice president of culture and engagement. So far, more than 200 employees have taken part in FlexRetirement."

Let's not just give retirees a gold watch and away they go. Instead, let's create a track around their legacy and have them continue to thrive in new ways.

Sources: Julie Jason, "Still Working After Age 65 and Thinking of Moving?," *Forbes*, November 14, 2021, https://www.forbes.com/sites/juliejason/2021/11/14/still-working-after-age-65-and—thinking-of-moving/?sh=5da991d25402; Patrick Coate, "Latest Trends in Worker Demographics," NCCI Research Brief, March 2021, https://www.ncci.com/Articles/Documents/Insights-LatestTrendsWorkerDemo.pdf; "Number of People 75 and Older in the Labor Force Is Expected to Grow 96.5 Percent by 2030," US Bureau of Labor Statistics, November 4, 2021, https://www.bls.gov/opub/ted/2021/number-of-people-75-and-older-in-the-labor-force-is-expected-to-grow-96–5-percent-by-2030.htm; Diane Eastabrook, "Ageism in the Workplace: Companies Breaking the Mold," Next Avenue, February 26, 2021, https://www.nextavenue.org/ageism-in-the-workplace-companies-breaking-the-mold. Note: The labor force is expected to increase by 8.9 million, or 5.5%, from 2020 to 2030. The labor force of people ages sixteen to twenty-four is projected to shrink by 7.5% from 2020 to 2030. Among people age seventy-five years and older, the labor force is expected to grow by 96.5% over the next decade.

were nearly nonexistent, and there were no tools or processes to enable managers to manage their people well.

While this problem affected both men and women, it disproportionally affected women because of the lack of informal systems working for them. With technology still a traditionally male-dominated field, women either were being shut out of the "boys' club" or were being asked to adapt to a more male-influenced culture. Combine this with the lack of effective people managers, who didn't have the tools to coach their people into optimal performance and career growth and who were disconnected from the intricacies of gender inequity dynamics, and it's no wonder women were leaving at a higher rate.

The firm implemented management and leadership training, but-tressed with specific DE&I training on gender-related unconscious biases. In addition, measurable accountabilities for effective people management were put in place. Finally, policies that allowed for greater work–life flexibility were enacted, as an important—but now under-stood as secondary—line of defense, to increase the retention of both women and men.

The learning: sometimes we need to look for the root causes of a symptom in a much different place than anticipated.

TRIP UP 3: FORGETTING ABOUT ACCOUNTABILITY

Say you have all your talent systems scrubbed for unconscious bias. You have built an inclusive recruiting strategy. Your development, succession planning, and promotion processes take the diversity of your talent into consideration. And let's add that your managers have been trained in these inclusive processes and have learned about unconscious biases as part of their manager training. Your leaders have made it clear that a focus on diversity and inclusion is important to them.

And yet, at the end of four years, there is not much progress to show for all this effort. What's missing?

If you want to effect true behavior change in your managers, you can't forget about *accountability*. Just as leaders and managers are held accountable for their sales targets, they also need to be held accountable for any metrics and goals set for DE&I. Without goals and accountability, you are banking on the personal goodwill of managers to institutionalize inclusion. On the other hand, holding managers accountable signals that you mean business. (For more detailed information on how to set your organizational metrics, see chapter 6, "How Do We Know It Works?")

In the next chapter, we will discuss how organizations can leverage their DE&I efforts to master the logistics of managing the bottom line.

4

Discipline 4: Master the Logistics

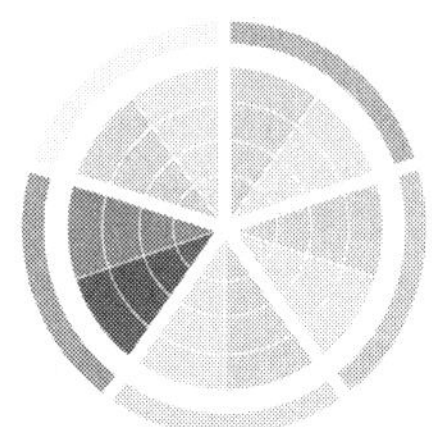

Maturity measure: the extent to which DE&I is integrated with all business operations.

Without logistics the world stops.

Dave Waters, Senior European Supply
Chain Manager at STERIS Corporation

SIX MONTHS INTO THE COVID-19 PANDEMIC, GERMANY-BASED medical technology company Siemens Healthineers needed to ship 15 million COVID-19 rapid antigen tests from China to France so that schools there could reopen with their mandated regimen of weekly COVID-19 testing.

Typically, this wouldn't be a challenge, but the nearly worldwide shutdown in commercial airline travel meant there were no passenger planes available to retrieve the tests from Shanghai and bring them to France. Siemens Healthineers managed to source an armada of twelve empty cargo planes, but as the planes were about to take off from Europe, they all were grounded.

The dearth of commercial planes and an upcoming holiday in China led Shanghai airport authorities to temporarily reduce staff on the ground and in all the handling areas that would be needed to load the massive number of test kits into the planes for delivery to France. Airport authorities subsequently canceled landing permissions for hundreds of incoming cargo flights, including those for the Siemens Healthineers planes. Further complicating the situation, the tests and approved customs papers were already on their way from the manufacturing labs to the Shanghai airport—where the reduced workforce would not be able to receive them.

The Siemens Healthineers team faced an urgent dilemma. "We needed to find a way to reinstate the landing slots. There was no other solution—and we only had two days to do it," says Joerg Berner, CFO of Siemens Healthineers Point of Care Diagnostics.

Here's where Siemens Healthineers harnessed the power of colleagues' collective experiences and expertise to kick problem-solving into high gear. The multinational team quickly got on a crisis call to brainstorm the various contacts each had who could possibly help with reinstating the landing slots, calling back workers, and changing flight plans to get the COVID-19 tests to France on time. They also troubleshot all the potential logistical challenges if the permissions issues were resolved—with no guarantee they were going to be.

The Siemens Healthineers team in China worked hard to get in contact with federal, city, and airport authorities to prepare the ground for receiving the potentially reinstated flights and to secure workers and resources required for customs processing and ground logistics. Given that the antigen tests were intended for use as part of a public health measure to reopen schools in France, crisis team members reached out to the French minister of health and asked for support with efforts in China. Simultaneously, they also called contacts at the German Ministry for Foreign Affairs and at the British embassy in Washington, DC, since half of the cargo fleet was from British Airways, and asked the British government to work with officials in China.

Together, the Siemens Healthineers team leveraged connections from all over the globe, working in cross-culturally competent ways to keep all team members informed about progress, and to use that progress to increase momentum toward their goal. Eventually, they were successful. Landing permissions for Siemens Healthineers' twelve flights were reinstated.

But this was only the first step. Myriad hurdles remained to actually pull off full delivery of the tests.

Even before the Siemens Healthineers crisis team was able to resecure landing permissions, the airlines required confirmation that the company still needed the planes, so that crews could be reserved. It was a go/no-go decision. At stake was a seven-digit airline cost that Siemens Healthineers would have to pay regardless of whether they were able to resolve the other logistical challenges to fill the planes with the tests and get them to their destination. Given the diverse experiences, backgrounds, and perspectives of the Siemens Healthineers colleagues, they leaned in to their collective intelligence and intuition. It was this inclusionary climate, in which all voices were heard, that allowed them some measure of confidence to take the gamble and say yes.

Fortunately, it paid off. Crews were contacted and redeployed back to the airport. The mechanisms to transfer hundreds of pallets of tests from the arriving trucks and onto the planes were reactivated. The multiple permissions for arrival and departure of the planes were reapproved. The flight plans were reprogrammed. With all these logistics in place, the planes landed in Shanghai, loaded up, and within two days arrived at the airport in Bordeaux, France, where idling trucks were ready to rush the tests to schools throughout the country so they could open on time.

"I know for a fact that without the team's breadth of experience and the inclusiveness of all working together collaboratively and listening to each other, we would not have been able to pull this logistical feat off," says Berner. "That was the power of diversity—where every idea counted."

Siemens Healthineers' story brings to life the fourth discipline of inclusive organizations: Master the Logistics. Inclusive organizations are not just diverse, equitable, and inclusive as an end in itself. They are exceptionally effective at leveraging the DE&I of the organization to get collectively smarter about how to improve processes to improve their bottom lines.

In the case of the Siemens Healthineers story, they leveraged their DE&I to solve a massively complex, continent-spanning dilemma that was going to have long-range implications for an entire country's ability to educate its students. In other instances, DE&I may also be leveraged to more effectively harness the diversity of acquired companies in a variety of operational events, such as a merger and acquisition; to improve safety on the factory floor; or to improve product quality and delivery.

Poor logistics can prevent the most breakthrough, necessary products, such as COVID-19 vaccines, from reaching the people who need them on time and in good condition. Poor logistics can lead to errors in assembly lines and distribution systems, as seen in the global supply chain meltdowns in the wake of the pandemic. They can lead to dangerous conditions for workers and result, for instance, in the deaths of construction workers during stadium construction for the 2022 Qatar World Cup. They may result in explosions in underwater pipelines, like the Deepwater Horizon platform in the Gulf of Mexico, or nuclear reactor meltdowns, like Chernobyl, Fukushima, and Three Mile Island. Or they may result in the presence of lead in drinking water pipes, as seen in Flint, Michigan, and many other cities.

They also can increase the everyday drudgery for millions of workers who must contend with backlogs and rework, as well as stressed-out colleagues and irate customers, because their organizations cannot get things from point A to point B in a timely way.

Logistics are not the most alluring part of running a business. So much of the cachet is in slick branding and social media campaigns. Oscar night–worthy high-end product rollouts get all the attention. Yet it's logistics that almost always saves the day.

MASTER THE LOGISTICS—STRUCTURALLY

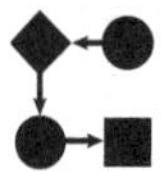

BASIC

When we look at Master the Logistics structurally, we consider the integration of DE&I into the structures of business operations focused on internal efficiencies, such as finance, procurement, or quality assurance.

Organizations that operate at the Basic stage of Master the Logistics do not recognize DE&I as a driver of business results and will therefore not be set up to seek diversity or leverage the diversity they currently have. DE&I is seen as a topic "handled" by the legal or human resources teams, the focus being on doing the right thing by everyone and not leaving others out. Business functions and their leaders act as the "recipient" of DE&I initiatives, such as training or invitations to DE&I events. At this stage, there is no expectation that DE&I will be leveraged to directly increase the bottom line and there are no dedicated DE&I resources allocated to logistically critical business functions such as finance, procurement, or quality assurance.

PROGRESSING

As organizations progress, they begin to integrate DE&I into select business functions where a link is initially seen. For example, as leaders become more cognizant of the link between diversity, equity, and inclusion on the one hand and innovation on the other, a business function such as research and development will be tasked with integrating DE&I into its operations. In fact, much research has been published about the link between diversity and innovation. According to a study by Boston Consulting Group, inclusive leadership—essentially, the art of leveraging diversity for business results—leads to 19% higher innovation revenue.[1] It follows that functions like R&D would be the first to understand the benefits of inclusively managed diverse teams.

ADVANCED

In the Advanced stage, DE&I becomes integrated into more business functions. That is because more mature organizations are able to make the link between being inclusive and better business outcomes as a whole, even for functions where a direct link to DE&I may not be obvious. It comes down to believing that diversity, when well managed and leveraged, will allow the organization to yield better outcomes, and then codifying that belief into the operational structure. At this stage you may see the formation of "innovation labs," made up of intentionally assembled diverse teams for the sole purpose of creating more profitable processes and systems.

For example, the US Marine Corps was able to intentionally leverage its gender diversity to maximize its operational effectiveness in Afghanistan. In 2010, the Marines, traditionally a male bastion, realized there was a better way to leverage its women Marines than in the support or technical roles they had occupied in the past. In rural Afghanistan, Afghani women are crucial to the fabric of society and the passing of information. But how could the Marine Corps access this information, given the villagers' strict adherence to Muslim rules that require women to operate in the background? It turns out that women Marines were the key.

Building on the Lioness program pioneered in Iraq, which used female Marines to search Iraqi women at checkpoints, the Marine Corps in Afghanistan trained women Marines to connect with Afghani women by handing out supplies and sharing tea, thereby gaining their trust. According to Captain Matt Pottinger, an intelligence officer based in Afghanistan at the time, one elder told him, "Your men come to fight, but we know the women are here to help."[2] The women Marines were often able to gain crucial information on Taliban movements in this manner, which led to important inroads.

And then there's the Highland Park "pawfficer." The City of Highland Park, Illinois, recently added a new member to its police force: the service dog Vinny, a highly trained walker hound. Vinny has started to accompany police units on missions of community engagement, domestic abuse calls, and mental health check-ins. His primary focus will be to reduce stress and fear in victims of crimes or other emergency situations. The four-legged pawfficer has already proved successful in deescalating situations, and the community has reacted positively. In one of his first missions, Vinny's presence alone easily coaxed out a child who had rebelliously ensconced himself into a clothes dryer. Chief of Police Lou Jogmen comments, "As a department, we are committed to implementing innovative ways to serve our community and enhance our ability to respond compassionately to crises and stressful situations. Our new community service dog will provide critical emotional support to individuals in need and accompany our officers in their visits around the community, engaging with residents of all ages."[3]

Integrating the concept of a service dog into the police force is an instructive example of leveraging new thinking—and diversity and inclusion—into operational effectiveness, making police procedures more effective in reaching its goal of public safety and well-being.

LEADING EDGE

Leading Edge organizations master their logistics with full integration of DE&I into everything they do. In those organizations, DE&I is embedded within the operational ecosystems, with dedicated resources standing ready to assist leaders within their own functions. Leaders and middle managers understand that diverse teams give rise to increased innovation, profitability, collective intelligence, and problem-solving capabilities.

At this stage, leaders are evaluated based on how they integrate DE&I into their business processes and decisions. Those efforts may include building mechanisms to encourage respectful dissent and to invite and explore different opinions. There may be regular events, such as *Shark Tank*–like settings where all voices are heard, intended to solicit innovative ideas around a variety of subjects. These organizations may publicize the implementation of nontraditional ideas or ideas from a variety of different employees that have led to a better business outcome, stronger teamwork, or accolades from a customer. They may establish a recognition program that spotlights those ideas and their sources.

Procter & Gamble took this concept to a whole new level when it redesigned its R&D function in 2000, embracing what they call a "connect and develop" innovation model. The company realized that even with the best researchers on staff, it was still missing out on input from potentially millions of people with great ideas elsewhere in the world. Using a crowdsourcing methodology, P&G invited people from all over the globe to submit their ideas. The plan paid off. P&G's research and development productivity increased by close to 60%, its innovation success rate doubled, and its costs fell. Within a few short years, P&G launched more than one hundred new products for which some aspect came from outside the company.[4] Add to this a system to publicize crowdsourcing goals through a variety of channels and in a variety of media and you have a shining example of what leveraging the power of diversity and inclusion for business operations looks like in a Leading Edge organization.

Leading Edge organizations understand that DE&I is a business imperative and increases operational efficiencies and therefore the bottom line. Hence, they build structures that encourage the leveraging of diversity, and they demand that their leaders and managers utilize these structures as part of doing business.

The Japanese methodology of *kaizen* is a structural way ensuring inclusive operations. Kaizen is a Japanese term meaning "change for the better" or "continuous improvement that improves operations and involves all employees." It encompasses a wide range of ideas and involves making the work environment more efficient and effective by creating a team atmosphere of improving everyday procedures, ensuring employee engagement, and making jobs more fulfilling, less tiring, and safer.

While kaizen has been deeply embedded into what is known as the Toyota Way, another longtime user of the kaizen method is Trader Joe's. Since 2007, the grocery company has used a strategy of incremental and continuous improvements over time to improve its customer service and product placement in stores, which has led to it being one of the most successful grocery chains. Additionally, Trader Joe's employs the kaizen strategy of cross-functional teams, which breeds loyalty and high morale grounded in employees feeling heard and valued. Another example is Japanese car manufacturer Subaru, which utilizes kaizen strategies for small, incremental changes. Through this approach it receives more than one hundred employee-implemented innovations and saves more than $4,000 per employee per year.[5]

Ironically, Japanese culture is one of the most homogeneous in the world, and overall, Japanese companies operating in Japan tend to be in earlier stages of DE&I maturity. But this does not take away from the fact that kaizen is an inclusive methodology that can be applied to including and empowering employees at different levels of the organization. It just goes to show that really no one has the perfect story. Every culture and company is in the maturing process, and even when they are strong in one discipline of inclusive organizations, they may have a long way to go in others.

MASTER THE LOGISTICS—BEHAVIORALLY

BASIC

In organizations at the most Basic stage of Master the Logistics, business leaders do not make the link between harnessing the diversity of their teams and improving the way the business is run. Rather, they see a focus on DE&I as yet one more thing taking their time from getting "real" business done. They don't see the diversity on their teams as anything but just that—diversity on their teams. In their minds, diversity is a nice thing to have, and "tolerating" differences is the right and decent thing to do. But merely tolerating differences does not activate the full potential of the team. Who wants to be just tolerated?

Far from leveraging the diversity of the team to make things more efficient, leaders in organizations at this stage may actually suboptimize

KAIZEN (改善)

Translated to "good change" or "continuous improvement," kaizen is a Japanese efficiency methodology established in the 1980s and is often credited with being the "building block" of lean production methods, including Six Sigma. The focus of the kaizen method is to eliminate waste by improving productivity and sustaining constant improvement of processes. The idea is that small, incremental changes continuously used over a sustained period will result in large, significant improvements.

To institute kaizen practices, an organization requires an open culture in which employees are empowered to identify and resolve challenges. Once this is achieved, an organization can implement a kaizen improvement process. Most companies individualize their improvement process, but there also is an overarching kaizen structure. The first step is to identify the process to be improved, which often includes administration or product development processes with significant bottlenecking or barriers.

Then, within the process, a specific waste elimination area must be chosen for improvement. Once the process and problem area are identified, a cross-sectional team is assembled. A hallmark of the kaizen process is a cross-functional team that leverages employees from throughout the business, especially frontline workers, to hear and enable new perspectives.

When the team is ready, it then works to solve the problem and create a solution. This may be done using Toyota's Five Whys method (which consists of asking a set of why questions to drill down on a problem area) or value stream mapping (a flowchart method). After a solution is implemented, a key part of any kaizen strategy is the follow-up, in which teams reflect on and track the solution to identify any further waste elimination opportunities.

Source: "Lean Thinking and Methods—Kaizen," US Environmental Protection Agency, September 29, 2022, https://www.epa.gov/sustainability /lean-thinking-and-methods-kaizen.

their team interactions and dynamics by having an "I treat everyone the same" attitude. They don't believe in different treatment for people who are different, and they make comments such as "Nobody did anything different for me and I still made it."

"The challenge here," says Victoria Russell, Chief Diversity and Inclusion Officer at Beam Suntory, "is that when managers don't tailor their management and coaching to the various individuals, with the mistaken notion that it's the most fair thing to do, it actually produces the opposite results."

PROGRESSING

It is at the Progressing stage of Master the Logistics where the benefits of inclusive behavior start to become top of mind for leaders. At a high level, leaders and managers understand the business case for DE&I, and it's not just the business case for retaining talent to avoid costly turnover. Instead, it's the *actual* business case that diverse teams are higher performing and more innovative if the team members feel accepted and appreciated and not merely tolerated.

At this stage you will hear leaders talk about the benefits of DE&I in all the right words. There is no longer a need to convince them that DE&I is necessary; they get that. Where they struggle is in knowing how to do it. We run into this gap a lot. It shows that we're at an inflection point of DE&I maturity, that after quite a steep climb, we are past the stage of having to convince. "But many leaders at this point confuse getting it with doing it," says Toyin Ogun, Chief Human Resources Officer at global logistics firm HAVI. But Ogun has been able to witness the breakthrough into transition, as exemplified through their work with people with disabilities.

ADVANCED

At the Advanced stage of maturity, organizations apply the discipline of Master the Logistics behaviorally in day-to-day decision-making. They consciously ensure that they have diverse teams (in terms of identity, experiences, functions, geographies, and thinking styles) in every area of the organization that enables it to run most effectively and efficiently. To make sure this is happening, the organization holds the teams accountable for this.

Since leveraging diversity to master the logistics requires mastering inclusive behaviors, organizations at this level of maturity make skill building through various forms of learning experiences part of the yearly cycle of development for leaders, managers, and employees.

Take the well-known hospitality service provider Marriott. All members at its properties—from bellhops to front desk workers to

ENABLING PEOPLE WITH HEARING IMPAIRMENT TO DRIVE FORKLIFTS IN A WAREHOUSE

As a global supply chain operator in the quick-service restaurant space, HAVI is charged with transporting hundreds of millions of items to restaurants and kitchens around the world. Pivotal to the massive logistics are twenty-four-hour warehouses buzzing with forklifts and conveyer belts quickly moving pallets of products. To keep things on schedule and the workers safe, constant verbal communication is essential—seemingly making it impossible for people with hearing impairments to work there.

Given its commitment to diversity and inclusion, however, HAVI was not willing to accept this as a truism. The company challenged itself to master the logistics to operationalize being an inclusive organization. To this end, it partnered with Salva Vita in Hungary, a nonprofit organization that designs training for the differently abled. But this time Salva Vitae needed to go beyond training, and it now partners with HAVI to design for those who cannot hear, enabling these workers to operate forklifts in a way that is safe for them and for everyone else while also keeping up with HAVI's rapid operational pace.

The process started not by looking at the limitations of being unable to depend on sound and but instead by looking at how to optimize the use of other senses, such as sight, for both the hearing impaired and those who are not.

According to Daniel Tomasetti, Chief People Officer, HAVI Supply Chain, this led to the following design elements:

- Make it easy for everyone to know who needs a nonverbal approach. Special yellow vests make that easy to spot.

- Equip each forklift with signals that can inform everyone which way the forklift is moving. In this case, yellow flashing lights indicate upward movement taking place, while blue flashing signals a downward movement.

- Position those who are hearing impaired in lower-traffic areas.

- Provide a sign language interpreter and teach sign language to those hearing colleagues who haven't yet learned.

(continued)

ENABLING PEOPLE WITH VISUAL IMPAIRMENT TO DRIVE FORKLIFTS IN A WAREHOUSE

(continued)

- Establish safety protocols to provide the most effective emergency help in a mixed-ability environment.

- Everyone is offered ongoing career development through performance management, continuing learning, and mentorship.

"I'm proud that our business has been certified as a 'disability-friendly' employer, which means our workforce keeps growing with great talent with hearing impairment," says Tomasetti. "We look forward to exploring more inclusive ways of supporting the enablement of every member of our community, regardless of ability."

---

housekeeping—participate in daily back-of-house meetings to figure out how they can get things done quicker and in ways that elevate the guest experience. The late Arne Sorenson, former Marriott president and CEO, expressed it like this: "We are a collection of people from everywhere, of every faith, race, sexual preference, and identity. . . . We welcome a million people every day from every walk of life. How anyone in this industry can be anything other than fully embracing of diversity of inclusion is lost on me, because you can't understand our business otherwise. . . . There are always advantages to having diverse voices in the room. You have to make sure that you pull that together."[6]

LEADING EDGE

Organizations at the Leading Edge of behavioral maturity apply their inclusion skills to all major operational decisions. They have the awareness, the motivation, and the skills to do it—all of which is demonstrated in how their leaders and teams function. They eagerly seek out a diversity of perspectives and nurture inclusive environments. A speak-up culture is their default way of operating. Ensuring that all employees feel a sense of belonging and know the value of their voices benefits not only the individuals but also the collective output of the organization, and it boosts the bottom line.

These organizations do what Siemens did in its crisis moment *all the time.*

Leading Edge organizations have leaders who intentionally deploy diverse-by-design teams with the sole purpose of coming up with better business results. The difference between Advanced and Leading Edge? Leaders, managers, and employees seek diversity and leverage it without thinking about it. It is no longer a separate step but is integrated into their mindsets. Call it inclusive business acumen.

TRIP UPS

Operations, by nature, are complex, with plenty of things that could go wrong. In Mastering the Logistics, however, the most common trip ups we have observed are sins of omission: overlooking the impact of DE&I on the bottom line and overlooking the power of inclusive teams.

TRIP UP 1: OVERLOOKING THE IMPACT OF DE&I ON THE BOTTOM LINE

While the first three disciplines, Manage the Risk, Explode the Awareness, and Maximize the Talent Systems, are a somewhat intuitive part of understanding the benefits of DE&I, Master the Logistics often gets overlooked. The business case for DE&I is often cited as supporting an organization's talent as opposed to its ability to increase productivity, be more innovative, increase safety, or bring about a successful merger and acquisition—essentially, to improve the bottom line. And because DE&I is not seen as a true business enabler, budgets and resources often are not allocated toward this goal. This is how organizations miss out on one of the biggest payoffs of embracing DE&I.

When businesses view themselves as the recipients of DE&I initiatives, rather than the key instigators, leaders don't assume responsibility for creating inclusive business functions. They don't make the hard link between the diversity in their business units and an inclusive culture, on the one hand, and enhanced operational results, on the other. What a loss!

To get out of this trap, business leaders must make the most of the diversity of their teams to address their day-to-day operational

US NAVY AND UKRAINE ARMY LEVERAGE DIVERSITY TO PROTECT THEIR COUNTRIES

Megan Eckstein

Commander of US Naval Surface Forces Vice Admiral Roy Kitchener believes that doubling down on diversity and inclusion can help the force gain further advantage over potential adversaries in multiple ways. No surprise, then, that the surface force is the most diverse of all the navy's major warfare areas.

"Our adversaries think differently than we do," Kitchener told *Navy Times*, after speaking at the first-ever Surface Force Diversity, Equity and Inclusion Symposium in Norfolk, Virginia, on April 7, 2022. "We have a lot of people in our country with a very diverse thought process, and that is a real strength when you're teaching people tactics.

"When people can say, okay, what do you think the opponent is going to do? . . . Your opponent is not necessarily thinking like you, and what I found is that, if you can have people on our team that can think out of the box, perhaps different than the conventional Western way to think, it really is a game changer.

"It's a proven fact that the more diverse you are, you're going to be a better and more high-performing organization. But I just see it simply from the warfare perspective, where being able to have a team that can think with that kind of agility against an opponent that probably doesn't have that agility is a huge advantage."

During the same interview, he cited an old navy saying: "People matter more than guns in the rating of a ship."

Rear Admiral Brendan McLane, the commander of Naval Surface Force Atlantic, offered up the Ukrainian military and territorial defense forces' ongoing performance since 2022 as an example of the need for agile thinking.

"I think if we look at what's happening in Ukraine right now, we can definitely see it's the people that are making the difference, not the warfighting equipment. . . . The way they are fighting—the thoughts that are going into asymmetrically battling a much superior force and winning—I think that really shows you the difference people can make in combat."

Kitchener and McLane say several factors are at play when looking at how to increase the performance of the surface fleet. As they

(continued)

aim to eliminate gaps in at-sea billets, boosting retention is one key to solving the problem. Sailors tend to stay in the service when they are happy with their jobs and working in high-performing units, meaning the navy needs to do whatever it can to keep top performers around to serve as tomorrow's leaders. In some cases, that means building an inclusive environment where all sailors can feel welcome, as well as perhaps giving some sailors additional mentoring or training so they can achieve their full potential and help create a diverse leadership team down the line.

"Our people are our critical strength, and that's going to make the difference for us in the strategic competition that we're in," McLane says. "And having the greatest amount of talent available on our ships and in our fleet is going to be the difference."

Source: Megan Eckstein, "Surface Navy Tackling Diversity as Part of Push for Better Retention, Leadership," *Navy Times*, April 11, 2022, https://www.navytimes.com/news/your-navy/2022/04/11/surface-navy-tackling-diversity-as-part-of-push-for-better-retention-leadership. Excerpt courtesy of Sightline Media Group, LLC, publisher of *Navy Times*. Megan Eckstein is the naval warfare reporter at Defense News.

objectives. This is not something you can do if DE&I is only under the domain of HR, for example.

"HR and the DE&I team are there as consultants, advisers, and subject matter experts—even the conscience—but they are not the general managers of the business," says Andy Sullivan, Executive Vice President and Head of US Businesses at Prudential Financial. "That, as in all things, belongs to us business leaders."

TRIP UP 2: OVERLOOKING THE POWER OF INCLUSIVE TEAMS

The traditional ways of organizing enterprises are not working anymore. Agility, fluidity, and spontaneity are needed more than structures, process, and in-person meetings to respond to the minute-by-minute barrage of challenges, opportunities, and knowledge dumps.

Diverse and inclusive teams make better decisions 87% of the time and are better at solving complex tasks.[7] However, as we mentioned in the first book of this series, *The 5 Disciplines of Inclusive Leaders*, diverse teams are not necessarily the most efficient. They can take longer to go through the Forming and Storming stages. When diverse teams get to the point that they are operating inclusively, however, greater innovation happens. We must now make the straight-line connection between the evolving, transformative nature of teams today and the innovation imperative—and the inclusiveness of diverse teams is that line.

The trip up for organizations seeking to leverage diversity and inclusion for business improvement is that they often overlook the role of teams—and the new reality of how teams operate. Today, teams—not practices, lines of business, or offices—are the key organizing principle through which work gets done in organizations. Agility in a fast-changing world warrants much less top-down decision-making. Diverse teams led by inclusive leaders must be empowered with more decision rights. Input, ownership, and action by all—it's the whole point of an inclusive organization.

Now that we have mastered the logistics, let's explore how inclusive organizations conquer the marketplace.

5

Discipline 5:
See the Marketplace

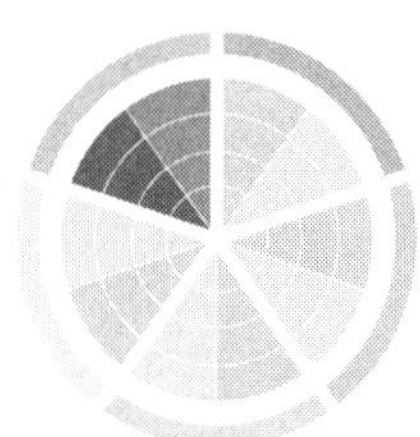

Maturity measure: the extent to which DE&I is integrated with markets, customers, and communities.

Sometimes the questions are complicated but the answers are simple.

Dr. Seuss, American author

WHEN NIKE DECIDED TO STAKE ITS BRAND on a controversial sports figure, NFL quarterback Colin Kaepernick, it was seen as a massive risk. In 2019, Kaepernick began kneeling on the field during the playing of the American national anthem as a protest against police brutality toward Black men. The public, both in the stands and watching on TV, were deeply polarized about this symbolic act, and even the president of the United States at the time weighed in, speaking disparagingly of Kaepernick and the many other players who joined him in silent protest.

But Nike went ahead and launched a massive marketing campaign on the thirtieth anniversary of its "Just Do It" slogan, which featured Kaepernick making this final statement: "Believe in something. Even if it means sacrificing everything."

Those outraged by the ad featuring Kaepernick predicted that Nike would suffer in the marketplace for this stance. The news media showed people burning their Nike shoes in protest. For a few days it seemed they had been right, as Nike's market cap lost $3.75 billion in value.[1]

But Nike stuck to its stance. In fact, this was not first time Nike had taken an inclusion and diversity stance in its marketing. Soon after the United States Congress passed Title IX in 1972, a landmark bill mandating that high schools and universities had to spend the same amount on female and male sports, Nike launched a women's clothing line and became the first sporting goods company to make clothing for women athletes that was not about fashion but about optimizing their athletic performance. Today, Nike is the largest provider of athletic gear for women in the world.

All of this has led to a full range of transformational support for female athletes. The company not only launched the Serena Williams Design Crew sport gear line but also built the Serena Williams Building, the largest edifice at Nike World Headquarters in Eugene, Oregon. In addition, Nike is recruiting and training more female coaches, creating digital tools to help coaches and empowered adults create safe and inclusive environments, and donating apparel and equipment "so girls can play with confidence, and striving for 50% girl participation in sport-based community programs."[2] In 2022, Nike's market cap was $178.6 billion, $50 billion higher than that temporary dip in the wake of the ad. In the United Kingdom, 30% of respondents at the time said that the Kaepernick ad made them view the brand more favorably, and 24% said they would buy more Nike products as a result.

As the Nike example shows, See the Marketplace must go beyond seeing just the segment that we feel comfortable with, the one that is most like us. That's when we can reap the benefits of DE&I to our top lines.

This chapter features many examples of organizations from all over the world, at various stages of seeing the marketplace. In the United States, though, many efforts to apply this discipline take the form of seeing the *Black* marketplace, even though many other groups also have been historically overlooked. Following society's tendency to overindex in this area, therefore, you will see our US examples also tend to be overweighted in this direction.

SEE THE MARKETPLACE—STRUCTURALLY

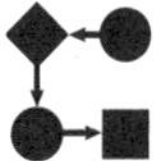

BASIC

Organizations at this stage do not take a strategic and culturally competent approach to serving new and diverse markets. While they may be interested in expanding into different regions of the world, or even to different demographics in existing regions, they very much approach these expansions like it is doing more of the same.

With DE&I separated from marketing and outreach efforts (and metrics), and the notion of cultural authenticity considered simply "nice to have," it is no wonder there are so many examples of market expansions gone wrong. Very often, branching into new markets at this stage involves taking what is currently being done in an organization's core market and simplistically replicating it for the new market. No thought is given to the culture beyond, perhaps, the language and branding needed to make the expansion.

Take Parker Pen Company, which wanted to market a ballpoint pen in Mexico. The initial ads were translated from the English "It won't leak in your pocket and embarrass you," except the translation used for *embarrass* was *embarazar* (to impregnate), so the ad ended up reading, "It won't leak in your pocket and make you pregnant."[3] That poor one-to-one translation, known as a "false friend," could have been easily avoided had culturally competent systems been in place.

In the case of the impregnating pen, Parker Pen actually publicized its mistake for others to learn from. And not only that, based on these types of experiences, the company's former vice president of worldwide marketing, Roger E. Axtell, published the book *Gestures: The Do's and Taboos Around the World.* Nice recovery!

In some cases, the cluelessness exhibited by organizations at this stage manifests as exploitative and triggers backlash. For example, in 2022, the Children's Museum of Indianapolis invited the public to celebrate Juneteenth with a Juneteenth Jamboree celebration. On the menu in its food court: a "Juneteenth watermelon salad." After intense backlash, the museum apologized for perpetuating stereotypes and took the item off the menu.[4]

And then there was Abercrombie and Fitch, whose exclusionary culture and marketing is now well documented in *White Hot: The Rise and Fall of Abercrombie & Fitch*, released on Netflix in 2022. While Abercrombie's transgressions are many, one stands out. In the early 2000s, the retailer produced a line of T-shirts featuring Asian Americans with caricatured faces, slanted eyes, and conical rice hats. One such design had the tagline "Wong Brothers Laundry Service—Two Wongs Can Make It White" and featured two smiling figures rendered in the stereotyped style of early 1900s pop culture depictions of Chinese men. There were many examples of similar shirts. The kicker though? Following the inevitable backlash, Abercrombie's public relations firm went on record as saying, "We personally thought Asians would love this T-shirt."[5] Clearly, the retailer could not have been further removed from actually seeing the marketplace.

PROGRESSING

As organizations progress on their journey and their structures become more inclusive, the need for more cultural competency in their core outward-facing functions, such as marketing and sales, becomes clearer. But even at this stage, See the Marketplace is about more than using a few images of different-looking people in ads. Rather, it's about understanding the cultural context in which people operate. For example, ads created at Christmastime, depicting a happy nuclear family under a Christmas tree, may work well for the traditional Anglo culture in which the nuclear family is the center of all activity. But it isn't relatable to people in Latin American cultures where the Christmas holiday is celebrated with a large extended family. In this case, swapping out White actors for Latino-looking ones will be seen as a poor attempt at being culturally inclusive.

At this stage, there is an increased understanding that in order to grow a presence in different markets one must actually listen to and seek to understand the culture. Official listening channels may be established to become knowledgeable about one's diverse potential customers, partners, and even communities at large. Organizations may host regular listening forums in different communities, not just after something goes wrong but even proactively, to be on the forefront of understanding trends, needs, and concerns within these communities. An organization may start small, expanding in one particular market and focusing its learning there.

When cries for equity were amplified following the uprising for racial justice and equity in the United States in 2020, many financial institutions promised to do their part to narrow the wealth gap. Chase Bank, for instance, opened a community center in a predominantly Black neighborhood in Los Angeles. They hired Jordan King, who lived in South Los Angeles as a child, to be branch manager. The community center offers space and equipment for community meetings and financial literacy sessions and has staff that leads a community home lending group, advising previously unqualified borrowers on home ownership. King explains, "We want to give people that access to those bankers, to those experts that we know have been missing in South LA, at least at this scale, and be that change and be that ecosystem to support the folks that are here now."[6]

Germany is home to almost 3 million people of Turkish descent, many of them second- or third-generation descendants of Turkish "guest workers" originally invited to Germany during the economic rebuilding in the 1950s and 1960s. Many of these people still send large portions of their wages to family still in Turkey. Inclusively thinking companies like Deutsche Bank have long seen the value of reaching out to this market.

Over the years, Deutsche Bank has marketed to the 700,000 Turkish households in Germany to influence them to invest their wages in Germany. Under the brand name Bankamiz, Deutsche Bank opened eighteen locations with bilingual customer service representatives, knowing that Turks are more comfortable talking about pension planning in their first language. Brochures about checking accounts, credit lines, and saving plans are also available in Turkish. There is a Turkish hotline and the ability to make a number of fund transfers into Turkey, free of charge.[7]

Of course, no organization goes to such lengths for purely altruistic reasons. They do the work to see the marketplace in the hope that these racially and ethnically different markets will see these banks as worthy of their trust.

ADVANCED

Organizations that are Advanced in See the Marketplace from a structural perspective seek to expand their relationships with their diverse markets, customers, and communities, to upgrade these from merely transactional. Their go-to-market strategies are intentionally inclusive; in fact, inclusion becomes part of the organization's brand. All advertising is done with an inclusion lens, meaning even ad campaigns for a "local market" sees the diversity in the local geography. DE&I metrics are applied to measure success.

To make the shopping experience more inclusive for a broader swath of the population, makeup megastore Sephora in Europe offers two types of shopping carts—a red one that signals it is okay for a salesperson to come up and offer assistance, and a black one that indicates the shopper prefers to be left alone. A genius idea to allow introverts to shop at their own pace. And because inclusive ideas, while designed for one purpose, often benefit a much larger group, there was an added benefit. People of color, who often feel targeted and "followed around" in stores, were now able to pick the "introvert" basket and have a much less anxiety-inducing shopping experience.[8]

Like Deutsche Bank, Mercedes has been targeting the Turkish market in Germany since the early 1990s. Mercedes is one of the most popular car manufacturers among Turks. That's no accident. Their ads don't just air in Turkish; their inclusive thinking has actually incorporated Turkish traditions into the creative. One ad, for instance, shows a family in their car, ready to leave for vacation. A bucket of water is emptied in front of the car—which is how you wish someone a good trip in Turkey. The tagline: "Mercedes-Benz ist immer gut" (Mercedes-Benz is always good).[9]

Judging from the brand loyalty Turks show Mercedes, seeing the market, too, is always good.

LEADING EDGE

Leading Edge organizations have DE&I expertise distributed throughout all outward-facing functions—marketing, sales, and customer service—as well as through the functions that only tangentially touch the marketplace, such as legal. DE&I metrics are embedded into all lines of management in all markets, and business outcomes are regularly evaluated to ensure sustainability and to course correct when needed. It is at this stage that internal employee resource groups are used to coming up with innovative solutions for their respective communities of customers. These groups may be used for product, market, and trend research, and ads are run by them for cultural input.

In 2021, Pizza2Go partnered with Red Crescent of the United Arab Emirates (the UAE affiliate of the Red Cross and the Red Crescent Societies) to tackle one of the biggest problems during the holy month of Ramadan: food wastage. During this time, approximately 25% of all food generated during *iftar* (breaking of one's fast) in the Middle East is wasted. In their joint campaign, Pizza2Go introduced a three-quarter version of its classic pizzas, which resulted in 25% less iftar waste. In addition, the company donated 25% of the earnings to the Emirates Red Crescent, thus supporting those in need within their communities.

The diversity angle: by seeing the marketplace and its unique needs and issues, Pizza2Go created a welcome campaign that solved a problem for its customers. In addition, it appealed to a new generation of more climate-conscious and purpose-seeking people, while doing good for society and the planet.

Gap Inc.'s product-inclusion initiative the Color Proud Council is another example of how seeing the marketplace has opened the doors to new markets. The company now embraces a product-to-market inclusivity model driven in part by ideas coming from the council.

In addition, the Gap Collective celebrates the spirit of activism with featured artists with Down syndrome or Black artists honoring moments such as Black History Month.[10] The Old Navy's Project WE, featuring limited-edition graphic tees designed by non-White artists, honors cultural moments such as International Women's Day, Pride Month, and Hispanic Heritage Month.[11] Meanwhile, the True Hues collection from its Banana Republic brand challenges the industry's definition of the word *nude* by offering a range of products, from bodysuits to camisoles to intimates, in eight shades, ranging from pale to dark espresso brown.[12] And its Athleta All Powerful brand has an inclusive sizing extension that ranges from 1X to 3X (or 18 to 26) to accommodate all body types, instead of a separate, stigmatizing "plus size line." The brand further stands out in the language it uses to describe its apparel. While its competitors are more prone to use "slimming" and "flattering" to describe larger sizes, Athleta uses "confident" throughout its catalog, regardless of size.[13]

The results? The True Hues collection beat expectations by double digits in the months after launch,[14] and Athleta's inclusive approach brought in growth despite a revenue decline among competitors.

"We felt there was an opportunity to have more diverse voices in the room impacting the products we make and sell every day," explained Bahja Johnson, Color Proud Council cofounder and Head of Customer & Community Belonging & Enablement at Gap Inc. "Customers are voting with their values as much as their wallets and are more outspoken than ever when they feel a company has missed the mark. That said, their ask isn't egregious—they just want to see themselves reflected in their clothes, and I truly believe it's our job as retailers to make that happen. In order to do that, inclusion must be at the forefront of every product decision—from concept all the way to marketing and the online/in-store experience—and the decision-makers must reflect the changing demographic of the customer base."[15]

None of this happens without truly diverse workforces that represent the marketplace. And the insights and skills they bring must be heard, valued, and implemented. It's the only genuine and effective way in which inclusive organizations can see the marketplace.

SEE THE MARKETPLACE—BEHAVIORALLY

BASIC

Leaders and employees at this stage usually have not been very exposed to cultural differences. They likely see the world only from their own vantage point. They may understand that the market is broadening and that there is a benefit to exploring these different markets; however, they do not yet have the cultural competency to approach diverse markets and customers in an authentic way.

At the Basic stage, you might see salespeople getting impatient with customers whose English is accented or treating as stereotypes customers who appear different from them. We have all seen storefronts decorated with the "culture of the month" decor, whether it's the rainbow flag in June or Martin Luther King quotes in February, even while the sales staff customarily treats openly gay shoppers with disdain or not-so-subtly follows Black shoppers around out of fear they might steal something.

In fact, as the study "Shopping While Black," published in the *Journal of Consumer Culture*, details, 80% of fifty-five middle-class African Americans interviewed in New York City reported experiencing racial stigma and stereotypes when shopping, such as being followed around in stores, being directed to the Sale section, or being ignored, made to wait, or skipped over in favor of nonminority customers. Cassi Pittman, the study author and an assistant professor of sociology at Case Western Reserve University, said, "Many shoppers feel their race undermines their credibility in stores. They're treated differently, but not wholly denied access. In many ways, this is a microcosm of racial exclusions embedded in American society."[16]

This lack of authenticity and the performative aspect of inclusion is readily transparent to customers and does not contribute to truly seeing the marketplace. No amount of black squares posted on the store's Instagram page can make up for it.

PROGRESSING

As organizations progress, business leaders start to explore how to utilize inclusive and cross-cultural competencies to deliver better outcomes to their customers. They may also expand outreach into the communities in which they operate. For example, intentionally deployed bilingual sales staff is prepared and eager to serve customers in areas with large immigrant populations.

Advertising to specific communities is becoming more adept because the leaders and teams responsible recognize the need to perform relevant market research to understand the culture and then to pull together a diverse team that includes members of the target community, for input and guidance. The ads that emerge from these collaborations have authentic story lines and messaging that makes consumers feel seen and heard.

Often, it takes a wake-up call to start listening. On a Virgin Atlantic flight from London to Mumbai, one customer was so displeased with the food he was served that he wrote a tongue-in-cheek disgruntled letter about the quality of his meal to the founder and CEO, Sir Richard Branson. After describing in detail how wrong the food was in presentation, cultural plating standards, and taste, leaving it all inedible for the diner, the passenger wrote, "By now I was actually starting to feel a little hypoglycemic. I needed a sugar hit. Luckily there was a small cookie provided. It had caught my eye earlier due to its baffling presentation . . ."

Here, he attached a photo of a cookie in what looks like Ziploc bag.

"It appears to be in an evidence bag from the scene of a crime. A CRIME AGAINST BLOODY COOKING. Either that or some sort of back-street underground cookie, purchased off a gun-toting maniac high on his own supply of yeast. You certainly wouldn't want to be caught carrying one of these through customs. Imagine biting into a piece of brass, Richard. That would be softer on the teeth than the specimen above."

The letter went viral. How did Branson respond? He accepted the input and called the man directly. And he offered him a job of suggesting improvements to Virgin's in-flight meals, making him part of Virgin Atlantic's food advisory board.[17] Behavioral inclusion nicely played, Sir Richard.

ADVANCED

In an organization that is Advanced, leaders and managers actively influence change by embedding inclusive and cross-cultural competencies across markets and initiatives. As organizations intentionally build their brands around the values of diversity, equity, and inclusion, their leaders and managers build inclusive leadership and management into the very function of brand building. Because all advertising is expected to be inclusive starting at its creation, leaders pull in diverse-by-design teams with representation from the communities they want to reach.

But in Advanced organizations, creative directors and brand managers go further. They use the very platform of their brand to ask underrepresented talent or groups to share their differentiated lived experience in order to create the most appropriate marketing messages. By tying the brand to the value of diversity, these leaders build trust among new market segments. This is how Adobe won the coveted Mosaic Award in 2021. Their "When I See Black" ad showcased the work of twelve Black creators: Lawrence Agyei, Temi Coker, Shani Crowe, Aurélia Durand, Yannis Guibinga, Asia Hall, Crystal Kayiza, Joshua Kissi, Esther Luntadila, Devin Wesley, Barry Yusufu, and Ismail Zaidy.

In a statement published by the company, Ann Lewnes, Executive Vice President and Chief Marketing Officer at Adobe, said, "Seeing creators like yourself, especially for this next generation, is absolutely crucial. We are proud to be celebrating the vibrant spectrum of creativity that exists in the world, because we all benefit when more perspectives are shared."[18]

LEADING EDGE

In Leading Edge organizations, there is a virtuous cycle between an organization's integration of DE&I and culture into their outward-facing work and the inner workings of the company that produces those offerings. In the same way, the inclusive manner in which the marketing and sales functions collaborate internally results in brands that more effectively and authentically reach a broader audience. This continuous and fluid cycle is automatic and built into the design, and thus the DNA, of the organization.

Furthermore, branding strategies and advertising produced by Leading Edge creative teams go beyond product advertising to shine a light on social injustices. P&G has distinguished itself in this way by releasing a series of short films spotlighting racial biases against Black Americans in daily life. In 2017, the company released a commercial called "The Talk," which focuses on the conversations Black parents have to have with their children to ready them for a world of racism and to keep them safe. No product was advertised in the commercial, which aired on the internet as well as on national television and won an Emmy.

The company followed up in 2019 with "The Look," which follows a Black man as he goes about his day encountering hostile or suspicious looks from White people, whether he is in an elevator, teaching his son how to swim, or shopping in an upscale store. The reveal happens when the man enters a courtroom in a judge's robe.

"Empathy can be a particularly effective antidote to bias, and we created 'The Look' to change perspectives, prompt personal introspection, and bring people together for a conversation to ultimately change hearts and minds," said Marc Pritchard, P&G's Chief Brand Officer. "We believe we have a responsibility to use our voice in advertising as a force for good by addressing issues like bias. As it has already done for so many who have seen 'The Look,' we hope this film leads to constructive conversation, understanding and positive action."[19]

SEEING ABORIGINAL PEOPLES AND TORRES STRAIT ISLANDERS IN AUSTRALIA

It is no secret that Indigenous peoples around the world have struggled with discrimination, cultural erasure, and invisibility in many countries. The Indigenous peoples in Australia have fared no better in this regard. Concepts of Indigenous self-management or self-determination have been debated for decades. Since the early 2000s, the commonwealth's policy has been to affirm "the fundamental right of Aboriginals to retain their racial identity and traditional lifestyle or, where desired, to adopt wholly or partially a European lifestyle."

More recently, corporations in Australia have shown increased support for Indigenous businesses and communities by "building relationships, respect and trust between the wider Australian community and two Indigenous groups, the Aboriginal and Torres Strait Islander peoples," according to Reconciliation Australia, a nonprofit promoting and facilitating reconciliation.

The desire to become more inclusive has led to a changing attitude in the corporate world, says Reconciliation Australia CEO Karen Mundine. "These are hard-nosed businesspeople who need to see value, and there is value in better recruitment policies, and new business opportunities," she said.

For example, in a community where 80% of all jobs require a driver's license, the Australian car insurance company NRMA set up free lessons for young Aboriginal and Torres Strait Islander people to get driver training. So foundational was this skill to being able to function successfully in the economy that of the thirty participants in the driver training in 2018, twenty-seven were employed afterward.

In another example, the carpet company Ontera partnered with the National Aboriginal Design Agency to develop and create a piece of contemporary interpretation carpet artwork, featuring a design by Brentyn Lugnan that describes and signifies the artist's connection to his ancestral land of Gumbaynggirr and its people. The artwork is called *Water Yuludarla*.

Shelley Reys, CEO of Arrilla Indigenous Consulting, believes that many organizations really want to make a difference in fostering

(continued)

reconciliation. "They're driving courageous conversations with their staff base and delivering innovative solutions to closing the gap well beyond their core business."

Sources: "Changing Policies Towards Aboriginal People," Australian Law Reform Commission, August 18, 2010, https://www.alrc.gov.au/publication/recognition-of-aboriginal-customary-laws-alrc-report-31/3-aboriginal-societies-the-experience-of-contact/changing-policies-towards-aboriginal-people; Liz Keen, "Corporate Australia Ups Support for Indigenous Businesses, Communities: Reconciliation Australia," *ABC News*, November 23, 2018, https://www.abc.net.au/news/2018-11-24/corporate-australia-supports-indigenous-businesses-communities/10549314.

TRIP UPS

There are many blind spots when organizations seek to see the marketplace. Among the common trip ups are concentrating on the external message while neglecting the internal work, promising something impossible, and not viewing the marketplace with an intersectional lens.

TRIP UP 1: CONCENTRATING ON THE EXTERNAL MESSAGE WHILE NEGLECTING THE INTERNAL WORK

While many organizations start their DE&I journeys by focusing on awareness building and only later direct their efforts toward See the Marketplace, there are some that start with this discipline.

We once worked with a nonprofit organization whose very mission consists of ensuring equity and inclusion in all aspects of life around the world—education, access to resources, civic engagement, and internet freedom, to name a few. As such, their employees are highly clued in to issues of social justice and equity.

Our work revealed that the organization showed up strong on two of the disciplines of inclusive organizations: Explode the Awareness and See the Marketplace. It approached DE&I from an awareness perspective, regarding it as the right thing to do. At the same time, it had mastered See the Marketplace with its external messaging, seeing DE&I as key to achieving its mission of a fairer and peaceful society.

Yet a closer look also revealed notable gaps related to the discipline of Maximize the Talent Systems. A lack of women and minorities in leadership had been plaguing the organization for years. This visible gap threatened to undo its credibility as an exceptional champion of DE&I. Not only was the gap apparent, but they did not have the right processes in place to change that reality.

Recognizing this gap encouraged the nonprofit to pull back a bit on its forceful and confident media-attractive declarations about the power and value of DE&I and instead to put more energy into ensuring it was living up to these high standards itself. In this case, an inward look was needed to advance on its DE&I journey. The organization needed to systematically strip out unconscious biases from its very own talent management tools and processes and create congruence between its outside message and the lived experiences of its employees.

TRIP UP 2: PROMISING SOMETHING IMPOSSIBLE

When it comes to DE&I there are certain promises that can sound so right and yet be so wrong.

In our DE&I consulting work, we partnered with one asset management company that suffered from a lack of diversity in terms of women and minorities in management and senior management. But this was not for lack of trying. In an industry notorious for its slow progress on the DE&I journey, this company had a solid DE&I strategy, with concrete objectives, a well-established and respected chief diversity officer, and local DE&I councils and employee resource groups in place. In addition, the company had rolled out unconscious bias training at the corporate level for all people managers. It also had excellent people managers and supportive talent development tools and processes.

Unfortunately, even with all these efforts aimed at creating upward mobility and advancement opportunities, the diversity in management did not increase. And the frustration among those not advancing was particularly acute.

The issue? A combination of long tenure, a flat organization, and offices in smaller cities meant that advancement opportunities for all employees were limited. But increasing the diversity in leadership was made more difficult because managers with long tenure were typically White males, and thus the lack of advancement opportunities perpetuated the status quo. In short, people in management positions were not leaving and so there was very little upward movement in general, not just for underrepresented groups.

In looking at this company's employee value proposition, we identified a major disconnect between what it had promised employees at hire time and what it could deliver. It had promised "come here and advance"—had, in fact, promised the impossible for most, and for too many. As the years of dashed expectations passed, the frustration mounted.

How to resolve? Its employee value proposition needed to change. Rather than promising "advancement," the promise became "growth." The organization rebranded as a "learning organization" where employees are given plenty of development opportunities that lead to professional or personal growth, which they can utilize there or take elsewhere. The company continued to press toward increased diversity at the top levels by promoting upward as much as it could and, at the same time, being a net exporter of exceptional talent outside the organization.

Greater transparency here was the key. It allowed employees to fully understand the realistic and still inspiring career experience the organization was promising, and with that, feelings of marginalization decreased significantly.

TRIP UP 3: NOT VIEWING THE MARKETPLACE WITH AN INTERSECTIONAL LENS

"Let's go after the Latino market!" is just one of the rising rallying cries within organizations as they seek to tap new market segments. In the case of the "Latino" market, however, organizations have to ask themselves, "Which Latino market?" Do they mean the Boomers and Gen Xers that came from Latin America to the United States many years ago and yet hung on to their culture and language as part of their identity? Or the second- or third-generation Latinos who grew up in the United States, comfortably navigating both cultures, and who fluidly switch between English and Spanish, or Spanglish? Or the recent immigrants whose journey has shaped their outlook and needs differently from those who have been here for decades? Or is it Afro-Latinos?

The same can be said about the Asian market. Which Asians—those of East Asian descent, such as Chinese, Japanese, or Koreans? Or is it the Southeast Asians, such as Vietnamese, Malaysians, or Filipinos? Immigrants from India or Pakistan? How many generations have they lived in the country they're in? Which immigration wave did they arrive with?

To see the marketplace without an intersectional lens is to not see the market at all.

We have now run through the five disciplines of inclusive organizations, with examples of strategies, systems, and actions that inclusive organizations can take at different stages of maturity. But how can we be sure that all this activity is leading to change? The only way is to measure, as you'll see next.

*   *   *

6

How Do We Know It Works? Measuring Success of the Five Disciplines

One accurate measurement is worth a thousand expert opinions.

Grace Hopper, US Navy Rear Admiral
and pioneering computer scientist

W E OFTEN GET ASKED, "WHAT MAKES LEADERS *really* care about practicing the five disciplines to become an inclusive organization?"

The answer is simple, though making it happen is not: measure their results and hold them accountable. Let people know what they need to achieve and how they are doing, and reward them or ding them based on their results.

While vision and strategy provide the road map for the way forward, it is measurements and metrics that indicate whether a plan is working and how to course correct when it is not. DE&I metrics have always mattered, but with the rise of environmental, social, and governance reporting and stronger demands from boards, investors, employees, and customers for greater progress and accountability, effective DE&I metrics have become even more critical.

CEOs are under increasing pressure to move from inclusive words to inclusive actions that deliver tangible results. To show progress, they need to apply the same rigor they use to monitor the financial health of their organization, make projections, place bets, and compensate talent. But *what* to measure?

We have seen many companies get lost in the weeds or fall into the "one fell swoop" trap when working with DE&I measurements. When it comes to DE&I there are hundreds of possibilities, and in their multiplicity, the conversation around metrics can devolve into analytical, nonactionable paralysis. Conversely, DE&I metrics can be reduced to a rashly made representation goal with no understanding of what is causing the underrepresentation in the first place.

The key to avoiding these traps is to establish a meaningful DE&I scorecard. But here's the caveat: the only meaningful scorecard is the one that has metrics that are meaningful to your organization. The best scorecard is not a generic best-in-class tool but one that is grounded in your organization's values and that reflects your stage of DE&I maturity and desired pace for change. To create your own best-in-class scorecard, you can follow the detailed methodology outlined in appendix A, "How to Create Your Own Best-in-Class DE&I Scorecard."

By the way, the five disciplines consist of the structures, mindsets, behaviors, and accountabilities required to drive the increased DE&I maturity of organizations. But the maturity model, outlined in the introduction, is the tool for leaders of inclusive organizations to stay the course in a methodical and disciplined way. Hence, you will see us refer to the DE&I *dimensions*, not *disciplines*, when discussing metrics and measurements.

And with that ends part 1. We've looked in depth at each of the disciplines and at what behavioral and structural inclusion looks like across four levels of maturity. We've provided a tactical road map for progress that meets you where you are on your organization's journey. But even if you're a Leading Edge organization across all five of the disciplines, there's still unfinished DE&I business to take care of. After all, if you have truly embraced the value of DE&I, then what matters more than leveraging all the benefits you have received from becoming an inclusive organization to make your community, city, nation, and the world at large a more diverse, equitable, and inclusive place?

No longer can we pretend that our actions—or lack of actions—have no consequences outside our organizational boundaries. And as we will show in part 2, if we want to be truly inclusive, our efforts must extend beyond transforming our companies. We must use our power to begin transforming the world.

THE FOUR VITAL TASKS

THE FOUR VITAL TASKS

For decades, academics, economists, business organizations, the United Nations, and social justice activists have been talking about the connection between people, profits, and the planet using concepts like the "triple bottom line" and "conscious capitalism." Over the past twenty years, the United Nations has launched various major initiatives to create global synergy around these transformational concepts. The field of DE&I is at an inflection point, so that its reach now overlaps with these other major forces that together will create a diverse, equitable, and inclusive world for all.

ESG (the inelegant acronym that stands for environmental, social, and governance) is the clarion call for businesses to realize that they can no longer maintain financial viability at the expense of the planet and its people. As we will unfold in part 2, without DE&I, many of the vital goals of ESG cannot be achieved.

We call the intersection of DE&I and ESG "inclusive sustainability." While many think of sustainability as an ecological concept, sustainability, at its core, is about people. You can't take care of the planet if you aren't also taking care of your people. When you put it that way, the connections between DE&I and ESG become glaringly obvious. (For a deeper exploration, see appendix B, "How DE&I Enables Environmental, Social, and Governance.") The world's social, political, and ecological fracturing have created a dire urgency that requires the full wisdom, practices, and mobilization of DE&I to come to the rescue.

In part 2 we seek to show how inclusive organizations can leverage their DE&I powers toward their ESG goals and, more expansively, toward transforming our world. To illustrate this important point, we have selected what we consider four of the most vital tasks (and vexing challenges) we have in the world:

1. Diversifying leadership. If we want people to lead differently, we need different types of people in leadership.

2. Eradicating polarization. If we can't agree on anything, we can't get anything done.

3. Achieving justice. If we care about the fair and equal treatment of employees, we must ensure their fair and equal treatment outside the office as well.

4. Saving the planet. Climate change is everybody's—and every organization's—problem.

In the next four chapters, we will explore in detail how the DE&I mindsets, processes, and systems that inclusive organizations have in place can be used both inside and outside their boundaries to create real, positive change in this world—change that benefits their people, their bottom lines, and the planet. All five disciplines will be key for inclusive organizations to soar in all four of the vital tasks, yet all five are not equally needed for each of the vital tasks. As you will see, each task may require the application of different disciplines, and to different degrees.

Completing these four vital tasks will be hard, ongoing work. They require significantly widening the scope of DE&I to much more than hiring more diversity and creating inclusive cultures. They require reaching out into our communities, partnering with like-minded government and nongovernmental organizations, and a commitment to inclusive sustainability.

There likely are other vital tasks confronting us for which inclusive organizations are needed. Yet, because of what we see in society and in our clients' environments, the ones discussed here are the ones keeping us up at night. As long as the four vital tasks remain festering and unresolved, we face existential threats to our societies and our world. We know that if they are not addressed, the inequities that exist in our systems will never go away.

7

Vital Task 1: Diversify Leadership

Infinite diversity in infinite combinations . . . symbolizing the elements that create truth and beauty.

Commander Spock, *Star Trek*

LET'S GET REAL HERE.

For all the emphasis over the past fifty years on diversifying leadership, we still have not made much progress. Diversity in leadership is the ultimate true metric. If we can't show change here, then what difference have all our efforts made? The World Economic Forum reports that at our current pace of change, gender parity on issues such as economic opportunity, political power, education, and health will take *135 years*—you can thank the pandemic for adding thirty-six years to that already embarrassing, but not surprising, number.[1] In 2021, only 8% of Fortune 500 CEOs were women,[2] and as of 2019, 44% of companies in a McKinsey study include women in their C-suites.[3]

When we look at racial and ethnic diversity in leadership, the numbers are even worse. In 2022, there were six Black and twenty Latino Fortune 500 CEOs,[4] representing 5% of all CEOs. If we add the thirty-eight Asian/Asian American Fortune 500 CEOs,[5] the percentage climbs to 8%. Said another way, 92% of leaders of the most powerful corporations in the United States are White males.[6]

In the various EU nations and the United States, women make up nearly half of the entry-level workforce, and in some industries even half of the managers. Yet, in 2020, women made up only 29.5% of boards of the largest publicly traded companies in the European Union and 26.5% of boards in the Fortune 500.[7]

This is not to say that there has not been progress.

Angela Merkel, Jacinda Ardern, Najla Bouden, Mette Frederiksen, and Sheikh Hasina Wazed are only a few of current or recent women world leaders today. They are the former chancellor of Germany, the former prime minister of New Zealand, the prime minister of Tunisia, the prime minister of Denmark, and the prime minister of Bangladesh.

As of September 2021, there were twenty-six women serving as national leaders and 21% of ministers worldwide were women.[8] In the United States, the 117th Congress in 2021 was the most ethnically and racially diverse ever, with 23% of voting members from racial or ethnic minority backgrounds.[9] Even Latin America, a region with a long-standing machismo culture, can boast more than eleven female heads of state.[10] Compare this to 1966, when Indira Gandhi became the prime minister of India and was the only female head of state at the time.

But the numbers are still way too low in both the political and corporate fields. It seems that knowing and applying the best practices for advancing underrepresented talent—mentorship, sponsorship, work–life flexibility, employee resource groups, diversity councils, heritage celebrations, unconscious bias training for everyone—has not been enough.

So what's the problem?

LET'S CRACK THE CODE

In the many root cause DE&I diagnostic projects we have done for our clients, we conduct what we call a talent flow analysis, which identifies barriers to hiring, advancement, and retention of underrepresented talent by looking at how talent moves in, through, and out of an organization, all by demographic group and by level.

The story is often the same. At the entry and lower levels, the demographic mix has become relatively equitable. Sometimes, women and racial and ethnic minorities or immigrants are even overrepresented at the lower levels. But then, as we look higher in the organization, the field very quickly gets thinner, until, from the director level and up, the numbers of underrepresented talent can be counted on one hand. Our analysis usually finds that this is not necessarily a hiring issue, as in the patronizing excuse of "I can't find a qualified [fill in the blank] to hire." Rather, the problem lies with consistently lower performance ratings and therefore lower promotion rates for people of color. Not surprisingly, exit rates are higher.[11]

In a global DE&I survey conducted by Korn Ferry in 2021, which drew 4,500 survey responses worldwide, the responders from participating organizations told us they have ramped up their DE&I activity and that they know what they need to do to fix representation. Yet they keep falling back into old habits and not enough action is taken to tackle the root causes of why they have not been able to diversify leadership.

What are these old habits?

- Still blaming the lack of talent supply
- Limited focus on inclusive leadership
- Thinking culture will take care of itself
- Underestimating the commitment required

Let's look at each in turn and how to crack the code on breaking out of the bad habits.

STILL BLAMING THE LACK OF TALENT SUPPLY

There's some truth to the fact that certain roles that have traditionally required specialized education are not representative of the different groups within the overall population. Engineering is one example.

But the reality is that even with this being true in some professions, leadership is not even close to reflecting *that* available labor pool. So there are still plenty of strategies and tactics that can be deployed to narrow the diversification of leadership.

Cracking the code means looking at where there is diversity and demolishing the "one job away" excuse.

Look at Where There Is Diversity

Dive deep into layers of the organization, where more diversity exists, and make it a point to find hidden talent. It is a fact that we all tend to see talent more readily if it looks and sounds like us. To counteract this, leaders and managers need to deliberately identify high-potential, underrepresented talent in the various talent pools. Look for individuals who have distinguished themselves through new and innovative ideas, who have been able to energize others and bring teams with them, who have proved to be agile and strategic.

Once these people are identified, leaders and managers need to ensure that this talent receives the development, mentorship, and sponsorship needed to stretch and develop, but also to receive the exposure needed to shine. Offer stretch assignments, provide guidance and feedback, but also autonomy for unique success paths. Be intentional. Find out what your high-potential team member coming from an underrepresented group needs to be successful. Remove potential barriers to participation in stretch assignments such as travel or meetings outside of business hours. Create a psychologically safe environment for this talent to thrive and opportunities to move across functions and lines of business.

Demolish the "One Job Away" Excuse

Why are there not enough people of color to promote to senior leadership? It's because they aren't being given opportunities in the lower ranks.

Here's how that plays out. When many talk about White male employees, it's about their potential to do good work. When many talk about talent that has been in the minority, however, most often it's only about how they've already performed. Nowhere is that more evident than in the way leaders determine who gets selected for stretch and high-visibility assignments and development opportunities, all of which are essential to be considered for promotions.

With those who have been members of the majority, the approach is often, "You've never done this before; go for it!" With underrepresented talent, it's often, "You've never done this before, so you're not ready." In addition, they often are not given helpful feedback out of fear on the part of the majority of being accused of being racist, sexist, or xenophobic.

How can talent of color elevate their game and prove their potential if they've never been given the chance?

It's now time for organizations to do their part, and to do so on a large-scale basis.

LIMITED FOCUS ON INCLUSIVE LEADERSHIP

Most leaders are neither assessed on nor held accountable for leading inclusively. In the Korn Ferry survey, only 28% of global companies assess their leaders for inclusive leadership skills.

The problem continues at the middle level of the organizations, where inclusive leadership training for people managers is limited or nonexistent. Despite lots of "activity," less than 45% of North American survey respondents said their organizations offer inclusive leadership training for people managers. In other regions, the percentage is even lower: 41% in Asia-Pacific; 40% in Europe, the Middle East, and Africa; and 40% in Latin America.

Cracking the code requires assessment and development of inclusive leadership.

Inclusive leadership is not just about good intentions. It's not just about traits such as empathy, openness to differences, and trust, as vital as these are. It's about marrying these traits with increased awareness around DE&I issues and actual leadership skills, such as managing conflict, collaboration, talent development, nurturing innovation, and driving results. All are required to lead transformation—and all must be measured.

Without inclusive leadership assessment and development, leaders and managers, try as they might, will be limited in their effectiveness to diversify the leadership of their organizations. Our first book, *The 5 Disciplines of Inclusive Leaders*, explains the full Inclusive Leader model and is replete with stories of these types of leaders and the difference their skill building had on their organizations' efforts to diversify leadership.

THINKING CULTURE WILL TAKE CARE OF ITSELF

Hiring diversity brings the mix in the door. But inclusion is making the mix work. Translation: Yes, there are enough qualified candidates to hire. But, in order for these new hires to be successful, organizations need

SHOULD PAY BE LINKED TO DIVERSITY, EQUITY, AND INCLUSION?

Tom McMullen

Linking pay to diversity, equity, and inclusion sounds like a good idea, but does it work?

While it can telegraph to both internal and external communities that the organization is serious about DE&I and is putting its money where its mouth is, these pay programs haven't always been successful when tried.

We have mixed feelings about them. Many DE&I strategies and the pay programs linked to them have been poorly designed from the outset. There can also be potential for gaming the system. Pay is a powerful clarity and reinforcement mechanism. If there is no clarity and executive alignment in the DE&I strategy, priorities, metrics, measurement processes, and governance, linking compensation to the program should be the last thing an organization does.

For pay-for-DE&I plans to work, they must consider the following five design principles.

1. Focus less on hiring goals and metrics and more on creating broader talent pipelines. Since organizations have indeed gotten better at sourcing and hiring diversity, especially at the entry and early career levels, target lower levels of the company to broaden talent pools, and consider incentivizing midlevel managers to more rapidly identify and develop high-potential, underrepresented talent.

2. Reward for nurturing inclusive cultures. Benchmark and assess whether employees in general and in underrepresented talent groups are engaged, have clarity in their roles, have a high degree of trust in leadership, and feel welcome, along with other factors that broadly measure inclusiveness. Then reward leaders for sustainable positive changes and ongoing inclusive practices in those metrics, while also delivering on the action plans to close gaps in these areas.

3. Align with the organization's compensation philosophy and mechanisms. Is focus on the DE&I agenda (or within an environmental, social, and governance context) one of the organization's

(continued)

> key strategic priorities that should be reinforced via the compensation program? There are many competing priorities that vie for the attention of leaders, managers, and employees. Is this one of them?
>
> 4. Inclusive by design: inclusive rewards require inclusive behaviors from leaders and managers to be successful. This involves ensuring the right stakeholders (for example, managers, employees, and underrepresented talent) have the opportunity to provide input on compensation strategy and to design and help pilot test change in programs and communications. It also suggests transparent communications with regard to the principles and design provisions of the compensation program design, as well as periodic reporting of results.
>
> 5. Make it meaningful. There should be material financial impact on reward opportunities (for example, at least a 15% weight on the metric for incentive purposes) to focus adequate attention on achieving these goals. If this is not in place, you likely are better off not attempting to tie compensation to DE&I initiatives.

to ensure they have the conditions and culture in place to make their workplace a place where they can develop, thrive, and advance. Because if that's not the case, they will leave for greener, more inclusive pastures.

Building an inclusive culture doesn't happen on its own just because there is a diverse employee population. It requires rolling out training that helps the entire organization become self-aware of where conscious and especially unconscious bias may show up in interpersonal dynamics and performance management interactions.

Cracking the code requires becoming aware of organizational unconscious bias and being cross-culturally agile.

Become Aware of Organizational Unconscious Bias

Unconscious bias will distort much of what leaders and managers assume about their underrepresented talent. It will weigh in how they evaluate a person's speech, body language, and clothing, and how they get things done. When unconscious bias is unchecked in an organization, underrepresented talent systemically gets overlooked, is given lower performance ratings, is and less likely to be given special assignments that offer opportunities for visibility, learning, and development. And, very often, mistakes made by members of an underrepresented group are amplified and seen as further proof that the person wasn't ready (often met with an "I told you so" attitude), while mistakes made by a "traditional" person (i.e., White male) are regarded as learning opportunities, with second chances given much more easily.

Why, in many organizations, are those who come from cultures that are more direct in their style of communication often dinged for being too confrontational, while those who are from the majority group, with a similar style, are seen as "straight shooters"? Why are tall, White males seen as leaders but tall, Black males are seen as a threat? Why are Latinas judged as being too social while their White counterparts are praised for their networking skills?

Often, the unconscious biases of leaders and managers are the roadblock for underrepresented talent to succeed and advance. Systemically these leaders and managers need to question their own biases and preconceived notions of "talent" and "potential." Many need greater exposure to those who are different from them. It is one of the most effective ways to challenge unconscious biases.

Be Cross-Culturally Agile

We often get asked what have been the hardest companies to work with in terms of the DE&I transformation. Our answer uniformly is organizations with strong cultures. Their very strength is their Achilles' heel when it comes to DE&I.

Organizations have their built-in worldviews shaped by their values, legacy, and who their leaders have been. The more well developed that worldview, the more prescribed the ways of getting things done—and the easier it is to reject perspectives, behaviors, and preferences that don't exactly line up. And who usually doesn't exactly line up and has different ways of getting things done? Those who are different from the legacy workforce.

Cross-cultural agility requires expanding one's knowledge of others, their preferences, and their worldviews, but it begins with awareness of one's own preferences and worldviews. Only with both sets of information in hand can we make fair compare-and-contrast evaluations. Being able to evaluate behavior through a cross-cultural lens will help reduce misunderstandings and open the door for a diversity of ways to get things done.

UNDERESTIMATING THE COMMITMENT REQUIRED

This work is hard. CEOs consistently underestimate the length of time, amount of money, and amount of their own personal effort it will take to get minorities more represented in leadership roles.

It is not simply a matter of hiring a few women or ethnic or racial minorities at the leadership level. Diversifying leadership is deliberate work that requires high-level value calibration as well as detailed scorecard tracking. It starts with a statistically validated understanding of where the organization currently stands in terms of diverse leadership and how it got there. Then, like everything else in business, comes the hard, daily work of setting priorities and timelines, allocating resources, and establishing success measures and accountabilities. It requires laser focus and a long-term commitment to moving away from the status quo regardless of how uncomfortable it may be.

Sure, this is a heavy lift. Diversity at the leadership level runs counter to our human preferences to gravitate to people like ourselves. But those within underrepresented groups have been doing the heavy lifting every day of their lives, dealing with a discriminatory system that has disproportionately benefited the majority. We can do this. We can undo the systemic inequities that are products not only of unjust people but also of unjust systems. We can challenge the very structures that make the world go around. We can do this and we must.

Cracking the code requires that we employ quotas as a short-term fix, develop different people differently, and start much earlier.

Employ Quotas as a Short-Term Fix

We have yet to find anywhere in the world where addressing a systemic lack of representation occurred without first a change in legislation or organizational policy. Throughout history, the oppressed and their allies have had to fight for new laws that allowed them to vote, own property, work, and even to be considered fully human. But even after those laws become ratified, correcting the balance of power doesn't happen organically. That's why quotas are such an effective tool. Power is never relinquished, or even shared easily. This is why in democracies term limits, balance of power mechanisms, and elections are in place to move leaders along their terms of service. When these safeguards are weakened or eliminated, democracies run the risk of being authoritarian regimes whose power cannot be challenged.

Quotas dilute the stranglehold on power that certain groups have historically held. Individuals in these groups usually are both unwilling to give up their own power and reluctant to allow the power of people in their group to be diminished. So much of succession is a subjective process in which one leader taps the next, and almost every time it is someone who looks like them.

Quotas break this homogeneity of leadership cycle with the lever of enforcement. In politics, the proportion of women members of parliament grows three times faster in countries with quotas. In the six quota countries (Austria, Belgium, Germany, France, Italy, and Portugal) considered in the European Institute for Gender Equality analysis, the share of women on boards has increased 3% per year since the quota was introduced. Previously, the rate of increase was 0.9% annually. In the six quota countries, the average share of women on boards is 37.6%. In European countries without quotas, the share of women on boards is 24.3%.[12]

The Brazilian quota system mandates that businesses with more than one hundred employees fill 2% to 5% of positions with employees with disabilities, and as of 2016, the quota system has had positive results, leading to increased requests for workers with disabilities, which has led to many businesses surpassing the quotas, particularly in the retail, transportation, and financial services industries.[13]

So yes, quotas work exceedingly well to increase diversity. But they also create a great deal of backlash and can sometimes backfire entirely. In the United States, for example, backlash against affirmative action led to a watershed Supreme Court case (*Regents of the University of California v. Bakke*, 1978) that struck down quotas in universities and corporations.

Admittedly, quotas are a brute mechanism that can lead to bad behaviors. If the goal is simply to fill a certain number of positions with members of underrepresented groups, the need for qualified talent may be overlooked. On the other hand, even qualified talent may have their credentials questioned because others assume they are there just because of the quota. Another critical trip up is when quotas are confused with tokenism. For quotas to have an impact, there will have to be meaningful representation (and inclusion). It can't just be about hiring or promoting one "different" person to meet a requirement or because it looks good.

In the United States, it is a settled issue that quotas cannot be used proactively. In other parts of the world, they are allowed and are being used to move the needle. In 2003, Rwanda dictated that 30% of legislators had to be women, and ten years later, 64% were.[14] Chinese Taipei, known for electing its first female president, Tsai Ing-wen, in 2016, required candidate quotas, reserving seats at the national level as well as 1 in 4 seats for women at the local level. This has resulted in 38% of elected positions being filled by women.[15] And despite criticism, resistance, and attacks on female politicians, Timor-Leste instituted a gender quota in 2006 requiring a third of candidates be female. As of 2018, the country surpassed this goal, with 40% of positions filled by women.[16]

The reality of our world today is that race-based quotas trigger exponentially more intense backlash than gender-based quotas. Therefore, quotas for women are more likely to be implemented and less likely to be challenged than those aimed at having more racial/ethnic diversity. The proof that racial diversity is seen as more threatening to the status quo is in the statistics. Women as a talent pool have made measurable strides (with still a way to go, for sure), but when we disaggregate the data, it's clear that the majority of progress has been made by *White* women and women of color remain as woefully underrepresented as ever. While representation of women in C-suite positions has been slowly rising, reaching 24% in 2021, 20% of these positions are held by White women, versus 4% by women of color. The pattern looks the same even for lower levels of leadership positions.[17]

This is why we see the value of quotas in the short term but not as a long-term solution to the problem of homogeneous leadership. The backlash is real and fierce and holding it at bay for a long period of time is not sustainable. We recommend that organizations early in their inclusive organizational maturity use quotas to get a jump start on changing course, mindsets, and systems. They are effective in generating enough of a jolt that in combination with the many other tactics addressed throughout this book, they can fuel the organic, self-generating quest toward diversifying leadership in the long run.

Develop Different People Differently

This concept drives the disciples of meritocracy crazy.

The meritocracy mantra goes like this: "Treat everyone the same—in how they are hired, how they are developed, in how they are assessed—and let everyone rise up to the fullness of their potential regardless of their gender, race, disability, sexual orientation, etc. This is color-blind and gender-blind. And therefore the most fair and inclusive!"

We would love to believe this is true. While we embrace its intent, in practice our nearly fifty DE&I organizational assessments have proved over and over again that organizations fall significantly short of being true meritocracies. If they were, there would not be underrepresentation of specific groups. There would not be pay disparities or performance assessment disparities . . . unless people from underrepresented groups are actually inherently less able.

But since few would claim that—and there is zero evidence that this is true—let's get to what organizations need to do to truly level the playing field. This requires taking into account the impact that being "different" has on how people are treated, how they show up, and how they can develop and grow.

It matters if someone has been the victim of discrimination and unconscious bias, if they have heard a lifetime of messages that they are *less than*, or if they have continuously been bypassed for opportunities for promotions. This continual marginalization has a proven effect on people's self-confidence; it makes them more likely to second-guess themselves or less likely stretch their skills to get to the next level.

For these reasons, developing leaders from marginalized groups often requires differentiated development strategies that address the headwinds they have faced their whole lives and careers. Differentiated development does not and should not mean preferential treatment. In the end, all should compete fairly for the opportunities that exist. But if the field is tilted (it is) and everyone is not at the same starting line (they aren't), then corrections must be made.

So, what does differentiated development look like?

It offers management and leadership skills development like everyone gets. But it also addresses people's lived experience. It surfaces how a lifetime of messages of discrimination may have led some to take fewer calculated risks or to feel they need to meet every single criteria in a job posting before they apply for it, rather than just raising their hand because they're up for the challenge.

Korn Ferry research shows that people from underrepresented groups often will internalize the negative expectations of others, impacting their confidence. We have also found that when individuals understand that they have power over how their career progresses and can make choices about how they react to the barriers they face inside and outside work, they go on to achieve great things. These findings have formed the basis of Korn Ferry's The Power of Choice program, which for many years has empowered individuals from underrepresented groups with the insights, strategies, and tools they need to successfully advance their careers.

With programs and approaches like these, underrepresented talent can have an equitable chance to show what it can do. In a Korn Ferry longitudinal study, The Power of Choice participants demonstrated a greater degree of confidence after participating in the program, with 99% of alumni agreeing that they now can solve difficult problems, know how to handle unforeseen situations, and can deal with whatever comes their way. These numbers far exceed those of our Korn Ferry global norms database. And for more tangible proof that differentiated development works: a survey of The Power of Choice alumni showed that 39% had been promoted, and 47% said the programs had helped them transition into a higher or more desirable position.[18]

Inclusive organizations know the value of differentiated development and make no apologies for offering it. They know that in doing so, they are truly living up to the meritocracy principles that undergird so much of the workplace today.

Start Much Earlier: Pipeline Development
Through Early Childhood Education

By the time companies fan out to colleges for their annual new graduate recruiting, so much of the battle for more diversity has already been lost.

For example, it's no secret that the entire field of science, technology, engineering, and math (STEM) has traditionally been male-dominated. To this day, women are not equitably represented in this field at any level, let alone in leadership. For organizations that want to change this, it's not a matter of simply adding a few women at the top—especially since the field of available candidates is truly slim. Here, the responsibility to diversify leadership starts much earlier.

A SUCCESS STORY IN ADVANCEMENT: FAST PROMOTIONS AT A CONSUMER PRODUCTS COMPANY

When one consumer products company realized that its women-of-color employees had lower job satisfaction, lower manager trust scores, and slower time-to-promotion, it set out to find out more about the headwinds this group was facing. And once it became aware of the gaps, it sprang into action. Mentoring programs and differentiated development programs were instituted. One-to-one coaching for success was provided, and managers were trained to manage the headwinds of their women of color so they could optimize the performance of their teams.

Within a short amount of time, results took hold. There was a 100% reduction in attrition among participants in the program. Turnover was down from 42% to less than 2% in three years. Average onboarding time for new reporting relationships decreased by 25% to 40%. Advancement for participants increased by 75%. Time-to-promotion was accelerated by six to ten months. And one of the key objectives in diversity—representation of women of color leaders—increased from 4% to 7% at the senior manager, director, and vice president levels in two years. All this led to the organization winning the coveted Catalyst Award in recognition of its Leading Edge inclusion efforts.

While some progress has been made at the high school level to develop the pipeline of women in STEM, even by that age, stereotypes have already kicked in and gendered tracking paths have been carved that will make it harder to interest girls in these subjects. Companies need to get involved much earlier in the lives of girls to engage them before they have internalized the gender stereotypes that steer them away from STEM.

This can take the form of partnering with organizations dedicated to exposing preschool- and elementary-age girls to STEM subjects, partnering directly with schools to offer girl-centered STEM programs, providing interested girls with exciting opportunities such as summer camps, following up with internship opportunities, mentoring, and careful and intentional pipeline development.

The smartest play, however, is when competitors in the same industry band together to address the pipeline issue that affects them all. For example, Intel, Takeda, Boeing, and NASA have banded together with other corporations and nonprofits to engage 1 million more girls in STEM learning opportunities through afterschool and summer programs, provided over a five-year period by the Million Girls Moonshot. This initiative seeks to "inspire and prepare the next generation of innovators," including those from racially and ethnically underrepresented and under-served communities, by helping them to experience robotics, drones, coding, and artificial intelligence.

As laudable as this and similar programs are, and while 1 million sounds like a lot, the World Economic Forum has estimated the STEM skill shortage will be 1 *billion* by 2030[19]—a gap that we cannot even come close to filling if girls and women, as well as talent from racial/ethnic minorities, are not developed as part of this pipeline, beginning from early childhood education.

The message is clear: sometimes inclusive organizations will have to play the long game to achieve the ultimate goal of diversifying leadership.

8

Vital Task 2: Eradicate Polarization

It's hard to hate up close.

Brené Brown, *Braving the Wilderness*

POLARIZATION IS CLEAVING SOCIETIES AROUND THE WORLD. Elections are being decided by the narrowest of margins. Voting results are being questioned. Coups are being attempted. People on different sides are screaming at each other, or worse, inflicting physical and emotional harm. In the midst of this rending of the social fabric, can inclusive organizations help eradicate polarization? We believe so. In fact, we believe they must get into the fray, not only because they can offer a third way through the conundrum of seemingly irreconcilable differences but also because civil unrest and lack of social cohesion are simply bad for business.

While tempers and even violence flare out on the streets and within legislative bodies, there is plenty that inclusive organizations can do within their boundaries to significantly lower the heat and to contribute to cooling things down beyond their borders.

Let's look at how inclusive organizations can mitigate polarization within the enterprise by leveraging three of their key assets: organizational structure, a business case for sociopolitical stability, and investments in DE&I.

ORGANIZATIONAL STRUCTURE

One major advantage organizations have over societies at large is that there is a shared expectation among employees that they need to work together, regardless of differences, toward agreed-upon objectives. Usually, there are systemic informal and formal accountabilities tied to these objectives, and so if someone chooses to act out in a way that jeopardizes these shared interests, they can be let go. But societies don't have, nor should they have, the lever of "firing" constituents.

Organizations can leverage this asset of organizational structure by setting the expectation that employees must not let their differences get in the way of getting things done. Whatever one's opinions and beliefs around the various political and social issues currently polarizing society, organizations cannot allow those to result in the gridlock we see in various legislative bodies—and definitely not the contentious, disrespectful, and unproductive fighting we see on cable news and in demonstrations.

BUSINESS CASE FOR SOCIOPOLITICAL STABILITY

Capitalism and democracy go hand in hand. At its purest form, capitalism is premised on the freedom to innovate, borrow money to invest, and set up a business or mission-oriented organization. This horizontal, democratic approach requires an equally horizontal, democratic political structure that enables people the freedom to choose their leaders and make their policy preferences known.

This is why the economies in democracies are more robust than those of authoritarian regimes. In "Democracy Does Cause Growth," a paper published in the *Journal of Political Economy*, the four authors (who include experts in economic and government policy) present evidence from a group of countries between 1960 and 2010 that show a robust and sizeable effect of democracy on economic growth. They write, "Our central estimates suggest that a country that switches from nondemocracy to democracy achieves about 20% higher GDP [gross domestic product] per capita in the long run (over roughly the next 30 years). These are large but not implausible effects and suggest that the global rise in democracy over the past fifty years (of over 30 percentage points) has yielded roughly 6% higher world GDP."[1]

Why may this be? Democracies protect civil liberties as well as economically related rights (via contracting, property ownership, court systems to ensure compliance, and so on) that can be easily perverted by the cronyism of an authoritarian regime. Also, authoritarian systems govern top down, which can squelch the entrepreneurial spirit fueling capitalism. Companies—as well as the vast number of nonprofits that have emerged out of this entrepreneurial spirit—depend on a stable democratic system to thrive. "Polarization threatens this entire system," a CEO of a major financial institution shared with us. "We can't be passive and not address it because social viability consequences become business viability consequences."

We're aware that neither capitalism nor democracy operates so purely in real life and that there are plenty of weeds of corruption in the garden. But that just means that we cannot allow the system to break down even further than it has already. It is in the best interest of capitalism to stop polarization from furthering the discord we are facing now: distrust of the very democratic institutions established to enable capitalism, subversion of the electoral process, rules that lead to voter disenfranchisement, and the weakening of voter rights.

From a purely internal perspective, the business case for sociopolitical stability is even clearer. It creates a more happy and productive work-force. The authors of "Democracy Does Cause Growth" declare that a divisive environment, on the other hand, can negatively affect employee sentiment—and performance. To prove their point, they cite a 2016 survey by the American Psychological Association, taken in the midst of the 2016 US presidential contest between Hillary Clinton and Donald Trump. The survey found that 24% of workers said a divisive political environment led to negative work outcomes, including poor work quality and lower productivity. According to the report, "Men were more likely than women, and younger workers (ages 18–34) were more likely than older generations, to have experienced negative consequences of political discussions at work this election season. . . . Similarly, these groups were more likely to say that because of political discussions at work, they feel more isolated from their colleagues, have a more negative view of them and have experienced an increase in workplace hostility."[2]

It's also an internal organizational issue. For all the emotional froth churned by polarization, it is not created by the majority. According to More in Common, an organization that "develops initiatives to address fracturing within society," 70% of Germans and 86% of French people are concerned about increasingly hateful public rhetoric. And *Harvard Business Review* references a 2018 study that placed 67% of Americans in the "'Exhausted Majority,' who say they feel fatigued by politics and feel forgotten in current debates." Therefore, "these employees may feel unwelcome in a highly politicized environment."[3]

INVESTMENTS IN DE&I

All of which brings us to the third asset. For a generation, many companies have been describing the importance of DE&I to the organization from a multiplicity of angles—such as acquisition of the best talent, talent optimization, corporate reputation and brand, the right thing to do, innovation, expanding markets—to make the business case for investment in their DE&I pillars and strategies. This investment, these pillars, and these strategies also can be turned to forcefully counter polarization within the organization, because DE&I is the opposite of what polarization stands for.

Leveraging their organizations' DE&I resources, training, and structures, leaders can make efforts to bridge gaps and foster cooperation among employee groups in the workplace. The approaches need to include both pragmatic and strategic takedowns of polarization. The pragmatic takedowns are to foster listening sessions, set reasonable norms, and seek joint projects. The strategic takedowns are to embrace commonality (up to a point), fight disinformation, and relentlessly communicate why polarization is bad for business.

A PRAGMATIC TAKEDOWN OF POLARIZATION

Given all the shouting, snarkiness, and meanness on the mild side of the spectrum, and outright violence on the extreme side, polarization may seem impossible to mitigate or manage. But it can be done by following some low-key, commonsense, people-centric, inclusive approaches. We realize that for some readers, these approaches may come across as naive and idealistic. But we have seen them work time after time.

While inclusive organizations are very limited in their ability to affect the deepest political and societal fissures, they have quite a bit of agency and power to significantly lessen, and even approach the eradication of, polarization within their boundaries. In the process, they foster a workforce of more empathetic people who are more invested in mending the rifts in our larger societies.

1. FOSTER LISTENING SESSIONS

Research by Boston Consulting Group shows that, not surprisingly, the fewer overlapping perspectives within groups, the more polarization there will be.[4] In our experience, one key way to narrow the distance between different groups and their differing positions is to engage in carefully designed and executed listening sessions with individuals from groups that usually don't interact with each other.

To do this, at Korn Ferry we have developed an approach called Real Talk. Thousands of our clients have experienced some version of this approach, through either public webinars or facilitated small-group sessions for clients.

The goal of these sessions is to listen to understand, not to debate. Our breakthrough in figuring out how to do this came in the immediate aftermath of George Floyd's murder in May 2020. When emotions were their hottest and polarization at its most extreme, we stepped into the fray with a call for this type of listening. Within a week of the release of the video of Floyd's murder, which unleashed street protests all over the world, Korn Ferry launched a six-part webinar series over ten working days called *Raceism Matters: Eradicating Racism in the Corporate World*. A cumulative 100,000 people worldwide Zoomed in and, through honest conversation, listening, seeking to understand, and empathy toward people of color as well as Whites, these webinars were a balm in the midst of the conflagration. They fostered connection and also offered pragmatic steps all of us could take to navigate the pain of that time and embark on a more transformative journey. For those who participated, the webinars went a long way toward eradicating polarization during this very polarizing time.

What we learned from these webinars, combined with nearly fifty years of legacy work of fostering inclusion in organizations, led to a solution we called Race Matters and another called Real Talk. While the webinars

KORN FERRY RACEISM MATTERS WEBINARS

Hear Me
Black Voices on Their Pain and Anger
Recorded June 4, 2020
Four Black professionals from three generations share what the tragic killings of George Floyd, Breonna Taylor, Ahmaud Arbery, and many other Blacks meant for them and their families.

Stand By Me
How Whites Can Become Authentic Allies
Recorded June 9, 2020
White privilege has always been difficult to explore. Without accusation, we talk about how Whites can leverage racial privilege to be effective allies for achieving equity.

In My Shoes
Addressing Systemic Racism Through Structural Inclusion
Recorded June 10, 2020
The emphasis of diversity, equity, and inclusion over the past few years has been to tackle people's behavior with unconscious bias training. But while this is worthwhile, it's not enough. In this webinar, we discuss how organizations are tackling the systemic racism in their existing talent systems.

Don't Talk, Do
Creating a Racially Equitable Future as Inclusive Leaders
Recorded June 11, 2020
Organizations need CEOs to be champions of racial equity. But to lead their businesses to become truly inclusive and equitable, they also need to be highly skilled in a multitude of ways. Here, we talk about what inclusive leadership looks like in action.

Power in the Boardroom
What Board Directors Can Do to
Eradicate Racism in the Corporate World
Recorded June 18, 2020
Eradicating racism is now on the corporate agenda. And leaders have the responsibility to act and the power to make a difference. What can they do?

Source: "Raceism Matters," webinar series, Korn Ferry, https://infokf
.kornferry.com/race-matters.html.

were more of an immediate response that had a lot to do with creating awareness, empathy, and understanding, Race Matters and Real Talk offered very pragmatic, structured guidelines, scripts, questions to ask and answers, and templates for how to prepare for difficult conversations. Thousands of people have participated in these programs and more have utilized the tools we supplied to have conversations with their teams on their own, multiplying the impact.

Participants gave us an average score of above four on a five-point scale on our postsession feedback form rating the program's effectiveness, enabling us to confidently say that through our work, combined with the work of tens of thousands of major competitors and boutiques elsewhere, the concepts of inclusion and the sessions conducted around them indeed have served to cool things down in polarized societies.

It gives us hope that even while the political body and society seem impossibly and destructively divided, inclusive organizations can make a difference in eradicating polarization.

2. SET REASONABLE NORMS

Earlier, we talked about how organizational structures serve to prevent polarization from jeopardizing shared company objectives. But one on one, we actually want conversations to happen so that maybe, just maybe, our understanding of another's opinion will broaden our horizon and bring us closer together.

One thing that the listening sessions and consequent Real Talk and Race Matters conversations taught us is that talking about what divides us is hard. But without these conversations, these divides widen. We found that the *how* really matters. Organizations can and have to set reasonable norms and rules for how employees interact with one another and how to approach our differences in a manner that will allow us to learn from one another rather than fight to get our point across.

Here are the norms we ask participants to agree to before we start a listening session:

It's about learning. Be sure that you come from a place of seeking to understand the other side, not to convince them that you are right. Acknowledge that it's okay to not have the answers, not have the "right" words, and not have an "action step" right now.

Learning starts with listening. Practice active listening by assuring you are fully present and giving full attention to what the other person is saying. Don't start formulating your retort before the other person is finished speaking. Pause and process what you've heard.

Respond rather than react. Resist the temptation to jump in with your argument. Reacting impulsively might come naturally, since most polarizing issues have a very strong emotional component. Be thoughtful in your response to make it clear you listened to the other side.

Challenge the idea, not the person. There is a lot to disagree with in today's society. Issues of social justice, civil rights, climate change—these are big-ticket items. It is easy to paint the person who thinks differently from you with a negative label. *Backward, elitist, racist, misogynistic, weak* . . . you name it. Remember, no good conversation has ever been had when calling each other names. Be sure to focus on the topic.

Keep calm and carry on. Closing the distance between two polarizing points of view requires cool heads. No matter how infuriating you find an idea, no matter how much the other person may antagonize you, please stay calm.

It's okay to disagree. Acknowledge that you may not change the other person's mind; remember the purpose was to learn, not to win. And if the conversation was calm and both sides listened actively, that's a step closer to eradicating polarization. We don't have to like or agree with what we hear or see, but if we can walk away with a better understanding of where people are coming from and why, our amygdalae can be calmer and our interactions with each other less stressful, charged, or even violent. That's a pretty good payoff.

3. SEEK JOINT PROJECTS

Much of the polarization in our society stems from the simple fact that everyone tends to move in their own circle. Whether we are politically left-leaning or right-leaning, chances are that those we all choose to be around carry similar views. We move in like-minded circles, are exposed to the same news, and share in the views of our circles on social media, with every Like confirming what we already know: that we are right about a certain issue. Tony Malinauskas, an Associate Principal at Korn Ferry who has done extensive research on political polarization, explains, "This type of repetition is called the 'mirror effect.' It's when a person believes information that they've repeatedly been exposed to, even if it's false. This is why many politicians have taken to the practice of continuing to repeat lies despite their having been debunked by credible sources."

Very rarely do we have to think about the accuracy of our position, since everyone around us has the same beliefs. If "everyone" agrees that undocumented immigrants are overrunning the country, vaccinations are dangerous, or mask mandates are unnecessary, there is no need to probe these notions. Conversely, if "everyone" agrees that burning fossil fuels, cutting down forests, and industrial farming cause an increase in earth's temperature, then there is nothing to argue about. There is harmony, the opposite of polarization.

When we are then confronted with people who think differently, vote differently, pray differently, or love differently, we can be quick to wonder why we should spend time with them. Their difference is "wrong," after all. We know this to be true because all of our friends—our entire eco-system—confirms it. And when things get really polarized, we often go a step further: not only are the others *wrong*, but they are naive, ridiculous, stupid, ignorant, or hateful for thinking the way they do. So we stay away, never socializing with the other side, thus widening the distance between the poles. The opposite of what we want.

In order to eradicate—or at least lessen—polarization, we suggest that organizations leverage the contact hypothesis, which suggests that contact between different groups can reduce prejudice. Gordon Allport, who first came up with the concept, highlights four conditions that need to be in place for this theory to work: equal status, common goals, cooperation, and institutional support.[5]

This is where inclusive organizations come in. Many organizations have started to support and encourage corporate volunteer work, going beyond monetary donations to their favorite charity. Sponsoring an employee volunteer program has proved to have many benefits, including giving back to the communities in which an organization is located, boosting moral and engagement among employees, and also increasing productivity and lowering absenteeism. And here's another one: reducing polarization.

Corporate volunteer projects fulfill all the conditions Allport high-lighted. Take Habitat for Humanity, where employees of an organization come together and build houses for people in need, for example.

Equal status: People of all organizational levels come together to build a house. Differences among directors, vice presidents, analysts, and receptionists vanish. Everyone contributes.

Common goals: Everyone wants to build a house for a family in need.

Cooperation: This is a team project; no one can do this alone.

Institutional support: None of this could happen without the corporate partnership of the organization with Habitat for Humanity. By allowing employees to take time away from work and contribute to a greater cause, the organization is lending the necessary institutional support.

Joint projects promote contact among different types of people and reduce prejudice by lessening feelings of anxiety and increasing empathy for others.[6] The result is a meaningful shared experience independent of whatever differences of opinion we have.

A STRATEGIC TAKEDOWN OF POLARIZATION

1. EMBRACE COMMONALITY (UP TO A POINT)

For those unfamiliar with our Korn Ferry point of view on being open and valuing differences, we caution strongly against minimizing differences as a default way of managing the complexity of diversity. Given the polarization of our times, we recognize that this inclination needs a tactical and situational adjustment.

First, let's discuss why focusing too much on commonality, referred to as "minimization"—where differences are seen as inconsequential and what matters most is what we have in common—has served as a barrier to inclusion.[7] The problem is that it can act as an erasure of the unique elements that make up a person's self-identity. For all their apparent surface egalitarianism, statements such as "I am color-blind" or "I am gender-neutral" ignore the reality that people of different races and gender identities have very different experiences in the world.

Erasure is the enemy of inclusion. It goes against the fundamental DE&I premise that we can achieve greater innovation and business results by leveraging the diversity in our organizations. How can we possibly leverage that diversity if we are minimizing it?

That said, we are now amid a dangerous polarization based on political and social ideology that in many ways intersects with different dimensions of diversity, like age, gender, race/ethnicity, and abilities. That means we can't lose sight of the power of surfacing differences and must also double down on seeking out our common humanity. What are the places where we have comparable aspirations for successful lives, healthy families, and a prosperous place to work?

While we may not agree on the best way to curb rising violence, we can agree that we want our kids to be safe. While we may not agree on immigration policy, we can agree that labor shortages are hurting our ability to deliver goods and services to customers. While we may not agree on what is causing climate change, we can agree that we want our loved ones and our neighborhoods and the businesses within to be protected from natural disasters. We may not agree on the causes, but maybe we can agree on the outcomes.

The *All That We Share* ad campaign by TV2, the most watched TV network in Denmark, did an excellent job treading that line of celebrating differences and focusing on the things that unite us in these divisive times. In the video, people who share some form of visible identity are grouped together inside boxes painted on the floor. A facilitator asks them a series of questions about experiences or passions they have, and they are asked to respond by moving to an empty box, where they will be joined by those who also share that characteristic.

The questions continue and new empty boxes are filled: those who were the class clowns, those who are stepparents, those who are spiritual, those who love to dance, those who were bullied, those who were bullies, those who saved lives, those who are lonely, those who are brokenhearted, those who had sex the past week. We see people who were originally separated from others based on one set of visible differences finding themselves now in boxes with those others. The message is obvious: it sure is a lot harder to feel leery of someone visibly different from us when we are standing side by side in the same box of brokenhearted souls.

The last question spoke to the power of being part of a larger entity, in this case, a country: *Who loves Denmark?* Of course, it was everyone.

This ad turned out to be one of the most shared ever, with more than 8 million interactions and more than 284 million unpaid views. Viewers also translated it into more than thirty languages. The best result? A 27% increase in the number of those who believe "we have more in common than what separates us."[8]

2. FIGHT DISINFORMATION

Disinformation is rampant in our current Orwellian world. This plays out as propaganda, information warfare, and psychological warfare, and it's corroding the public's trust in governmental, religious, and corporate institutions, undermining societies' abilities to maintain cohesion and keep chaos at bay.

It is being used to pit groups of people against one other through hate speech that leverages humans' proclivity to not trust people who are not like them. This is done by creating mechanisms that, via decentralized, untraceable, anonymous bot farms, flood mass media channels with unflattering disinformation, untruths about a group already seen as not trustworthy due to its differences. This onslaught by artificial intelligence disinformation armies then metastasizes *fear* of the other into *hatred* of the other.

"Hate speech and information disorder are weapons of war and enablers of conflict, used to create and reinforce sentiments of mistrust, exclusion, fear, and anger toward perceived enemies, and simultaneously to unite allies," write four social scientists in a research report commissioned by the Social Science Research Council. Especially worrisome, they continue, is that when online hate speech "is appropriated and shared by ordinary citizens, [it] is used to support open confrontations between nations or blocs, and can be approved or encouraged by state governments. While the involvement of governments and powerful organized groups (such as terrorist organizations) is striking in concerted disinformation campaigns and propaganda, these tactics also turn ordinary users into active participants in the spread of hate and disinformation."[9] And it's these ordinary users who then can turn their disinformed fear and hatred into violent confrontations on the street or into votes cast for corrosive candidates who augment polarization.

Organizations must take an active role in detecting, labeling, and countering disinformation, because their employees are not immune to these destructive societal forces that from the outside in are actively working against diversity, equity, and inclusion. Organizations can counter this by harnessing their scale and their already formidable information creation and dissemination powers.

Corporations and large nonprofits are information factories. Whether they are part of the knowledge economy or not, all organizations gather and disseminate information. They conduct research, sift and test their findings for new insights. They carefully curate the story they want to tell about themselves and they educate their consumers in ways that influence their shopping behaviors and choices. While this can be done manipulatively, here we are speaking to the righteous side of corporations who truly believe they have a product or service that would make people's lives better if they knew about their solution and how to attain it.

Corporations spent $837.5 billion on advertising globally in 2021 and are expected to surpass $1 trillion in 2026. And when it comes to research, "corporate funding across disciplines has grown and 41% of researchers expect it to grow over the next two to three years." For example, when it comes to solutions to climate change, it is predicted venture capitalists will invest a record $26 billion in 2021 for climate tech–focused funds and $58 billion for climate tech companies.[10]

This means there are deep pockets to create information. Strategically, companies now need to harness their resources to counter disinformation. They can do so "by promoting the cause of independent, fact-based journalism" as the authors from Boston Consulting Group and More in Common urge in their *Harvard Business Review* article on the topic.[11] This will help protect the integrity of factual information.

Think about how unprepared the government and pharmaceutical companies that created COVID-19 vaccines were to counter antivaccination disinformation. Consider how this led to a critical public health hazard and further polarization within our society.

To counter disinformation, organizations can seek partnerships with the social media platforms that have become the conduits of disinformation parasites. Companies can pressure social media companies such as Meta, Telegram, and others that they do business with to screen for disinformation and the excessively corrosive language coursing through their feeds. Examples of this pressure are working.

In 2019, in response to both external and internal pressure, Instagram developed the Restrict feature to decrease online harassment and bullying. The feature allows users to categorize other accounts as restricted, which hides those accounts' comments and messages from the user. Once the user restricts an account, they also will no longer receive notifications when that person comments on a post, though they are still able to manually approve whether content can be shared. During the testing period, the Restrict feature "significantly reduced the number of unwanted interactions and experiences of bullying" because it gave users control of the content in which they were tagged. Additionally, Instagram rolled out a new feature to identify comments as "mean-spirited" before they were posted, in order to prompt users to reconsider making or sharing hurtful posts.[12]

3. RELENTLESSLY COMMUNICATE WHY POLARIZATION IS BAD FOR BUSINESS

We have made the case that polarization is simply bad for business, and so, if for no other reason than their economic best interests, inclusive organizations should be relentless in strategically eradicating polarization from their workplaces.

Ignited by the antiracism protests in the United States in 2020, the executive team of a large health diagnostics laboratory wanted to do its part in closing the gap between the polarized factions of society and inside their organizations. They participated in our Korn Ferry executive version of Real Talk, called Conversation—part of our *Raceism Matters* offering. Once they understood the business implications of sustained polarization, they asked their most senior leaders, several hundred people, to participate.

The rollout of the Real Talk sessions was just the beginning. What followed were inclusion and diversity performance metrics that were incorporated into all people leader reviews. In fact, according to Caitlyn Dipierro, Senior Principal at Korn Ferry, 20% of people leaders' performance metrics counted toward their willingness and ability to lead the eradication of polarization. Additional initiatives premised on common interests and objectives that people generally agreed upon made the task of eradicating polarization part of how business is run, from offering nutrition classes in their communities to collaborating with schools in writing health curricula, teaching kindergarteners to cook, or launching a health segment in collaboration with a children's TV show.

Also using Real Talk was Russell Investments, which took this approach globally to more than 1,300 of its people worldwide. Appropriately, the polarization topics varied by country. In Japan, the conversations addressed gender polarization while in countries like Australia and the United States, race was the center of gravity. Russell now touts this and various other efforts in its proposals as it pitches for new business, and the company reports that it offers a competitive advantage.

Before continuing, we want to make a fine but important distinction between this vital task of Eradicate Polarization and the related one, Achieve Justice, which we explore in the next chapter.

If we eradicate polarization without seeking to also achieve justice, we may create a safer culture, but not a more inclusive one. We may create environments in which things get swept under the rug, left unaddressed, to fester. Or the organization may become so disengaged from the issues that really matter in society that it loses relevance. Conversely, to achieve justice without eradicating polarization is to heat things up so much that there is no room for imagination and courage. That's no way to live—or to run a business.

We see Eradicate Polarization as a vital task that organizations must focus on internally, while Achieve Justice requires them to fully engage issues both outside and inside the organizational boundaries. In the next chapter, we'll explore how.

9

Vital Task 3:
Achieve Justice

Remember that hope is a powerful lesson even when all else is lost.

Nelson Mandela,
first president of South Africa

WHEN DISCOVER CEO ROGER HOCHSCHILD HEARD A speech by university professor and activist Ibram X. Kendi challenging corporate America, he took it to heart. What had caught Hochschild's attention was Kendi's point that very few companies were addressing inclusion in sustainable ways, such as investing their assets in under-served communities.

Hochschild and his executive team made the decision to open Discover's next call center in Chatham, a cornerstone Black community on Chicago's South Side, where the unemployment rate of 15.7% was nearly double the city of Chicago's average. As a further commitment, 75% of the construction spend went to minority/women-owned business enterprises.

"Discover recognizes that traditional corporate site selection has contributed to issues of unequal opportunity in our society, and we want to be part of the solution," Hochschild told the *Chicago Tribune.*[1]

The response was overwhelming. Discover received more than 1,300 applications for twenty leadership roles in the first seventy-two hours after the company's announcement. The new center opened in June 2021 and quickly scored high marks for customer satisfaction and retention. By the end of 2021, more than two hundred people were employed at the Chatham center, and 83% of them lived within a five-mile radius.

Within the next three years, Discover expects to employ nearly a thousand people full time, with customer care representatives paid a starting salary of at least $17.25 per hour, with health insurance, a 401(k) plan eligibility, paid time off, and free college education for those who want it. The facility will also include space for community-based organizations and local businesses to host meetings and events and will serve as a training and meeting space for Discover employees.

CEO Hochschild wants the Chatham center to serve as a model for how Discover lives up to its values of diversity, inclusion, and equity—from the site selection to hiring practices to community engagement and procurement. He is showing that major organizations can help achieve justice in a particular community in a way that benefits the bottom line. But skeptics abound.

DO JUSTICE AND PROFITS MIX?

Justice takes many forms. In the legal criminal space, it's about holding law-breakers accountable for their actions. In legal civic cases, it's about financial restitution to those who were hurt economically, physically, or emotionally by the actions of others. In the political and governmental space, justice can come seismically for an entire nation through landmark legislation or supreme court and tribunal rulings that free slaves, confer voting rights to those excluded, and legalize marriage for those prohibited.

But what does achieving justice look like for for-profit organizations? Of course, companies should be and are held accountable for the fair treatment of individuals and for providing a safe environment free of physical or emotional harm. That's why policies, ethics, and human resources exist. This protection of the individual then rolls up into the protection of whole groups of people who, on the basis of a shared characteristic such as gender, race, disability, nationality, or the like, are measurably and systematically being treated unfairly.

Issues of justice and equity as they relate to the workforce have already been thoroughly addressed throughout the book. Here, we explore the role of organizations in contributing to justice outside their main purview by leveraging their brand, reputation, and economic prowess.

This is no easy task. Systemic injustice is deeply entrenched in our societies. Additionally, achieving justice in the broader society has traditionally been outside the scope of for-profit businesses.

Yet the tumultuous, polarized times we live in are demanding a shift—in part due to the raised consciousness that organizations themselves have been major contributors to the structural exclusion of certain groups. According to the Edelman Trust Barometer, 54% of employees globally believe that CEOs should speak publicly on controversial political and social issues they care about. And 53% of consumers agree that every brand has a responsibility to get involved in at least one social issue that does not directly impact its business.[2]

Some companies, such as Unilever (human rights),[3] Mars (removal of Uncle Ben's icon),[4] Nike (embracing of Black Lives Matter),[5] Marriott (standing up against the "Muslim ban"),[6] Ulta (pledge to source proportionally from minority-owned business),[7] and Patagonia (environmental racial justice),[8] have embraced this shift, but many have not. And others, such as Disney (LGBTQ+ issues), have been caught in the crossfire of their ambivalence.

Whether it's speaking up on behalf of voter rights, war and climate refugees, or transgender youth, or against hate crimes, more companies are trying to act consistently with their stated DE&I values. But they also see the importance to their business—failure to act hurts their ability to attract and retain talent, their brand reputation, and consequently, sales.

Disney learned firsthand that not having a stand can hurt its brand. Long known as an LGBTQ+ friendly Magic Kingdom escape, the company's silence regarding Florida's "Don't Say Gay" law brought on protests by employees and boycotts by consumers.[9] When the company finally spoke up against the law, its condemnations in turn invited protests from the other side, who showed up at the Happiest Place on Earth with angry signs attacking those who are LGBTQ+.

Given the polarization that often gets triggered when speaking up for justice, is it worth it for inclusive organizations to do this? And how much difference does it make when they do?

In the next section, we will go around the world, showcasing organizations that are addressing justice related to a variety of diversity issues, such as gender, sexual orientation and identity, disability, refugee status, race, and Indigenous rights. We will see how they are using their organizational brands and power to advocate for justice in broader society and government policies.

GENDER JUSTICE

Patriarchal societies—which is pretty much the dominant reality everywhere—sure don't like it when women gain freedoms and rise in power. It's not just the Taliban in Afghanistan keeping women and girls from attending schools and universities. In the United States—the birthplace of modern feminism—women's rights over their own bodies are being stripped away.

In the wake of this stark attack on women's rights, organizations are grappling with how to take a stand. In the past, organizations have stayed clear of issues that were perceived as too political; there are shareholders to consider, after all. But the crosscurrents are increasing in intensity. Inclusive organizations are starting to realize that having a responsibility for their employees does not stop at five p.m. when their workdays end. It extends to their well-being outside work as well.

The assault on the rights and well-being of female employees did not sit well with many. Organizations such as Amazon, Apple, Citigroup, Mastercard, Salesforce, Starbucks, Tesla, and Yelp have broadened their health benefits to include the coverage of travel fees for employees who are trying to seek an abortion if the procedure is no longer legal near their home.[10] In addition, rideshare companies Lyft and Uber announced they would provide legal resources for drivers should they be sued for driving passengers to an abortion.

But taking a stance on behalf of gender justice isn't just limited to US companies or women's bodily autonomy. Globally, the fashion industry employs more than 75 million workers. About 85% are women and most work without employment contracts or labor law protections.[11] In addition, in many countries, women face gender-based violence and limited access to health information and services. In Kenya, garment manufacturer Hela, which supplies major brands like Calvin Klein and Tommy Hilfiger, employs a workforce that is 75% female. That means that any way it supports its staff has an outsize effect on women in the community. Hela is working to achieve gender justice for its community by providing free on-site day care, a health clinic with a nurse midwife, and mobile health care services such as screenings for cervical cancer, blood pressure, HIV/AIDS testing and education, and nutrition education.[12]

Organizations like Hela are beginning to realize the impact this societal problem is having on their business. When women have to miss work or leave their jobs for health reasons, it directly affects their employers. This is the reason why gender parity by 2025 would translate into $28 trillion being added to the global economy.[13]

LGBTQ+ JUSTICE

At the 2013 annual Starbucks meeting in Seattle, CEO Howard Schultz was approached by a shareholder who complained the company was losing customers over its support of gay marriage. The shareholder in question described the company's earnings as "disappointing" after a boycott by the National Organization for Marriage. To this, Schultz responded that the company had in fact achieved a 38% shareholder return and, moreover, that the decision was not a financial one to him. The people Starbucks employed and their diversity were of more importance. Schultz ended by saying, "If you feel, respectfully, that you can get a higher return than the 38% you got last year, it's a free country. You can sell your shares in Starbucks and buy shares in another company. Thank you very much."[14]

To be one of the tens of millions of LGBTQ+ community members around the world is to risk being bullied, attacked, fired, fined, jailed, physically attacked, or even killed. Although some countries have protections against these forms of injustice, people still choose to harm those who are LGBTQ+—the law be damned. In other countries, these injustices can be lawfully perpetrated by the state itself.

It's no wonder, then, that LGBTQ+ individuals are more likely to experience depression and other mental illnesses, lack of stable housing, and food insecurity.[15] LGBTQ+ youth are more than four times as likely as their peers to attempt suicide,[16] and 45% of LGBTQ+ youth surveyed in 2021 had seriously considered attempting suicide in the past year.[17]

The injustices carry through into the workplace. LGBTQ+ workers, compared to cisgender workers, make 90 cents on the dollar. This pay gap grows with intersections of race (80 cents and 70 cents on the dollar for Black and Native American LGBTQ+ workers, respectively) and gender (87 cents, 70 cents, 70 cents, and 60 cents on the dollar for LGBTQ+ women, nonbinary and other nonconforming genders, trans men, and trans women, respectively).[18]

LGBTQ+ employees in more than half of the world lack legal protection in the workplace, meaning they can be denied jobs or promotions or be terminated based on their sexual orientation or gender identity.[19] In China, the Philippines, and Thailand, 21%, 30%, and 23% of LGBTQ+ adults, respectively, have faced discrimination, bullying, or harassment in the workplace. Their experiences ranged from derogatory jokes, slurs, and rumors to being denied jobs and promotions, with some job postings explicitly requiring non-LGBTQ+ applicants.[20] In Asia, 20% of executives interviewed noted that openly identifying as LGBTQ+ in the office is considered a "hindrance to one's career." In fact, 60% of survey respondents stated that their business's commitment to and investment in LGBTQ+ inclusion should stay the same or even be decreased.[21]

At the same time, India is losing roughly $32 billion yearly due to its attrition of and discrimination against LGBTQ+ employees. And in the United States, greater inclusion of LGBTQ+ employees translates to an estimated $9 billion annually that could be added to the economy. From a customer perspective, LGBTQ+ customers demonstrate some of the highest brand loyalty to companies that "have their back." The community also flexes significant spending power, with an estimated $800 billion a year in the United States.[22]

It can be difficult to maintain consistency in the call for LGBTQ+ justice. For instance, Adidas was the first sneaker brand to release Pride sneakers, in 2015, yet it also was one of the main 2018 World Cup sponsors in Russia, meaning it poured money into a country where those who are LGBTQ+ can be jailed for being gay.[23] In another example, even after debuting its Pride merchandise, Pink initially refused to hire a transgender model. After the backlash, it changed its position and has now done so.[24] When companies say they support LGBTQ+ rights in an attempt to be inclusive and to tap into the marketplace, they need to weigh how ready they are to see that commitment all the way through.

Professor Suen Yiu Tung, director of the Sexualities Research Programme at the Chinese University of Hong Kong, sums up the totality of benefits of LGBTQ+ justice: "Creating better workplaces for LGBTI employees will benefit the national economy, individual companies, organization and departments, and the economic and social well-being of LGBTI people and their families."[25]

There are companies that very much get all this. Accenture, for example, stands up for its LGBTQ+ employees and the global community. The firm established employee resource groups for LGBTQ+ employees in more than forty-five countries, along with an ally program over 110,000 members strong. To address the obstacles and understand the experiences of the LGBTQ+ community, Accenture has conducted its own research on inclusion and LGBTQ+ leadership in the workplace. It also developed a nonbinary voice assistant, Sam, to promote gender nonconforming diversity.[26] Outside the office, Accenture collaborates with the Partnership for Global LGBTIQ+ Equality to advocate for the community and support the UN's LGBTI standards of workplace equality.

Other companies are taking up the gauntlet by advocating for LGBTQ+ rights in the public arena. For instance, Apple signed a Supreme Court amicus briefing in 2019 arguing against the exclusion of LGBTQ+ people from federal civil rights law, and the company signed a Human Rights Campaign letter supporting the opposition of anti-LGBTQ+ legislation that same year.[27] Another company advocating for LGBTQ+ justice is Coca-Cola. In addition to offering transgender health insurance and providing leadership development to young LGBTQ+ individuals, Coca-Cola advocates against anti-LGBTQ+ legislation in multiple US states, including Mississippi, Missouri, and Tennessee, and partnered with other businesses in Georgia to defeat the Religious Freedom Restoration Act in 2020.[28] Especially noteworthy is Bharat Aluminium Company in India. In this country where there are far fewer protections for those who are LGBTQ+, BALCO has publicly committed to hire transgender employees. To create an inclusive, supportive environment for these employees, the company has also engaged in gender-sensitization workshops for the entire workforce of the company.[29]

WHAT IS IT ABOUT SOCIAL MEDIA THAT MAKES PEOPLE SO POLARIZED?

Apparently, echo chambers of like-minded individuals are not the main culprit in polarization on social media. Rather, the problem of polarization lies with "influencers." These are the people at the center of a network who are connected to every person in the group. While each person in an egalitarian network may be connected to only a few others, in a centralized network, the person or people in the middle (that is, the influencers) are connected to every person. This gives them a disproportionally powerful position—an outsize influence, if you will—over the group.

"In a centralized echo chamber, if the influencer at the middle shows even a small amount of partisan bias, it can become amplified throughout the entire group. But in egalitarian networks, ideas spread based on their quality, and not the person touting them," Damon Centola writes in *Scientific American*.

According to Centola, social media exacerbates polarization because "online networks are often organized around a few key influencers. This feature of social media is one of the main reasons why misinformation and fake news has become so pervasive."

Source: Damon Centola, "Why Social Media Makes Us More Polarized and How to Fix It," *Scientific American*, October 15, 2020, https://www .scientificamerican.com/article/why-social-media-makes-us-more-polarized -and-how-to-fix-it.

DISABILITY JUSTICE

Globally there are 1.1 billion people with some form of disability, making this the largest minority group.[30] Despite this, people with disabilities are often the most overlooked in terms of disparities. The injustices encountered by other groups may go unaddressed, but at least we are for the most part aware of them. For those with disabilities, the discrimination is often unaddressed and invisible to the larger society—a particularly sad reality when you realize that this is the one form of diversity that any person can acquire at any time, due to an accident or illness.

People with a disability have the highest unemployment rate of any group. Globally, 44% of people with disabilities are unemployed. Adding to the injustice is that even when they are employed, workers with disabilities earn 37% less than their peers. In 2011, they took in 63 cents for every dollar paid to workers without disabilities.[31]

"There is a societal belief that having a disability means you *can't* work," the late Marca Bristo, a disability rights activist, told Andrés a few years ago. "The whole system is based on a model that people with disabilities have to be taken care of because they can't take care of themselves."

So if disability does not equal inability, disability justice requires that we rethink the capabilities that are really required for a job.

In the case of neurodiversity, many neurodiversity advocates question the premise that it is even a disability. Companies such as Danish software-testing firm Specialisterne specifically seek out neurodiverse talent. They value people with autism for their sometimes photographic memories or obsessive attention to detail. In fact, there is a growing recognition that among the most brilliant people (Albert Einstein and Thomas Edison, for example), there is a high incidence of learning disabilities or autism.[32] Their minds roamed the outer fields of thought and brought back ideas no one had yet considered. With so many critical twenty-first-century problems to be solved the world over, it's time people pay attention to these outliers whose rare skills we urgently need.

Able-bodied people's beliefs about the requirements for performing a job are also riddled with assumptions that must be questioned. For example, a person who uses a wheelchair applied for a store manager job at a retail store, where the hiring manager's immediate reaction was, "You can't do this." The applicant responded by saying, "Give me a day-to-day listing of a store manager's responsibilities, and let's walk through them and see what a person in a wheelchair can't do." As they went through the list, the only thing that came up as an obstacle would be reaching a high shelf. The applicant said, "Okay, that's fair. But is that something I need to do, an absolute?" The manager answered, "No, it's not."

UNIVERSAL DESIGN = INCLUSIVE DESIGN

We are at the cusp of a golden age of addressing disabilities in unprecedented ways—through the mainstreaming of prosthetics controlled with the brain, wearables for addressing biological differences, and artificial intelligence to address cognitive differences. Inclusive organizations grasp this and own leadership into this new today.

But one-off efforts by organizations will not be enough. Structural justice demands concerted, coordinated, scalable effort. People with disabilities require more than just larger parking spaces and restroom stalls, though that's a start. A growing number of organizations, therefore, have been using an inclusive approach with a design principle called universal design, which benefits both their employees and their customers.

In a universal design building, the elevators open on both sides to eliminate jostling for wheelchairs, voice commands announce the floors, and light sensors automatically adjust as the sun moves across the sky, keeping lighting levels constant. All desks and chairs are easily adjustable, and restroom entrances are set up with long, curved entrances and without external doors, so people in wheelchairs can easily enter and exit while privacy is protected. Low-emitting carpet material that doesn't require detergents for cleaning eliminates air contaminants that may be harmful to people with chemical sensitivities. And low-pile carpeted floors provide the right balance between traction and gliding for wheelchairs and walking aids. To walk through a building designed this way is to realize just how much we've built nearly everything in the world only for able-bodied people.

Universal design for stores, airports, workplaces, streets, and blocks requires designs, materials, and processes that are the results of millions of decisions made by myriad stakeholders. Inclusive organizations must demand partners with the same commitment to disability justice and then coordinate action to make all the inclusive efforts come together synergistically. This means exercising the discipline of Master the Logistics with a great deal of organizational maturity. And if altruism isn't enough to motivate organizations toward disability inclusion, then let's talk about self-interest.

From a commercial perspective, disability justice means that the massive purchasing power of those with disabilities has yet to be capitalized. The global disability market has mushroomed to include nearly as many people as China. The market's 1.1 billion people control $4 trillion in spending power. If you include family and friends who have a direct and emotional connection to people with disabilities, the numbers nearly double, to a staggering 2 billion people who control $8.1 trillion.[33]

But the benefits don't stop at expanding into this burgeoning market. There are plenty of benefits for the not (yet) disabled, particularly as having a disability is a form of diversity any person can acquire, at any time, due to an accident or illness. That TV remote that allows you to effortlessly navigate more than five hundred channels without getting off the couch? That was originally designed for people with mobility challenges.[34] That high-contrast Kindle allowing you to read your page-turning thriller on the beach at high noon? Originally created for the sight impaired.[35] Alexa and Siri being at the beck and call of your voice? Created for the sight and mobility impaired.[36] Ramps for pushing your kid's stroller along from sidewalk to street? Built originally for those in wheelchairs.[37]

"Until we come to the realization that every single one of us is temporarily able-bodied, we're not going to make significant progress on this," says Deb Dagit, president of Deb Dagit Diversity LLC and formerly Vice President, Diversity and Chief Diversity Officer at Merck. "If we create a world where people with disabilities can fully participate, then we'll have created an insurance policy for ourselves and anyone we care about. It's not an 'other' issue. It's a 'self' issue."

REFUGEE JUSTICE

At the end of 2020, more than 80 million people were forcibly displaced due to persecution, conflict, or violence, among other reasons. The UN High Commissioner for Refugees reports that 1 in every 95 people in the world has fled their home.[38]

Most refugees come to their new home countries with nothing but the trauma of the life they left behind. And then they must overcome the hurdles of starting over. Complicated immigration and asylum laws make it hard for refugees to find their footing in their host countries.

Yet even with legal work permissions squared away, refugees typically have trouble finding employment due to limitations in the acceptance of foreign degrees, different educational and vocational requirements, and plain old prejudices and biases. A 2017 study in Germany found that an understanding of refugees' educational degrees, vocational qualifications,

TEN BUSINESSES SEEKING DISABILITY JUSTICE

These companies rank high on the Disability Equality Index because of their efforts to create a positive work experience for people with disabilities.

Accenture. Instead of looking for ways to just improve existing technology, the company collaborates with Microsoft to incorporate accessibility when creating new tools. Accenture has increased access by live captioning all of its streamed events and adding closed captions to video content.

Microsoft. Its neurodiversity hiring initiative ensures that the company proactively recruits for roles in which neurodiverse employees can excel. It includes a specialized recruiting and interviewing process that has helped Microsoft find neurodiverse candidates to work in various important positions, including as service engineers, software engineers, lab engineers, data scientists, and data analysts.

L'Oréal. The beauty and personal care company has joined various global initiatives, with the mindset of "One day to talk about disability inclusion and 364 days to do something about it." Their "Breaking the Silence" campaign encouraged twice as many of their workers to disclose their disabilities. "Building disability inclusion into the new normal is essential to our mission to create the beauty that moves the world," says their chairman and CEO Jean-Paul Agon.

Procter & Gamble. Through a partnership with Gallaudet University, the world's largest school for the deaf, and another with the Rochester Institute for Technology, P&G actively recruits employees and interns who are hearing impaired.

Cisco. The technology company created the Connected Disability Awareness Network, which works on several initiatives, including "Project Lifechanger," in which engineers with disabilities work to create technology that allows employees with disabilities more opportunities to work from home.

Dell. Through its Dell Autism Hiring Program, Dell recruits neurodivergent individuals. Realizing that the traditional interview process often excludes individuals with autism, it reworked its approach to remove barriers. Rather than viewing their differences as limitations, they leverage them as skills.

(continued)

Intel. The semiconductor chip manufacturer has pledged that by 2030 people with disabilities will account for 10% of its workforce.

CVS Health. The health care company combats a system that places low expectations on employees with disabilities instead of fostering their career development, by actively recruiting them and ensuring they receive ample opportunities for skills training.

Boston Scientific. The company supports employees with disabilities by providing physical and digital accommodations through a Universal Design section in the company's Global Design Guidelines, which details what an inclusive physical and digital workplace for individuals with disabilities should look like.

Inclusivity. A few years after implementation, more than fifteen thousand job candidates use Inclusivity to find job placements at employers including Comcast, Microsoft, and Salesforce. Job seekers on the platform include people with autism, PTSD, and mobility-related disabilities.

Sources: Adapted from Sarah Roberts, "Top 10 Companies Empowering Employees with Disabilities," Verbit, https://verbit.ai/top-10-companies -empowering-employees-with-disabilities. Used with permission. See also "Disability Equality Index," Disability:IN, https://disabilityin.org/ what-we-do/disability-equality-index/2022companies; "Driving the Accessibility Advantage at Accenture," Accenture, https://www.accenture. com/us-en/case-studies/about/driving-accessibility-advantage; "Microsoft Neurodiversity Hiring Program & FAQ," Microsoft, https://www.microsoft. com/en-us/diversity/inside-microsoft/cross-disability/neurodiversityhiring; "#BreakTheSilence: Our Employees Talk About Disability and the Group Renews Its Commitments," L'Oréal, https://www.loreal.com/en/news/ commitments/break-the-silence-on-disability; "People with Disabilities," P&G, https://us.pg.com/people-with-disabilities; "Creating a Culture of Inclusion and Collaboration," *DIVERSEability Magazine*, https:// diverseabilitymagazine.com/2017/08/creating-a-culture-of-inclusion-and -collaboration; "Neurodiversity@Dell Technologies," Dell Technologies, https://jobs.dell.com/neurodiversity; "Abilities in Abundance," CVS Health, https://www.cvshealth.com/about-cvs-health/diversity/workforce-initiatives/ abilities-in-abundance; "LEADing Change for Employees with Disabilities," Boston Scientific, September 9, 2021, https://news.bostonscientific.com/ LEADing-Change-for-Employees-with-Disabilities.

and competencies are of vital importance to their integration into the labor market.[39]

So what roles should organizations play in achieving refugee equity and justice in the societies in which they operate? And how can they do so in a way that's beneficial for the bottom line?

A PEOPLE FIRST PHILOSOPHY

Hamdi Ulukaya, founder and CEO of Chobani, is a Turkish immigrant to the United States from a family of nomadic sheepherders. He recounts making yogurt and cheese up in the mountains with his animal herds. He started Chobani (Turkish for *shepherd*) in 2005, with a "people first" philosophy. Realizing that his workers could not make a real living for themselves and their families on minimum hourly wages, he gave his full-time employees 10% of the company in 2016. He passionately believes that businesses need to step up for their own employees, but also for their communities.[40]

But then Ulukaya went further than that. When he heard that resettled refugees in upstate New York were having trouble finding employment, he purposefully started recruiting them. And Ulukaya did not stop there. Seeing the tragedy unfolding within the Yazidi community in Iraq in 2014, he realized that the business community, which he was a part of, needed to do more. And so the Tent Partnership for Refugees was born in 2016 with the goal of "mobilizing the business community to improve the lives and livelihoods of over 30 million refugees forcibly displaced from their home countries." As the founder, Ulukaya believes that "the moment a refugee gets a job, it's the moment they stop being a refugee. It's the moment they can stand on their own two feet; it's the moment they can make new friends; it's the moment they can start a new life." In 2019, about 30% of his workforce was refugees.

Ulukaya initially partnered with companies like Mastercard, Johnson & Johnson, and Airbnb to help refugees start over. Today, the Tent Partnership for Refugees is made up of more than two hundred large multinational companies committed to including refugees. These companies help train and prepare refugees to become part of their workforce, encourage their suppliers and vendors to hire refugees, commit to sourcing from businesses that employ refugees, support refugee entrepreneurs and small businesses by providing loans and facilitating their access to market, and engage refugees as customers by tailoring their products to better meet the needs of refugee communities.

Ulukaya saw injustice and engaged organizations to seek justice beyond their four walls. And he has proved that an organization can put people first and still do pretty well—today, Chobani is worth billions and has filed to go public. Many other companies are following Chobani's lead. In 2021, more than 100,000 Afghan refugees were airlifted out of Kabul after the Taliban took control, and almost half of them will be resettling in the United States. The Tent Foundation founded the Coalition for Afghan Refugees Network, with thirty-two companies announcing they would help Afghan refugees, among them Amazon, Facebook, and Pfizer. Even prior to the Afghan refugee crisis, Amazon hired refugees from all countries in its fulfillment and transportation centers and offered training and placement of highly skilled refugees in corporate roles.[41]

"We are committed to expanding and improving on these efforts and providing employment support for the refugee population," said Beth Galetti, Amazon's Senior Vice President of People, Experience, and Technology, "including the imminent need for Afghan refugees."

Barilla Group launched the Barilla Refugee Program in Sweden in 2015. It later expanded to Germany, France, and Italy, where refugees receive work experience and training to aid integration into the workplace. In 2019, the UN High Commissioner for Refugees lauded Barilla for its support and promotion of the professional development of refugees and their integration into the workplace.[42] In 2021, the company received the coveted Catalyst Award for its diversity, equity, and inclusion efforts.

And in 2022, Sodexo Australia graduated a class of ten as part of its first-ever refugee employment program. The course is designed to support Australians with refugee status in learning core skills to enter the workforce. Darren Hedley, Sodexo Australia Country President and CEO of Asia Pacific Energy and Resources, said, "Many refugee-status Australians experience barriers to employment such as cultural differences, limited social networks, relevant experience, language proficiency, and unconscious bias. Recognising the growing skills shortage, we have the responsibility as an employer to generate avenues to upskill and train people and provide equitable employment opportunities for everyone."[43]

RACIAL JUSTICE

"This time it's different!" was the rallying cry in the summer of 2020 as a racial reckoning of epic proportions swept through streets, workplaces, and other communal spaces in the United States, triggered by the murder of George Floyd.

The thing being held up as being different? A plurality of White Americans finally realized that racism is a pervasive and systemic reality in US society and that it requires collective accountability, ownership, and allyship on their part to truly break its back. People of all colors and socioeconomic backgrounds came together in the streets to shout at the top of their lungs, "Black Lives Matter!"

One year later, following the conviction of police officer Derek Chauvin, Floyd's murderer, had anything really changed?

The jury is still out.

There are some things that are indeed fundamentally different, as evidenced by the fact that Officer Chauvin was convicted on two counts of murder and one of manslaughter. Previous cases—of which there have been many—ended with acquittals, lesser charges, or the officers not even being charged.

The reckoning on the streets around the globe was so loud, intense, and disruptive that it also altered the vocabulary and mindset of many people in power. Historically, corporations have resisted the notion of systemic racism within their organizations, so it was unprecedented when CEOs began speaking out on the topic. They owned up to their responsibility to use their power to fight against racism. They acknowledged the pervasiveness of systemic racism, and they went on the record about rooting it out in their organizations.

In the five months right after Floyd's death, Russell 3000 companies appointed 130 Black board members, compared with thirty-eight Black directors appointed in the preceding five months; representation of Black directors in the United States tripled from 11% to 33% a year after Floyd's death;[44] and in the United Kingdom, 11% of Financial Times Stock Exchange companies' board members identify as a racial minority, with 61% of boards including at least one member identifying as a racial minority.[45]

And a significant number of companies remain on the vanguard, doubling down on the promises they made to have more people of color at the top; to develop their diverse talent pipelines; to create more inclusive environments; and to have honest, courageous conversations about inequity not only in society but also in their own workplaces. According to Korn Ferry's executive compensation practice, a growing number of companies are putting in place accountabilities with financial implications for their executives to achieve greater diversity, equity, and inclusion. For instance, the Future of Work Trends 2022 report predicts that the rate of S&P 500 companies that include DE&I and ESG metrics in their compensation will rise from 44% to 60%.[46] After all, business putting money on the line is what can turn short-term emotion into long-term action.

But the reach of organizations as they strive to see racial justice in society at large needs to be broader and outward facing to really move the needle. As we saw in the Discover Financial example at the beginning of this chapter, inclusive organizations can seek justice by supporting the economic development of Black communities. They may do this by choosing to locate their offices, factories, and call centers in communities of color with high unemployment, by awarding contracts to minority-owned businesses, and by offering training and education opportunities that give people a hand up and provide a path out of poverty.

WIDENING THE FOCUS ON RACE

In the United States, discussion of racial justice is very squarely centered on the historical and ongoing discrimination that African Americans face. Much like a lens zoomed to its maximum setting, we've been completely, and justifiably, fixated on the very real plight of one underrepresented group. Following the racial uprising in 2020, many eyes have been opened to the particular traumas of being Black in America and how African Americans suffer disproportionate levels of inequality and injustice.

While still maintaining the focus on deep discrimination against Black people, we must also open up the aperture to acknowledge the other racial groups that are suffering too. Each group's story of injustice, marginalization, and inequity is different in key ways and similar in others. As we widen the field of vision, it becomes clear that the discrimination against Latino families that has led to family separations, the treatment of Asian Americans as perpetually foreign, and the decimation of Indigenous people and their displacement from their ancestral lands are all rooted in the devaluation of people who are not White. This legacy has led to vast inequities for these groups throughout society, including their systemic underrepresentation in the upper echelons of the nation's business and public life.

After White people, Latinos are the second-largest racial or ethnic group in the United States, totaling 58 million, or 18% of the population. Yet US Latinos hold less than 3% of the board seats among the publicly traded companies listed in the Russell 3000 Index.[47] There are only sixteen Latino CEOs within the Fortune 500, slightly more than 3%, and even lower representation in other C-suite roles.[48]

There's a need to address this type of underrepresentation, for moral and economic reasons. After all, US Latino consumers alone are responsible for more than $2 trillion of the country's $19 trillion-plus economy and are driving growth in many consumer categories.[49] Asian Americans are a similarly fast-growing customer segment, with a $1.2 trillion consumer market that is projected to reach $1.6 trillion by 2024.[50]

So there's a clear case, but how can we work to achieve justice for all underrepresented racial groups? In other words, how can we put more effort into helping other underrepresented groups without taking away from the momentum to support Black Americans?

To be clear, expanding the focus to other groups, if done incorrectly, can alienate Black employees. We cannot lose sight of the fact that as soon as we start talking about opening up the aperture, Black employees could legitimately say, "Wait, now that we have your attention, we're going to lose it to other groups?" That worry is grounded in US history. The 1960s civil rights movement, which started as a focus on Black Americans, within a few years morphed into a focus on women. In the more than fifty years since then, White women have made significantly more strides than Black men or women in narrowing the equality gap at work and in corporate leadership.

We believe there are plenty of ways to keep talking about race and keep the plight of Black talent in focus. First, we need to engage the issue from the perspective of intersectionality. It's a little simplistic, for instance, to talk about a monolithic Black experience when Black men and Black women are often viewed and treated very differently. And what about the Afro-Latinos who also suffer from racism? Inclusive organizations need to talk to each group and learn about its unique experiences and challenges.

WHEN THE LATEST SOCIAL INJUSTICE STRIKES: PUBLICLY SPEAK UP OR NOT?

The CEO of a Fortune 100 company called one of us to urgently facilitate a conversation with his C-suite to figure out whether the latest social injustice travesty that was dominating the news cycle warranted yet another public statement.

This company had for the previous three years been consistent in speaking up against injustices affecting immigrants, various racial/ethnic minority groups, and those who are LGBTQ+—in fact, multiple times for each of these groups, since the violations were happening repeatedly. "But we are realizing these types of events, carried out by lone wolves, groups of people united by hate toward others, or even by elected officials, are going to keep happening," he said. "And now, given the precedent we've set, our employees and customers are expecting us to make a statement every time. Is that our role?"

His company's dilemma was that of many others. Given the case we've made that inclusive organizations must tackle the vital task of achieving justice—and given the reality, as we have seen in this chapter, that injustices around the world against groups of people, based on who they are, happen incessantly—this is a fair question.

When answering, let's keep in mind that at their core, the makers of cars, the providers of hospitality, and the chain store retailers are not social justice organizations. Yet not speaking up, if they're going to be true to their commitment to inclusion, would also be an abdication in the eyes of their employees and customers.

There is a way to navigate the dilemma: align who you are values-wise, industry-wise, and brand-wise with the kinds of causes you are most likely to speak up about.

Realistically, there are simply too many injustices against too many people to be able to speak to all of them, especially when social justice is not the core mission of the organization. Social justice and nonprofit organizations are usually focused on just one or two issues that then dictate what they will speak out about, and the same is appropriate for for-profit companies. Choose your social justice lane and commit to it. And the more it's tied to your core business, the better.

Second, we need to look at other ways in which skin color is used to discriminate against groups of people. While racism is about discrimination against another racial group, colorism is discrimination on the basis of skin tone *within* a racial or ethnic group, and it afflicts all communities of color. We must stay the course on addressing the depths of inequities of the Black experience within the US corporate world. At the same time, we can also make room to help bring along other groups as well.

Ultimately, this is all about inclusive organizations as allies, using their power and privilege to level the playing field for underrepresented groups (see figure 4). Injustice is about bad actors using their power to keep groups of people down. The vital task of Achieve Justice is for good actors to use their organizational heft to counter the abuse of power.

Figure 4: Movements We Support, Ben & Jerry external website, 2022. Reproduced with kind permission of Unilever IP Holdings B.V. *Source:* Ben & Jerry External Website, 2022.

10

Vital Task 4:
Save the Planet

We should try to be the parents of our future rather than the offspring of our past.

Miguel de Unamuno,
Spanish philosopher and novelist

"WHEN ASTRONAUTS ARE FLOATING ABOVE THE EARTH, they know exactly how much oxygen they have left and they do everything they must to conserve it, and especially not use it all up, since once it's all used up, that's the end," oceanographer Dr. Sylvia Earle shares on an MIT podcast. "Yet, us astronauts on spaceship Earth are not behaving as if every day we keep depleting our ability to survive on this planet."[1]

Spaceship Earth indeed is running out of all life-sustaining things, and just as astronauts can see their oxygen levels go down, we also are seeing our criteria for viability disappearing.

In a devastating World Economic Forum video, climate investigators mapped out how things could unfold in this century if we don't reverse the inexorable trends we are barreling through.[2] Although models may vary, based on scientific studies around the world, here's what awaits us in the next decades.

By 2030, melting ice caps and arctic ice sheets will swell sea levels by twenty centimeters (nearly eight inches); 90% of coral reefs—the most life-sustaining ecosystem on the planet—will be threatened, and 65% will be highly endangered; decimated crops will have pushed 100 million more people into extreme hunger; and climate-change-related illnesses will kill an extra 250,000 people per year.

By 2040, when the world shoots past its 1.5°C (2.7°F) Paris Agreement temperature rise limit, Bangladesh, Thailand, and Vietnam will be threatened by annual floods, sparking mass migration; 8% of the global population will see a severe reduction in water availability; the arctic will be ice free in the summer; and sea levels will rise sixty centimeters (nearly two feet) in the Gulf of Mexico, delivering an unprecedented number of hurricanes.

By 2050, 2 billion people will face temperatures of 60°C (140°F) or higher for about a month each year; masks will be needed not for disease prevention but to protect lungs from pollution; the US Northeast will experience twenty-five major floods a year, up from one in 2020; rising sea levels will cause island nations such as Maldives and Kiribati to lose two-thirds of their land, while populations in major coastal cities from Jakarta to Miami to New York will be living on "threatened land";[3] and 140 million people will be displaced by food and water insecurity or extreme weather events.

By 2100, severe drought will affect 40% of the planet; insects will have disappeared, causing massive crop failures due to the lack of pollinators; a quarter of the world's fish will be gone; Southern Spain and Portugal will become deserts; and Florida will have largely disappeared under water.

By 2150, climate change could force 216 million people across six world regions to leave their homes and become "climate migrants."[4] Climate change will also contribute to the threat to regional security and stability. Experts often cite the drought in Syria as a precursor to its 2011 civil war. Similarly, security experts see a connection between climate change and terrorism, as the decline in agricultural livelihood often creates a fertile recruiting ground for potential extremists.[5]

But we don't have to wait ten-plus years to see how climate change will play out. It is already making its presence known. Fires in southeastern

Australia, Siberia, and Southern California have destroyed beautiful desolate wild expanses as well as populated neighborhoods. Millions of climate refugees are fleeing drought-stricken areas in Central America and the Middle East. And thousands of families have watched all their belongings be swept away by floods and tsunamis, or their homes swirl up into the sky in tornadoes and hurricanes.

No wonder David Wallace-Wells titled his a bestseller on climate change *The Uninhabitable Earth.*

Climate change is everybody's problem, but as with most hot-button issues in society, it affects certain groups more—usually those who are already marginalized in some way or other. In American cities, residents of low-income neighborhoods and communities of color endure far higher temperatures—an average of 1° to 7°F (about 0.5° to 4°C) higher during the day—than people who live in whiter, wealthier areas. This is due to factors such as more buildings, less tree cover, and to a lesser extent, higher population density.[6] This is referred to as the heat island effect.

In fact, poorer countries across the globe experience the most adverse effects of climate change.[7] And to make racial and economic inequity even more stark, climate change is disproportionately affecting the African continent, despite its per capita carbon emissions being lower than that of any other continent (with the exception of Antarctica), as Vanessa Nakate of Uganda pointed out at the Youth4Climate summit in Milan, Italy, in 2021.[8]

If all this sounds apocalyptic, it's because it is. Meanwhile, our governments are dithering, disinformation is leading millions to dismiss the dire predictions, and efforts to fight climate change are falling victim to partisan politics, organizational denial, and short-termism. Collectively, our human species is simply not doing enough to save our world.

This is why it is so important for inclusive organizations to assume a larger role in mitigating what at this point feels like an inevitable environmental—and economic and social—collapse.

ARE CORPORATIONS THE FOX IN THE HENHOUSE OF CLIMATE CHANGE?

Why do we believe inclusive organizations have both the responsibility and the ability to do all they can to save the planet?

On the *responsibility* front, corporations must face up to the role they have played in creating a polluted and oxygen-depleting planet. The sins are multiple and at scale. But we don't seek to dwell too long on a well-deserved condemnation of carelessness and even wanton disregard for the toxic costs of production and "progress." The environmental, social, and governance movement is well on its way to holding organizations accountable through metrics, regulation, and most effectively, investment withholding.

Our thrust here is on the *ability* front. Just as the damage to the environment was collective, systemic, and at scale, the response can also be collective, systemic, and at scale. There are plenty of best practices and evolving best practices for how to do this, such as decarbonization technologies, clean energy installations, and recycling, as well as the manufacture of plant-based clothing, containers, and meat substitutes.

This is where inclusive organizations can have an exponential impact on countering climate change. They have the responsibility and ability to harness and reposition their structures, processes, capital, R&D, marketing, and people power in the service of saving the planet.

Here, we would like to narrow our focus even further, to the people power angle. New climate-saving technologies—the implementation of the emerging and the creation of the new—will require massive amounts of innovation not only on the scientific side but also on the change management side, given that consumers and employees will have to work and live with new habits to avert the oncoming disaster. And what do inclusive organizations excel at? Leveraging their diversity, inclusion, and equity to foster innovation.

We have identified five steps for inclusive organizations to address this vital task:

- Get the facts right
- Call out delusions
- Embrace the circular economy
- Empower all with urgency
- Go big

GET THE FACTS RIGHT

Businesses know how to address threats to the bottom line. By using ESG's triple bottom line concept, in which the externality costs are added to the ledger balance sheet, businesses can effectively add up the costs of not reversing course on climate change. They must then use their mega megaphone and deep pockets for branding messages that convey the truth.

While complete extinction is difficult to grasp, there are some "spreadsheetable" costs hitting bottom lines in organizations and national budgets. Some of the organizational costs incurred due to climate change include health issues and downstream implications, organizational issues, and environmental mitigation issues.

Health issues and downstream implications

- Smoke inhalation from perpetual forest fires[9]

- Neurological damage due to poor water quality[10]

- Fertility issues and complications of childbearing, along with increased dependent health care needs due to air, water, and land pollutants/contaminants such as toxic factory runoff[11]

- Increased insurance costs[12]

- Uninsurability[13]

How does this affect organizations? Our population—and with that, our workforces—will get sicker and will have to contend with worsening severe chronic illnesses. This will disproportionately affect employees from historically underprivileged and underrepresented communities because environmental regulations are the least stringent there, which makes these communities prone to becoming dumping grounds for contaminated production waste. Organizations will bear the brunt as sicker employees translate into more doctors' visits, which in turn drives up health insurance premiums for organizations.

Organizational issues

- Increased absenteeism

- Lost productivity

- Decreased morale and increased risk of publicly visible protest/ strikes/activism if workers believe their employer is contributing to or not advocating adequately for their well-being

How does this affect organizations? It follows that a sicker workforce means increased absenteeism, which then leads to lost productivity. According to a study by the IZA Institute of Labor Economics, based in Bonn, Germany, "a 1 percentage point increase in the rate of sickness absenteeism is estimated to decrease productivity by as much as 0.24%."[14]

Environmental mitigation issues

- Natural disaster recovery
- Designing and building for resilience, such as disaster prevention costs like the cost of building seawalls
- Loss of core feedstock in such areas as forestry, fishing, livestock, or agriculture; fewer overall resources
- Loss of the ways in which the ecosystem itself provides "ecosystem services" to the planet, such as cooling and sheltering benefits against extreme weather events, leading to increased need for air-conditioning and extreme weather–durable structures
- Loss of weather-dependent tourist destinations as a result, for example, of not enough snow for skiing, temperatures too hot to visit the beach, or areas becoming too prone to wildfires for hiking
- Interruptions to or loss of supply chains
- Talent migration away from employment hubs due to high-risk weather events making an area increasingly seasonal and inhospitable, with some regions unable to rebuild infrastructure

How does this affect organizations? After every natural disaster, whether floods, forest fires, or droughts, who pays for the cleanup and the mitigation? Yes, initially it's governments who step in, but those very same governments are quite adept at recouping those extra costs by raising taxes both on individuals and on organizations. Both affect the organizational bottom line, as tax increases on individuals eventually translate into reduced buying power and therefore potentially less organizational growth.

Fewer resources in agriculture, fishing, livestock, and other sectors also mean higher costs for organizations needing those resources to produce their products—costs that are then passed on to the consumer, who may not be able to pay.

To clean all this up, it's estimated, will take $300 billion a year in environmental mitigation efforts. It also requires a $3 trillion per year increase in all investment types, from governments, investment banks, development banks, and commercial banks, as well as consumer investments such as buying an e-car or more energy-efficient appliances.

In this politically polarized environment in which whoever is in power determines the strength of carbon emission regulations, Izabel Loinaz, a senior partner in Korn Ferry's ESG practice, sees corporations needing to step up even more:

> The volatile regulatory environment makes it even more of an imperative for the private sector to save the planet by taking full accountability for their own medium- and long-term economic interests. If the goal is true-cost, sustainable growth over the long term, strategies solely dependent on the regulatory environment are subject to short-term gains at the expense of long-term, resilient value creation. The urgency increases while the accountability levers are unstable. The responsibility and accountability for addressing climate change as a threat comes back to a societal obligation and the role of corporations in society.

As inclusive organizations grasp what Loinaz is indicating, they must clearly and compellingly inform all their stakeholders about what they see is at stake for the organization and what the organization, given who it is in the marketplace, can offer to do to help save the planet. All should be informed of the *what (the current state), the why (the urgency to address), and the how (the approach to reversing course).*

CALL OUT DELUSIONS

The quest to save the planet is rife with fantastic ideas, dire threats, myriad dilemmas, and various delusions. It's the delusions that can significantly take us off track. Inclusive organizations need to use their amplification and reputational power to call these out and to model what real inclusive sustainability looks like. Some of the biggest delusions with regard to climate are:

- we can keep focusing on "growth" while living on a finite planet,
- we can just pass responsibility for change on to the next generation,
- technology labeled "green" is automatically safe for the planet,
- we will figure it out in the nick of time, and
- the actions of many virtuous individuals alone are enough to save the planet.

DELUSION: WE CAN KEEP FOCUSING ON "GROWTH" WHILE LIVING ON A FINITE PLANET

One of the biggest delusions of our times is predicated on what we know to be the key driver of our economic life: growth. Growth is *the* metric of capitalism as we understand it, the North Star for for-profit organizations. It's based on the mantra and goal of "sell more stuff to more people."

The mantra has been so engrained in our business model that organizations have resorted to planned obsolescence to increase growth. When your smartphone seems to slow down after two or three years, it is because it was designed to do exactly that.[15]

Samantha Putt del Pino, Eliot Metzger, Deborah Drew, and Kevin Moss from the World Resources Institute explain the fallacy of continuing down this path in their working paper *Elephant in the Boardroom*. The world's population is set to exceed 9.5 billion by 2050, which means that under current consumption patterns, we will need three times as many natural resources as we did in 2000 to support human life . . . and we are already "at or close to the limits of the planet's ability to provide."[16]

The current model of selling more stuff to more people is simply not sustainable. We need to embrace different business models and rethink what growth means.

One organization that is capitalizing on this "new growth" is Rent the Runway, a clothing company that rents high-end clothing to its customers instead of selling it. The company accomplishes two objectives with this one approach: it does not consume valuable environmental resources to produce new clothing and it cuts down on fashion waste accumulated through our buy-and-discard-after-one-season shopping habits.

Organizations will need to be innovative to resolve the inherent clash between growth and being good stewards of the planet. But one thing is certain: innovation requires diversity leveraged by inclusion.

DELUSION: WE CAN JUST PASS RESPONSIBILITY FOR CHANGE ON TO THE NEXT GENERATION

"It's the young people who will save us," we hear. This is equal parts wishful thinking and negating one's own role. Yes, young people have been galvanized by the obvious and blatant disregard for our planet on the part of their parents and grandparents. They are marching. They are giving speeches. They are protesting. But all the Greta Thunbergs in the world cannot turn this apocalyptic tide around by themselves.

Why not? Let's run through some key questions. Who still holds the power in this world? Who has decision-making rights over budgets? Who passes laws? Who runs the corporations? The average age of the CEO of a Fortune 500 company is fifty-seven.[17] The story is the same in government. The average age of the 117th Congress of the United States is fifty-nine years old. Out of all 435 members, only thirty-eight members were born in the 1980s and only one was born in the 1990s.[18] The reality is that all of our power structures are still firmly in the hands of the older generation, so the onus still is on them.

What makes the continued involvement and leadership of our older generation even more pressing is that this very generation is to blame for the current state of affairs. They are ones who have allowed the depletion of nutrients from our soils, released unprecedented levels of carbon dioxide into the atmosphere, ordered mass deforestation, and saddled our young people with crippling debt. But they still have a chance to change their climate legacy.

Patagonia is showing the way. In 2022, Yvon Chouinard, the founder of the iconic brand valued at $3 billion, transferred his family's ownership to a specially designed trust and a nonprofit organization to ensure that all of the company's yearly $100 million in profits will be used to combat climate change and to protect undeveloped land around the globe. As Chouinard told the *New York Times,* "We are going to give away the maximum amount of money to people who are actively working on saving this planet."[19]

TikTok will not be enough to save the planet. But more leaders like Chouinard leading inclusive organizations will.

DELUSION: TECHNOLOGY LABELED "GREEN" IS AUTOMATICALLY SAFE FOR THE PLANET

Everything in the world comes with consequences—intended ones and also unintended ones.

To steer away from carbon dioxide emissions from cars and trucks, *voilà*—we got the electric car. It was immediately heralded as a green panacea. But even electric cars are not without environmental impact. For instance, the electricity used to charge electric cars often creates carbon pollution as local power is generated using coal and natural gas. In addition, the manufacturing of electric cars requires large-scale mining of cobalt and nickel in rainforests from the Philippines to Peru, adding to harmful deforestation and in some places fomenting civil unrest as aggressive mining company land purchases threaten the livelihoods and lifestyles of Indigenous populations.[20] And once those lithium-ion batteries run out, they add to the electronic waste stream and become a major environmental hazard.[21]

Or consider the quest to get rid of plastic straws. Starbucks has been lauded for eliminating 1 billion straws a year, but many disability activists advocate for the use of these plastic straws as a reasonable accommodation. They have fought to be included in the conversation about how to be green about straws without being exclusionary of those who need them.[22]

Given these counterintuitive realities, we need open minds to truly weigh the pros and cons of the solutions brought forth. Decisions need to be based on facts, with all the information at hand, rather than on emotion or the latest green fad.

DELUSION: WE WILL FIGURE IT OUT IN THE NICK OF TIME

We can no longer wait to do something "when climate change happens." Climate change and its destructive power are already here, and already causing massive catastrophe in the form of record heat waves, unprecedented floods, and raging forest fires.

Feeding this delusion is a mindset in the so-called developed nations (the Global North) that scientific advancements and a can-do mindset eventually will save the day. Yet there's no cavalry or superhero or mad scientist with the one antidote waiting in the wings to pull off a save.

In the Global South, the conversation has long passed the narrative of disaster avoidance. Ethiopia, Kenya, and Somalia, for example, are facing sustained droughts that have killed millions of animals. After four missed rainy seasons in a row, 18 million people in these three countries do not have enough food to eat.[23] It's estimated that every year around the world, with a heavy concentration in the Global South, 5 million people die due to climate change.[24]

In the Global South, life and survival are already disrupted, while the conversation in the Global North remains future-facing, allowing for the delusion that disaster can still be averted through better technology. Only a transformative adaptation of our current lifestyle at mass scale can save the planet—and inclusive organizations need to be at the forefront, leading the charge.

DELUSION: THE ACTIONS OF MANY VIRTUOUS INDIVIDUALS ALONE ARE ENOUGH TO SAVE THE PLANET

The days of personal "green practices," such as bringing reusable shopping bags on our grocery store runs or not using plastic straws being enough to save our planet, are over. Do we still need them? Yes, absolutely. But we are so deep in the climate change hole that personal action can only help if it's taken in tandem with systemic interventions at the hands of corporations and governments. Incremental and haphazard virtuousness is not enough. We need to go big, which we'll get to in a moment.

EMBRACE THE CIRCULAR ECONOMY

Loinaz says that for all its currency in today's vocabulary, "sustainability" is already passé: "At this point, *sustainable* is no longer an achievable target on its own—the target instead must be regenerative, where we are not only reducing dependence on natural resources and eliminating waste, but meaningfully investing in the restoration and replenishment of our natural ecosystems."

This is referred to as the circular economy. As the Ellen MacArthur Foundation describes: "In our current economy, we take materials from the Earth, make products from them, and eventually throw them away as waste—the process is linear. In a circular economy, by contrast, we stop

DTE: SAVING THE PLANET ALSO REQUIRES TAKING CARE OF YOUR EMPLOYEES AND YOUR COMMUNITIES

Detroit Energy (DTE) has committed to being a carbon-neutral energy company by 2050. DTE's massive transformation from fossil fuel to clean and renewable energy sources showcases exactly how diversity, equity, and inclusion and an environmental, social, and governance approach lead to inclusive sustainability.

Such a sea change in business operations and mindset requires a gritty and tenacious look at every single aspect of the organization. While the engineers are looking at how to shut down coal plants and transition to wind turbines, solar arrays, and other renewable sources of energy, business and human resources leaders are looking at how to reskill their employees so they too can make the transition.

For example, as part of its commitment to the social aspect of ESG, DTE has pledged to make this transition without laying anyone off. But producing green energy requires fewer workers than producing carbon-based energy, so how is it going to pull this off? Plans include managing retirements and turnover thoughtfully and not overcommitting to replacement hiring, in order to protect the jobs of those who stay. This is what taking care of your employees looks like.

DTE also recognizes its responsibility to contribute to the economic sustainability of the region it operates in and hires from. When organizations fail to honor this commitment, whole communities can end up being disenfranchised, and neglected neighborhoods with few breadwinners can become epicenters of despair that lead to higher addiction rates, suicides, and chronic health conditions—all of which contributes to social unrest. This cascade of events not only is detrimental to the immediate community; it also saps the economic and social vitality of the region and the company itself. To prevent this scenario, DTE is making sure that its talent sourcing and hiring taps into all the demographic groups in its talent radius.

This emphasis on a diverse hiring pool is also necessary for the unprecedented amount of innovation the transition to a carbon-neutral future requires—from the development of game-changing technologies to myriad microprocess improvements. A homogeneous workforce at different levels of the organization, from the board to the plant floor, would be severely constrained in thinking

(continued)

alternatively about the way forward. Those who are in charge have experience in an energy world that is going away. Many have never led or innovated in an era like today, with all its disruptions. DTE, and really all organizations, need diversity of backgrounds, experiences, cultures, income levels, education, thinking styles, and passions to envision—without a road map—a future that must be vastly different from today.

So DTE is on the march to source, recruit, hire, and onboard the most diverse talent force it has ever had. It is not content to have diversity just at the plant and field operations level—as important as that is and will continue to be. It also wants it among its engineers, technicians, managers, and executives. Currently, people of color make up 28% of DTE's overall workforce, including 30% at entry level and 40% at the next two levels up. To get the best out of all the people sitting at the table, it is ensuring that all voices feel valued and respected. All are invited to speak up, and all are advocated for.

waste being produced in the first place." A circular economy requires that we learn from nature's ability to generate life from decay. Nothing goes to waste because everything, even as it dies, contributes to life. "There is no waste in nature. When a leaf falls from a tree it feeds the forest. For billions of years, natural systems have regenerated themselves. . . . Waste is a human invention."[25]

The circular economy is based on three principles:

1. Eliminate waste and pollution. Rather than accepting waste as part of the production and consumption process, products should be designed so that their materials reenter the economy at the end of their use. Examples are either package-free products or products with plant-based packaging that reenters the earth after use.[26]

2. Circulate products and materials (at their highest value). This is about keeping a product in use, either as a whole or through its components or raw materials. It can be accomplished by reusing, repairing, repurposing, or recycling products.[27]

3. Regenerate nature. An example of nature regeneration is farming practice that allows the soil to rebuild itself by returning biological materials back to the earth. Conventional farming depletes the soil of natural nutrients, which we then replace with chemical fertilizers, which cause downstream pollution such as toxic algae, which then make lakes unusable and uninhabitable by wildlife. The holistic principles behind regenerative agriculture are meant to restore our soil and ecosystem health and leave our world in better shape for future generations.[28]

Puma is an example of an inclusive organization that has fully embraced the circular economy. Its goals include reducing its direct and indirect emissions by 35% between 2017 and 2030. The sportswear company has partnered with the First Mile Coalition, a network of self-employed refuse collectors in Taiwan, Honduras, and Haiti who remove plastic waste from ecosystems and sell it to make a living, according to environmental freelance writer Gina-Marie Cheeseman. When locals collect plastic bottles in their communities and bring them to collection centers, this is what is referred to as the First Mile.

"Further down the supply chain, recycling facilities grind these bottles into plastic flakes, which then become pellets and, eventually, fibers for textiles." As a result, "each piece of clothing in the [Puma] collection—ranging from jackets and training pants to T-shirts and leggings—contains 95 percent recycled plastic."

This approach, referred to as "social plastic," leads to more sustainable use of materials while creating income opportunities for people who have often been seen as completely marginal. The First Mile Coalition has many partners like Puma, and by 2020, it had diverted more than 30 million bottles, which adds up to 1.3 million pounds of plastic waste.[29]

In addition to private organizations, whole cities, such as Glasgow, Scotland, are pledging to be circular economies. Among Glasgow's myriad large- and small-scale initiatives is "Beer to Bread," where any spent grain from the brewing process can be used to replace up to 50% of the flour needed to produce bread in the baking industry.[30]

EMPOWER ALL WITH URGENCY

Both our personal experiences and the deluge of data show us the grave danger the planet and all living beings are facing as we keep depleting the resources that make the planet livable. One would think that should create urgency enough. But it hasn't, and inclusive organizations need to step into the breach, sound the alarm louder and incessantly, and take urgent action.

For all the direness of the situation, large segments of the public—the very public that must be kept engaged in this fight—have lost interest. Consumed by pandemic fatigue and economic worries such as high inflation, basic goods shortages, and economic uncertainties, climate change has pretty much dropped off the priority list. In a poll by the *New York Times* and Siena College, only 1% of respondents saw climate change as the most important issue facing the United States. You might think that the percentage would be higher among those under thirty years old. But nope. In that demographic, a mere 3% see it as our most pressing problem.[31]

How can inclusive organizations reverse this apathy?

When it comes to strategic direction, as well as motivation and inspiration at scale, governments create platforms that then allow for the optimization of private sector investments. That means both government and the private sector need to do their part in inspiring and equipping people, and in changing the narrative from saving the planet being a burden to it being a can't-miss opportunity.

However, governments around the world clearly are not doing enough. They can barely eke out collective agreements such as the Paris Accord of 2016, much less do the actual work of lowering carbon emissions. Political polarization and gridlock are at fault, but so is a lack of imagination and will. That's why corporations need to pick up the slack—for their own sake and, existentially, for the sake of the only planet we have, spaceship Earth.

Let's go back in time to 2005, when Hurricane Katrina swallowed New Orleans. That massive disaster was the first major flash point of the climate change crisis for the Global North. It also triggered a culture of transformation at Walmart.

When Katrina hit, Lee Scott, Walmart's CEO at the time, gave clear and urgent orders that every manager was empowered to do everything possible to help the evacuees from and in New Orleans: "Send people what they need and don't worry about cost. We will figure it out."[32]

This unleashed an unprecedented mobilization of help in every possible form: donating pallets of clothing and truckloads of merchandise, deploying drivers and trucks to transport relief provisions and water, assisting people finding their loved ones, making distribution centers available as shelters, providing laptops, giving away gift cards, fulfilling prescriptions for those who had lost their records, cashing checks for free, providing bedding for shelters, and collecting donations totaling millions of dollars.

The natural disaster also shaped Walmart's proactive response to climate change. Now, in addition to just helping people recover from natural disasters, the company has thrown its substantial financial support to businesses that are fighting the good fight to prevent more climate-change-related disasters.

"While we don't give mandates [on commitments to the planet], we express our values and our objectives [about climate change]. This means if you all have the same type of product and similar price and quality, the one who is going to get our business is the one, for example, that says they used sustainable packaging," Scott says.

In the hands of the behemoth Walmart, this simple decision is a really big, impactful one. With more than 100,000 suppliers, 1 million employees, and 220 million customers weekly, what Walmart does shifts the ground.[33]

GO BIG

Remember when, during the COVID-19 pandemic, everything suddenly shut down and businesses everywhere had to pivot overnight? CEOs got done in days what under normal circumstances would have taken months or even years to decide on and then implement.

We must harness that same energy to deal with the climate crisis.

In the same way that the pandemic was an immediate, quantifiable threat, so too is climate change. Just as we saw overflowing emergency rooms and mass graves during the pandemic, today we also are seeing mass deaths of people, this time through natural disasters or famine, plus the mass extinction of species.

But for the biggest polluters on the planet, the industrialized nations, this has not hit home acutely enough, mostly because they see it happening in the most egregious ways in developing countries. But the United States alone has cost the world more than $1.9 trillion in climate damages since 1990, according to a study from Dartmouth College.[34] There is an accountability that comes with that.

Incremental progress alone will doom us. So will moving at the pace of traditional cycle times for big projects, with their detailed strategic plans

MARS CALLS ON ITS SUPPLIERS, ASSOCIATES, AND CONSUMERS TO TACKLE CLIMATE CHANGE

#PledgeForPlanet is a Mars initiative to accelerate climate action within its business; the company has pledged to achieve net zero greenhouse gas emissions across its full value chain by 2050. The initiative highlights the shared responsibility of businesses, governments, and consumers to take action. The new initiative follows Mars's investment of $1 billion toward its Sustainable in a Generation Plan to accelerate progress against a range of global threats by looking beyond its own direct operations and into its extended supply chain. In fact, the company is calling on all its suppliers to set science-based climate action targets, to sign on to the Climate Group's RE100, and to embrace a future with renewable energy at the center of plans for direct operations. Olam, a Mars supplier of cocoa and palm oil, is already on board.

"Climate change is a real and tangible threat to society. For example, in our business, we already see it in the risk to livelihoods for smallholder farmers who provide most of our raw ingredients," Mars CEO Grant F. Reid explains. "Risks to the resiliency and sustainability of our supply chain and the future of the farmers we work with is top of mind. But, as a family business that thinks in generations and aspires to make a positive difference in the world, our responsibilities and our ambitions go beyond risk mitigation. We are committed to doing our part for the good of the planet.

"As a business, we've set ambitious goals to help deliver on the Sustainable Development Goals by changing the way we operate. We're also inspired by the youth movement demanding climate action and the role of all of us as individuals in driving change. With our #PledgeForPlanet initiative, we are calling for simple, everyday actions that anyone can take today to help create a better tomorrow."

Source: "Mars Accelerates Action to Tackle Climate Change With New #PledgeForPlanet Initiative," Mars Incorporated, press release, September 26, 2019, https://www.3blmedia.com/news/mars-accelerates-action-tackle-climate-change-new-pledgeforplanet-initiative.

and lengthy budget approval processes. Loinaz says the way forward is both big *and* incremental. She calls this "incremental in aggregate."

"This is not a time for making small plans," says Loinaz. "This will require bravery, integrity, and a willingness to rapidly ideate and implement despite the ambiguity while holding steadfast to accountability."

Let's look at single-use plastic bags. Americans use 100 billion plastic bags a year, which translates to 365 plastic bags *per person* per year.[35] These single-use bags end up in landfills, where they may not disintegrate for one thousand years. They also turn into toxic microplastic in the soil, which may be ingested by humans, or they pollute oceans, where they are eaten by fish, and in the logic of nature's food chain, eventually by humans.

Over the period of a generation, the percentage of US shoppers bringing their own reusable bags has risen to a respectable 39%.[36] But it required cities, municipalities, and states to ban the use of single-use plastic bags to generate real progress. In California, the ban led to a 71.5% drop in plastic bag consumption.[37] As this example shows, incremental gains turn into big ones when government and consumers get on the same page. Then, when you bring inclusive organizations into the fold, the wins get exponentially bigger.

In 2019, through a combination of grassroots pressure and a hard look at its own organizational values, Trader Joe's decided to eliminate the use of single-use plastic bags in all of its stores—that's 1 million fewer bags per year being consumed. The company also committed to replacing Styrofoam trays used in packaging, and to selling more loose produce rather than wrapping it in plastic. And that's just the actions of one inclusive organization.[38]

The same concept applies to composting. In the city of Highland Park, Illinois, about 10% of residents have participated in a voluntary composting program at a cost of $239.05 per season. Unfortunately, the high fee may have created a barrier for those who are motivated to help the environment but for whom the price is a deal breaker. In this case, incremental usage determined by personal decisions (and affordability) was not going to move the needle.

So, at the end of 2022, the Highland Park City Council approved a composting program for $3 a month, which was charged to all households whether they used the service or not. Charging all households a communally shared fee with a communal benefit is what allowed the price to drop so low. To aid in the change management, the city also enrolled volunteers, students in the local school districts, and its own staff to provide education, inspiration, and tips to composting newbies. It's a great, innovative example of how to go from incremental to big in order to accelerate scalable solutions.[39]

Similar solutions are happening with regard to many other products and services, such as with the phasing out of incandescent light bulbs to be replaced by significantly more energy-efficient LED lights, serving more plant-based meat alternatives in restaurants, and in the biggest *Go Big* of them all, the mandate by some states and commitment by most car manufacturers to phase out gasoline combustion engines in their cars in the coming years and evolve to all-electric fleets. The impact of these types of Go Big changes is easily visible.

Around the world, phase-outs of incandescent bulbs have been ongoing, and manufacturers such as Signify (formerly Philips) have been hastening the transformation by getting ahead of the regulatory deadlines. According to Wikipedia, Brazil and Venezuela started their phase-out in 2005; Australia, the European Union, and Switzerland in 2009; Argentina and Russia in 2012; and Canada, Malaysia, Mexico, and South Korea in 2014. The United States will make the transition in 2023. In the United States alone, this will cut carbon emissions by 222 million metric tons over thirty years and will save Americans $3 million per year on utility bills.[40]

Compared to conventional meat, plant-based meat uses 47% to 99% less land, emits 30% to 90% less greenhouse gas, uses 72% to 99% less water, and causes 51% to 91% less aquatic nutrient pollution.[41] Because China currently consumes 28% of the world's meat (50% of which is pork), a reduction in its meat consumption would have significant impacts. In fact, if China were to halve its animal agriculture industry, estimates report a carbon emission reduction of 1 billion metric tons. And it doesn't stop there. An increase in plant-based meat would lead to a reduction in water consumption and protect against animal-borne pathogens.[42] Companies have responded. The plant-based meat market, with products such as Impossible Burger and Beyond Meat, is expected to grow to 15.7 billion by 2027.

If car manufacturers' fleets in the United States were to be all electric by 2040, this shift would lead to a 92% reduction in greenhouse gases by 2050, generating $1.7 trillion in climate benefits by protecting ecosystems, agriculture, and infrastructure from rising sea levels and catastrophic weather events, including drought and floods. All this would help prevent more than 110,000 deaths, lead to 2.8 million fewer asthma attacks, and avoid 13.4 million sick days, according to the American Lung Association. Because communities of color and low-income neighborhoods suffer disproportionately from air pollution and climate disasters, they would reap the biggest benefits.[43]

Going big requires that inclusive organizations be stewards not just of their people but also of all people everywhere. We must join the ecosystem of governments, nonprofits, and individual consumers in doing our part to counter climate change.

In that spirit, let's revisit who we are saving the planet for. It's for all of us, present and future humanity, or else *kaboom!* There goes the marketplace. Activation of the final discipline of See the Marketplace brings everything around full circle. This is how we use our power to do right by all of our stakeholders, including our biggest stakeholder of all, Earth.

■   ■   ■

CONCLUSION

The Irrevocable Responsibility to Use Power for Good

Dream no small dreams for they have no power to move hearts.

Johann Wolfgang von Goethe,
German poet, philosopher, and scientist

THROUGHOUT THIS BOOK WE HAVE ENDEAVORED TO dream no small dreams, to embody the exhortation from Goethe, who was grounded in both the abstractions of art and the immutable laws of science.

We certainly have come across plenty of people who are cynical that inclusive organizations can transform the world, especially when corporate organizations often have been the perpetrators of inequity, both internally and externally, as a result of their own Faustian bargains between financial profit and justice, clean water and air, and sustainability.

Our work as DE&I practitioners requires a cold-eyed look at the facts and all the bad things that happen—*and* the ability to maintain an artist's hope that we can transcend the wrongs caused by greed, indifference, and pride to achieve the greater good. We have mapped the very brutal realities we face as a species, and yet we choose to lead with the hard-edged optimism that we can change course.

While there are plenty of organizations who are uninterested in changing course, we have chosen to highlight those dreaming no small dreams, those who want to leverage the power of their scale, influence, brand, and people to further diversity, equity, and inclusion, to transform the world.

THE NATIONAL GALLERY: PORTRAIT OF A NATION

The National Gallery of Art in Washington, DC, has had a long-standing organizational inclusion problem. In 2018, during the gallery's search for a new director, and after members of its security staff had complained publicly about a hostile work environment, a *Washington Post* article detailed the challenges the incoming director would face. Sources and experts described "long-standing problems of sexual harassment, retaliation, and favoritism," lack of accountability among managers and senior leaders, and missed opportunities to connect with younger, more diverse audiences. Employees openly hoped for "an agent of change." More than 90% of the artists represented in the collection were White men, its major exhibitions had almost exclusively showcased White artists, and there was little diversity among senior leadership or curatorial and other program staff. In short, the museum failed to represent the nation in its workforce, programs, collections, or audiences.

Understanding the urgent need for the National Gallery—funded largely by taxpayers—to better serve a changing nation, the board of trustees set diversity, equity, and inclusion as primary goals in their search for a new director. In late 2018, they appointed Kaywin Feldman, an experienced museum director with a track record of connecting with communities and putting people at the center of the museum's mission. Feldman, a self-described feminist, became the first woman to lead the National Gallery in its seventy-seven-year history. As she told *The Guardian*, her mandate from the trustees was "to put the 'national' back in the National Gallery and think about how we serve the American people."

The National Gallery now has its first vision statement—"Of the nation and for all the people"—and its top strategic priority is to "reflect and attract the nation."

"We will focus on diversity, equity, accessibility, and inclusion throughout our work—diversifying the stories we tell, the ways in which we tell them, and ourselves."

Feldman recognized early on that if the National Gallery of Art was to achieve its vision, she needed a diverse staff and an inclusive culture, starting with a senior cabinet of inclusive leaders who would own this vision and help embed it across the museum's operations. Feldman had inherited a leadership team that was entirely White; retirements and reorganizations gave her the chance to rebuild. Today, the ten-person executive team includes six people of color

(continued)

and six women, the most diverse in the National Gallery's history and a far cry from norm in the art museum field in the United States overall, in which approximately 88% of museum leadership is White. Among the new executive team members is the museum's first chief of diversity, inclusion, and belonging, Mikka Gee Conway.

This diverse team is planting seeds of the inclusive organization it aspires to be. Since 2019, the National Gallery has acquired major works by Black, Native American, and Latino artists, including Edward Mitchell Bannister, Theaster Gates, Carmen Herrera, James Luna, Faith Ringgold, and Jaune Quick-to-See Smith. It has diversified its exhibition program, expanding the range of stories told and the achievements celebrated as well as the roster of scholars and projects awarded valuable research opportunities by its Center for Advanced Study in the Visual Arts. And with support from the Mellon Foundation, it has partnered with Howard University on an innovative undergraduate fellowship pilot program to engage young scholars of color with museum theory and practice.

The National Gallery is also working on inclusion behind the scenes, engaging Korn Ferry to conduct a climate survey and assessment to bring employee and volunteer voices to the forefront and to diagnose the root causes impeding diversity, equity, access, and inclusion. The assessment asked staff and leadership to envision their future success, which one executive team member described as "creat[ing] the conditions for people to feel welcomed. We are here for you. This is the nation's gallery. It is for all people, all walks of life. You are welcome."

While still in the early stages of change, the National Gallery of Art is beginning to show what an inclusive organization looks like, starting with inclusive leaders who can make decisions that shape every aspect of the organization's vision to be "Of the nation and for all the people."

Sources: Peggy McGlone, "The National Gallery's Next Leader Will Have a Chance to Reshape the Museum. If the Museum Allows It," *Washington Post,* August 29 2018, https://www.washingtonpost.com/entertainment/museums/the-national-gallerys-next-leader-will-have-a-chance-to-reshape-the-museum-if-the-museum-allows-it/2018/08/29/bf3adc50-9b44-11e8-843b-36e177f3081c_story.html; David Smith, "Putting the 'National' in the National Gallery: Kaywin Feldman Wants the Museum to Serve the People," *Guardian,* December 25, 2021, https://www.theguardian.com/culture/2021/dec/25/national-gallery-kaywin-feldman-serve-american-people; Zachary Small, "National Gallery of Art Reopens With a New Vision: 'For All the People,'" *New York Times,* May 13, 2021, https://www.nytimes.com/2021/05/13/arts/design/national-gallery-washington-reopen-rebrand.html; Mariët Westermann, Roger Schonfeld, and Liam Sweeney, *Art Museum Staff Demographic Survey* 2018 (Andrew W. Mellon Foundation, 2019), https://mellon.org/media/filer_public/e5/a3/e5a373f3-697e-41e3–8f17-051587468755/sr-mellon-report-art-museum-staff-demographic-survey-01282019.pdf.

As we look back on the stories and arguments we've shared in this book, here are our final observations. We cannot achieve the audacious ambition of transforming the world without inclusive leaders, inclusive teams, and inclusive organizations. We need inclusive leaders to set the stage, inclusive teams to power all DE&I efforts, and inclusive organizations to scale empathy.

INCLUSIVE LEADERS SET THE STAGE

In the first book in this Five Inclusive Disciplines series, we shared a comprehensive view of what an inclusive leader looks like, and we provided various examples of exemplary inclusive leaders around the world. Here we make the essential link between those inclusive leaders and inclusive organizations.

Inclusive organizations generate outcomes that are only possible if the enterprise is led by behaviorally and structurally inclusive leaders. This requires leaders to care about more than their narrow scope of responsibilities; they must care about what happens to their people within the entire enterprise and about what is happening in the world outside the organization.

An inclusive leader isn't just focused on their title. They also are focused on the collective impact that leaders have and can have on their teams, on the whole organization, and on the people the organization serves. But without leaders who use their power this way, nothing will change to bring about the urgent changes our world needs. They must lead with self-awareness, be curious about truly understanding the wonder of differences in their people, and be courageous to challenge the very status quo they have traditionally upheld. The director at the National Gallery is an exemplar of this type of leader.

INCLUSIVE TEAMS POWER ALL DE&I EFFORTS

As we have mentioned, the traditional ways of organizing enterprises are not working anymore. Silos are in the way. Hierarchy is dead. Face-to-face is less of a reality. Teams are now the key organizing principle through which work gets done in organizations, and they are the ultimate morphing entity. They can be of any size, exist for any length of time, accommodate any person, be anywhere. They are disruptive, agile, and dynamic. They are the lifeboats for people drowning in the mega structures of big business and big government.

Within inclusive organizations, teams are the nexus of greater diversity, inclusion, innovation, and better business results. They are where employees have the greatest chance to feel they belong, can bring their full selves to projects, and can do their best work. Executive teams that understand why diversity matters have seen an increase of 15% in financial performance, and those that execute diversity initiatives have seen an increase of 21%.[1]

Currently, our DE&I practice is collaborating with the Korn Ferry Institute and the Team Effectiveness practice to unearth and verify what is necessary for diverse teams to be inclusive. We are testing our hypothesis about the secret sauce that leads to the already proven correlation between diversity and inclusion and greater innovation. Those findings will be reported in the next book in our Five Inclusive Disciplines trilogy, *The 5 Disciplines of Inclusive Teams.*

While we have more to find out, we know for sure that for inclusive organizations to mature in their DE&I transformation and be able to address the four vital tasks, they will need to empower and unleash the power of inclusive teams.

INCLUSIVE ORGANIZATIONS SCALE EMPATHY

Without empathy, we cannot achieve inclusion. But empathy at the interpersonal level alone will not help transform the world. Of course, there have always been sensitive managers and leaders whose eyes are open to internal and external inequities. But organizations cannot rely on empathy during one-on-one interactions alone to create a psychologically safe, equitable work environment, nor is individual empathy enough to address massive social and environmental disruptions.

Instead, inclusive organizations must create structures and processes that scale empathy.

To do this, inclusive organizations must break the default templates that exist in all arenas. Internally, they must systematically weed the biases out of their systems and processes—from recruiting and promotion to meeting etiquette and physical environments—so that every person who walks through their doors has the opportunity to thrive and contribute their best work. Externally, they must harness their entire enterprise to go after eradicating polarization, reducing social inequities, and achieving zero carbon emissions. This requires truly caring about socially marginalized groups and the future of the next generation and empathetically putting the organization's massive machinery and infrastructure at the disposal of this vital work that must be done.

INCLUSIVE GOVERNMENTS ARE THE NEXT FRONTIER

Can the five disciplines of inclusive organizations be applied to cities, counties, states, provinces, and even nations? In effect, are inclusive organizations a model and a platform for inclusive governments and a wholly inclusive world?

Andrés, who is currently serving as a city council member in Highland Park, Illinois, has witnessed the five disciplines transform at the municipal level. He and City Manager Ghida Neukirch have no doubt that the answer is a resounding yes.

Cities, counties, states, provinces, and nations have many similarities to corporate organizations. They have boundaries, governance, revenues, and expenses and obligations around risk management, security, fiscal health, care for their people, and so on. We believe governments can use the five disciplines in support of their own measures of success, including committing to equity and inclusion in an exceptionally diverse world. (Remember that diversity in some form or another is almost everywhere, and societies have a choice about whether or not to manage it inclusively.)

Let's look at each of the five disciplines of inclusive organizations and how they can apply to governments.

Manage the Risk. As everyday alerts on our smartphones remind us, our societies are rife with tensions due to diversity. From fear of immigrants that translates into unwelcoming policies and reactions that can turn violent to electorates polarized on the basis of religion, socioeconomic status, race, and ethnicity, there is risk everywhere! We are all anxiously holding our breath until the next social derailment takes place. So, yes, we need government entities that can effectively reduce the risk with inclusive policies and practices.

Explode the Awareness. Cities and nations have the opportunity to educate their populations about the makeup of the community's fabric. This not only allows for better policy that leaves no one behind but also helps everyone become more aware so they can, at the very least, better understand why certain policies that are not important to them are important to others.

Maximize the Talent Systems. Jobs, jobs, jobs! Employment is a major preoccupation of every city and nation. The workforce is the engine that propels economies. When people don't have opportunities to work or to access work, this suboptimized talent pool not only loses its own sense of dignity and ability to care for themselves; it also can become a burden on the city or nation. Inclusion means that all who want and need to participate in the workforce can.

Master the Logistics. At its most essential, cities and nations need to function. Water must come out of faucets when turned on, streets must be paved, garbage must be picked up, first responders must save lives and tackle disasters, construction must be authorized and overseen, and building applications must be reviewed and issued. While innovative policy and strategy is important in a city and a nation, a city's main job is to master the logistics for all of its citizens. Who is being systemically left out in the basic running of the city? How can we address this problem?

See the Marketplace. Cities and nations are the ecosystems in which businesses decide to invest. Inclusive cities as well as nations are able to see the unique assets they possess that will attract businesses and shoppers. They are able to understand the unique demographics within their boundaries and surrounding areas in order to leverage that diversity and provide differentiated retail and dining experiences. They are able to create financial incentives and bureaucratic streamlining to grow their economic prosperity by leveraging their diversity to attract diversity.

It's clear that inclusive organizations have something to model for cities and nations on how to be more inclusive. And given ESG's mandate for organizations to go outside their boundaries and take into account the impact they have on society at large, we can see there are plenty of opportunities for organizations to partner with cities and nations for a more inclusive society and a healthier planet.

Inclusive organizations of all types are precisely what we need to meet the moment.

WHEN THE UNTHINKABLE HAPPENS

Andrés Tapia

It took ninety seconds for the mass shooter to fire eighty-three rounds with an AR-15-style semiautomatic weapon, which took the lives of seven people and injured forty-eight during the 2022 Fourth of July parade in our city of Highland Park, Illinois. Families from Highland Park and other neighboring cities who lost loved ones were devastated, and entire communities were emotionally shattered. The strollers, wagons, bikes, blankets, purses, backpacks, and folding chairs chaotically left abandoned in the wake of people fleeing for their lives will forever be etched in our collective minds.

What happened next, though, was transformative. We witnessed a religiously, racially, ethnically, socioeconomically diverse community respond organically as an inclusive city through inclusive leadership.

As the shots rang out, Highland Park police immediately ran toward the shooter while other first responders as well as civilians helped parade attendees escape and tended to those hit by bullets and shrapnel. People's belongings left in the parade route were pro-tected, while ensuring the FBI could complete its forensic work. Overnight, with the help of the FBI's violent crimes victims unit, a trauma psychotherapy center was set up in Highland Park High School, with a bilingual and bicultural intake process and therapists.

Communication to a bewildered and scared population was fre-quent, transparent, and actionable. The mayor consistently provided updates and reassurances while not glossing over the city's trauma. Press conferences in English and Spanish were offered. Websites were created for fast information sharing and also for people to offer their services and make suggestions. Updates were sent through a variety of channels preferred by a variety of constituents: flyers, emails, Facebook videos, and even text messages. Spontaneous memorials went up, tended by grassroots groups, and are now maintained in collaboration with the city.

Within six days, the place where the shooting had taken place was restored—blood stains removed, shattered glass picked up, and the plaza repainted. The yellow CRIME SCENE DO NOT CROSS police tape was removed and the downtown opened up for people to begin to reclaim our communal space.

The city ensured that its day-to-day operations continued unin-terrupted even while it tended to the grief, the logistics, and the

(continued)

criminal investigation. It also moved into legislative activism as the mayor was the lead witness on a US Senate Judiciary Committee hearing on assault weapons and the Highland Park shooting.

Highland Park had to face the unimaginable. By doing it inclusively, residents, visitors, and workers felt seen, informed, and taken care of.

Inclusive leadership and inclusive cities are not just a nice concept. It is a hard-edged way of serving a community. In the most unimaginable of situations, it is what is needed to provide personal comfort, scalable help, and communal positivity. Inclusion is what is helping the City of Highland Park to not only recover but also regain, and over time, reinvent.

WITHOUT ACTION TODAY, THERE IS NO TOMORROW

As uncomfortable as it is to talk about violence in a book focused on organizations and on DE&I, there's nothing like a near-death experience to provide clarity about what truly matters. You might say we are collectively having a near-death experience, if we consider the COVID-19 pandemic and what is going on with our planet. With this clarity, then, we can operate with what Dr. Martin Luther King Jr. referred to as "the fierce urgency of now." This was his response to his own statement, "We are now faced with the fact that tomorrow is today. . . . There is such a thing as being too late."

People continue to be murdered for the color of their skin, mass shootings are an epidemic, and the planet is losing millions of species and millions of members of the human race due to climate change. Nature is voicing its fury at our neglect, through mass fires, superstorms, massive droughts, and flood deluges.

The inclusive organizations we have showcased in this book have what it takes to bring about the more appealing, inspirational-poster, uplifting aspects of DE&I: greater representation as well as more inclusive, engaged, and psychologically safe environments that offer everyone the equal opportunity to rise to the fullness of their potential.

But we see that these same organizations have also played a part in weakening or even gutting sustainable practices, leading to intensely dysfunctional and violent situations such as the hatred coursing through political rallies, the toxic rhetoric in ad campaigns, and the damage we are inflicting to our planet. All these trends have taken their toll. We know this because at least 25% of the US population in 2022—that's 1 in 4 people—and approximately 1 billion people globally are experiencing mental health illness.[2] And in low-income countries, up to 75% of those facing mental health illness do not receive treatment.[3]

The question confronting organizations, then, is simple but loaded: What will it take to transform the world?

For the longest time, wise women and men have told us to be patient, that things take time, that there's a process, that Rome wasn't built in a day. Good advice . . . for another time.

But for this time, "tomorrow is today." We cannot wait around to figure it out. We must get to solutions much, much faster. As we have shown through these pages, we know without a doubt that inclusive organizations led by inclusive leaders and powered by inclusive teams are key to transforming the world. Without these inclusive qualities embedded throughout every dimension of the DE&I Maturity Model, we won't be able to diversify leadership, eradicate polarization, achieve justice, or save the planet.

Inclusive organizations have the opportunity to lead with greater purpose, manage with deeper empathy, and redesign with heightened imagination. Many of them, across many different industries and geographies, are doing exactly that. They are acting fiercely in the urgency of now because they don't want us all to be too late.

We know what to do. The five disciplines of inclusive organizations provide the road map to execute on our irrevocable responsibility to do good.

But will we do it? It's now up to organizations seeking to be inclusive to have the courage to say *Yes*.

APPENDICES

How to Create Your Own Best-in-Class DE&I Scorecard

As framed in Chapter 6, when it comes to metrics and scorecards, one size does not fit all. In this Appendix we provide a detailed roadmap for developing your own scorecard. Our experience over the years..

A significant amount of the content in this appendix comes from a coauthored white paper, "The DE&I Metrics That Really Matter," written by the two authors of this book, with contributions by Korn Ferry colleagues David Herrera, Associate Client Partner, and Gustavo Gisbert, Senior Principal.

SET UP

1. DETERMINE THE ORGANIZATION'S CURRENT DE&I MATURITY

Measurement and goal-driven metrics always begin a comparison. A comparison between where you were and where you currently are. Between where you are and where you want to go. Between where you land and where your competitors land. Between what happens when you

10-step process

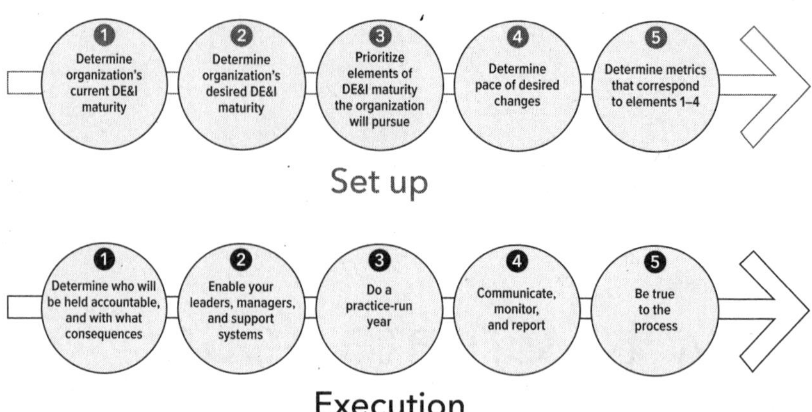

Figure 5: 10 Steps to Building the Right Metrics.

do *X* and when you do *Y*. Between the results in one context compared to another.

So when it comes to DE&I, the best place to start this compare-and-contrast work is by determining where the organization lands on its own current DE&I maturity (see figure 5). This is measured against the DE&I Maturity Model described in detail in the introduction of this book. Its five DE&I dimensions (Risk Management, Awareness, Talent Integration, Operations Integration, and Market Integration), and their behavioral and structural components, form the basis of the five disciplines we have discussed. While the five disciplines consist of the structures, mindsets, behaviors, and accountabilities required to drive the increased DE&I maturity of organizations, the maturity model itself becomes a tool for leaders of inclusive organizations to stay the course in a methodical and disciplined way. Hence, in this appendix, you will see us refer to the DE&I *dimensions*, rather than the *disciplines*, when discussing metrics and measurements.

The most effective way to determine an organization's DE&I maturity is through a comprehensive, data-driven DE&I diagnostic and root cause analysis in which the results are mapped against the maturity model.

Through classic diagnostic methodologies such as surveys, talent flow analyses, focus groups, social network analyses, psychometric assessments, and other data-gathering and analytical processes, organizations can measure their maturity. Through statistical analysis of this data, such as regression and driver analysis, the strongest relationships can be pinpointed, providing guidance for additional exploration of what may be causing what and why.

2. DETERMINE THE ORGANIZATION'S DESIRED DE&I MATURITY

The second part of the compare-and-contrast exercise is deciding where you want to go next on your DE&I journey. This is not as straightforward as it appears. Using the Korn Ferry model, you can see that there is plenty of organizational choice involved. If Company X is at the Advanced level of maturity in Awareness but only at the Basic level in Talent Integration, the organization can legitimately either choose to mature to the max on Awareness and make maturity in Talent Integration something that can wait another year, or vice versa.

The decision may be driven by other internal initiatives. For an organization that is currently focused on revamping its talent processes in general or is more specifically focused on one or two processes, such as talent acquisition and performance management, it might make sense to integrate an inclusive approach to the new processes and therefore to concentrate on Progressing in the Talent Integration dimension.

So determining the desired DE&I maturity in the various dimensions depends on the organization's overall DE&I strategy, with which all DE&I steps should be aligned. One thing to remember is that "best-in-class" can happen at any stage of the maturity model, in the same way that best-in-class in sports can be determined for different stages of physical development as athletes go from being kids to teens to adults.

During this process, we also recommend that the desired state is aligned to the business strategy and priorities. For example, if your organization has plans to open operations in new markets, Market Integration and Talent Integration might be relevant to support the success of your firm. Another example is innovation, where Operations Integration plays a key role.

3. PRIORITIZE THE ELEMENTS OF DE&I MATURITY THE ORGANIZATION WILL PURSUE

Once you decide where you want to go—what your desired DE&I maturity in the various dimensions is—it's time to determine priorities. What are the quick wins you can focus on first? Which areas of focus will need to be tackled before others?

For some organizations, the journey starts with their leaders. For them, step one is to assess and educate their leaders on what it means to lead inclusively so they can then lead the DE&I journey forward. For others, it's more grassroots. Their journey may start by pulling together a DE&I council or committee that will lead the effort and drive awareness, or by establishing employee resource groups. And yet others will start by educating the organization as a whole through distinct learning journeys. Priorities are usually set by considering what else might be going on in the organization; the level of leaders' and employees' preoccupation with other initiatives, such as a possible merger, for example; the general culture of the organization (whether hierarchical or more bottom-up); and of course, the budget available both presently and in the future.

Like determining the desired future state in step two, setting priorities is best aligned with the overarching business direction and strategy. If your business strategy involves expansion into new markets, for example, an inclusive hiring strategy targeting talent from this market or culturally aligned to the market will make sense. Culturally competent marketing will need to follow. If your business strategy is based on innovation and creative product development, a focus on embedding inclusion skills into operations—on Master the Logistics—is the logical place to direct one's effort.

Once you establish your priorities, you can determine the more granular execution goals you need to achieve your priorities. One thing to remember is to be realistic. Many organizations have established priorities and goals that do not reflect their current maturity or their organization's complexity. Supported by data from your DE&I strategy, a detailed analysis of resources is required, and opportunities per year should inform where and when to act.

4. DETERMINE THE PACE OF CHANGE

So now that you know where you want to go and have set your priority areas and the tactical goals to focus on, you will need to determine by when you will want to achieve your goals.

A timeline should be both ambitious—a true call to action—and realistic. Many factors will determine whether a timeline is realistic, such as competing priorities, staffing availability, leader buy-in, and last but not least, your industry's trends and other outside factors.

For example, we have seen many organizations set ambitious but seemingly arbitrary goals and timelines, such as aiming to "increase representation of women in senior leadership roles to 30% in two years." While on the surface this sounds like a worthy goal, it raises the question of whether it's realistic for each company or in each industry. Some industries are very much behind in terms of gender parity, something that often starts at the entry levels or even before that, meaning the number of girls and women pursuing careers in those areas in school or college is already lower than the number of boys and men.

What this means is that organizations focused on filling senior-level positions with women within a relatively short timeline will likely fall short and will lose valuable internal credibility. To achieve this goal, it might make more sense to create a longer timeline with built-in subgoals that include concentrating on an equitable pipeline of women moving toward leadership while at the same time committing to encouraging girls and young women early in the pipeline to pursue studies and careers in these traditionally male-dominated roles. When you build your DE&I strategy and timeline, the balance between ambitious and realistic is crucial to its success.

5. DETERMINE MEASUREMENTS AND METRICS THAT CORRESPOND TO ELEMENTS 1 THROUGH 4

Once your current state, your desired state, your strategic priorities, your tactical goals, and your timeline have been established, it's the right moment to ask yourself how to measure success. This is the point where meaningful and relevant metrics can be put in place. A DE&I balanced scorecard or dashboard consists of a set of metrics designed to capture data about the organization's performance with respect to its DE&I

initiative and to monitor trends over time. Based on the answers to the earlier questions, the "right" metrics are likely a combination of five different types: activity metrics, process metrics, lagging indicators, leading indicators, and predictive metrics.

In the preceding chapters, we have discussed the five disciplines; it follows that organizations will need to consider all five disciplines when they put metrics in place to mature in each of the DE&I dimensions. In our explanation of the different types of metrics here, we have focused our examples on metrics related mainly to the dimensions of Awareness (corresponding discipline, Explode the Awareness) and Talent Integration (corresponding discipline, Maximize the Talent Systems). For examples of metrics for all dimensions, see table 2.

Activity metrics tend to measure elements involved in DE&I initiatives, such as number of people who attended a DE&I training, number of employees who are part of ERGs, time dedicated to mentoring or sponsoring others, number of events attended, volunteer hours, number of new innovation ideas tracked back to diverse-by-design teams, and so forth. These tend to be helpful metrics early in a DE&I journey.

Process metrics evaluate the impact of the different activities on key processes, such as performance management, recruitment, and selection; supplier diversity; or whether DE&I training has made a difference in more equitable performance ratings or more diverse new hires. Measuring customer satisfaction or customer retention is another example of process metrics.

Lagging indicators usually capture a snapshot of the organization's current state and past efforts. Examples include representation data; engagement and employee perception of organizational DE&I maturity, cut demographically; recruitment, promotion, and termination/layoff rates; or advancement speed.

Leading indicators are a measure signaling whether the lagging indicator metrics will or will not be achieved if things continue on their present course. Talent pipeline analysis for women or underrepresented racial/ethnic groups is a common leading indicator of what the diversity mix of talent will be at different levels of the organization within a few years. These are some of the most overlooked metrics, and the most strategically important, since they can be an early warning that the efforts may or may not ultimately achieve the desired objectives.

Table 2 Sample Diversity, Equity, and Inclusion Metrics.

DIMENSION	WHAT TO MEASURE AND TYPE OF INDICATORS	EXAMPLE OF METRICS AND TYPE OF ACTIONS IMPLEMENTED
Risk management	Tend to be **lagging and leading** indicators to understand long-term trends. The intent is to have a snapshot to understand current state of "the mix" (focus on representation), mitigate legal risks, and even flag when trends are inching upward with discrimination claims.	Response and actions can be reactive as well as proactive. Reactive examples of lagging indicators include incumbency (headcount representation) versus external workforce availability analysis or number of claims related to harassment and discrimination, cases open, cases closed. Proactive leading indicator examples would be representation targets or quotas set (mindful of local laws, of course), or the number of people taking courses on discrimination, which can be a signal that the enterprise may become less vulnerable to an increasing number of claims.
Awareness	Tend to be **activity metrics, process metrics, and lagging indicators.** The intent is to see how leaders and employees are aware of and committed to the value of diversity, equity, and inclusion and of "making the mix work." The focus is on creating a culture of inclusion.	Response and actions tend to be inspirational and purpose-driven. Examples of activity and process metrics include percent of training attendance; time dedicated to mentor and sponsor; number of events attended; volunteer hours; perception of leaders committed to diversity, equity, and inclusion; inclusive behaviors demonstrated by leaders and rated by employees; engagement of different groups; and intent to stay and/or net promoter scores.
Talent integration	Tend to be **leading indicators and predictive metrics** signaling future trends and probability of changing conditions in the talent pipeline and talent systems. The focus is on accelerating movement, development in talent pipeline of high-potential feeder pools, broadening diverse sourcing pools, achieving parity levels in hiring, promotions, lateral moves, exits, and manager competencies.	Response and actions tend to be more proactive. Examples include talent flow analyses cut demographically (promotion rates, external hiring rates, terminations and turnover rates, voluntary versus involuntary exits, lateral moves, stretch assignments, performance ratings). Examples of predictive metrics typically include a driver analysis that seeks to find relationships between different factors that may not be readily apparent or provide statistical evidence to qualitative observations. Examples include the relationship between employee resource groups and retention and advancement; the impact of training on engagement levels; the impact of lateral moves on vertical advancement; skills and competencies that, when selected, can negatively impact underrepresented talent.

(continued)

Table 2 Sample Diversity, Equity, and Inclusion Metrics. *(continued)*

DIMENSION	WHAT TO MEASURE AND TYPE OF INDICATORS	EXAMPLE OF METRICS AND TYPE OF ACTIONS IMPLEMENTED
Operations integration	Tend to be more **lagging indicators, leading indicators, and predictive metrics.** The intent is to understand how the organization may leverage its diversity in an inclusive way to achieve bottom-line impact, reduce costs, create safety, create agile teams, and improve processes to increase margins.	Responses and actions tend to be more operational and tactical. Examples may include cost reduction and increased productivity correlated with increased safety as well as value creation in a merger or acquisition. A shocking 70% to 90% of all M&As fail, and the common denominator in those failed M&As are people and culture,* essentially failure to leverage diversity in an inclusive and innovative way. Metrics here also include supplier diversity volume and diverse-by-design team assignments to create more lean and efficient practices. Other metrics include procurement contracts with minority-owned business enterprises (MBEs), women-owned business enterprises (WBEs), and minority-owned disadvantaged business enterprises (DBEs) in Tier I and Tier II.
Market integration	Mix of **leading and lagging indicators.** The intent here is to have a snapshot to understand how successfully the organization leverages diversity, equity, and inclusion to enhance its customer experience, employee value proposition (EVP) as well as the overall company brand in the community. Focus is on top-line revenue and growth as well as brand enhancement.	Responses and actions tend to be strategic and innovative. Examples include growth due to diverse market share penetration, increase of consumers from demographics not previously well reached, enhanced customer satisfaction in online and in-store transactions, and retention of nontraditional customers. On the community side, measures include amount of donations of money and employee volunteer time.

Sources: *David Garrison, "Most Mergers Fail Because People Aren't Boxes," *Forbes*, June 24, 2019, https://www.forbes.com/sites/forbescoachescouncil/2019/06/24/most-mergers -fail-because-people-arent-boxes; Lisa DeWaard, "The 70%–90% Problem: Why Do M&As Have Such High Failure Rates?," Lisa's Insights, March 9, 2021, https://www.linkedin.com /pulse/70-90-problem-why-do-mas-have-high-failure-rates-lisa-dewaard.

Predictive metrics help identify the likely impact of specific variables on key DE&I outcomes, such as promotion and retention of diverse talent. Typical predictor variables include performance ratings, high-potential designation, mentorship or sponsorship, leadership development opportunities, involvement in critical projects, ERG participation, and more. The benefits of using predictive metrics is that it helps one to better understand the possible driving forces behind the organization's talent trajectory and to develop long-term initiatives that pull the correct lever for the desired outcomes.

With respect to the DE&I Maturity Model, a combination of these five types of metrics can be put in place for each of the dimensions. In the spirit of the model, we do not want to be prescriptive as to which metrics are better than others.

It is also important to add that there are multiple ways for an organization to set inclusive metrics. For instance, when analyzing DE&I-specific data and demographic groups, grouping employees under certain terms is a crude but necessary and helpful way for collecting and evaluating data. But it is not perfect. Performing intersectional data cuts—such as through self-determination questions and the ability to check multiple boxes in self-identification surveys—is the way to get closer to the reality of intersectional identities in the analysis and reporting.

For example, when looking at Asian + Female + Generation + In a Labor Union and then comparing to another combination where just one of the variables is different, such as race/ethnicity, we can begin to explore what dimension of identity is more influential in that group's experience in the workplace and create interventions accordingly.

Each organization will have to set its own metrics that are right for the organization at the present time.

EXECUTION

Now that the metrics have been identified, it's time to tackle the most difficult aspect of a DE&I scorecard: execution. And execution requires well-designed structures and processes, and regular, easy-to-read dashboards with actionable indicators and trends that enable leaders to make just-in-time adjustments.

Many organizations underestimate the importance of setting up structural systems that can help coordinate and collaborate with multiple internal and external stakeholders. The five steps here are a synthesis of the key steps to drive execution.

Keep in mind that following through on the steps ahead requires a clear governance structure that leaves no doubt as to who sets the key metrics and to whom stakeholders will be accountable. While ultimately all are accountable to the CEO, the question to answer is whether this will be governed by an executive DE&I council or the existing executive team structure. Only when the answer to this question is clear can the following steps be taken.

1. DETERMINE WHO WILL BE HELD ACCOUNTABLE, FOR WHAT, AND WITH WHAT CONSEQUENCES

Metrics need to stick like Velcro to those who are accountable for meeting them. Too often, metrics for bold DE&I goals are declared but then don't stick because none of the desired numeric goals were pegged to anyone to get them done.

Metrics need to be something that people can take action on, so they need to have the following characteristics:

- Be ambitious, driven by vision and aspiration, yet grounded in reality and not clouded by unrealistic wishful thinking.

- Be specific and addressable by the leaders being held accountable. Executives, managers, human resources, and employees all should have differentiated metrics that tie to different parts of the DE&I strategy to which they have the greatest line of sight. For example, hiring rates for women or members of underrepresented groups are typically metrics assigned to HR because they are the ones responsible for presenting diverse candidate slates. However, we found that when hiring metrics are assigned solely to HR, the success rate is often low, because even when HR presents a diverse slate, it is ultimately the hiring manager who makes the final hiring decision. In this case, the hiring key performance indicator would have to be assigned to both HR (to provide diverse slates) and the hiring managers (to ensure hires from underrepresented groups).

- Be time bound and specific as to when the goals are to be reached.

2. ENABLE YOUR LEADERS AND MANAGERS FIRST, BUT DON'T FORGET THE SUPPORT SYSTEMS

Preparation is key. Be sure not to just spring goals and accountabilities on your various stakeholders without giving them the tools to get the job done. It is important that leaders and managers are grounded in the business case for DE&I and that they know how it aligns with the broader business and talent strategies of the organization. Provide training on how to identify and manage unconscious bias in the hiring and performance management processes, as well as on ways in which the use of common talent systems and processes can perpetuate the lack of DE&I. (See chapter 3, "Maximize the Talent Systems," for more detail.) This will give managers the opportunity to gain the insights and skills they need to then take the necessary and courageous actions to achieve the goals and metrics they were given.

At the same time, support systems such as legal, compliance, human resources business partners, communications, and others need to be enabled and aligned. Their role in supporting managers is crucial, and often they do not have the competencies or resources to provide the right assistance. For example, corporate communications plays a key role in the rollout of the communications strategy; any leader should be able to reach out to this team to request support for a specific event or initiative. The communications department should then provide guidance and support, using the right DE&I lens, and ensure that all communication is aligned to the overall organization's strategy.

3. DO A PRACTICE-RUN YEAR

Putting leaders' and managers' bonus and pay at risk by tying it to achieving DE&I goals is not a light matter. Personal economics, as well as people's own sense of emotional well-being, are in the balance. Therefore, adequate preparation time before "playing for real" is warranted. A good way to do this is to have a practice-run year. Similar to learning a new card game, newcomers are given a practice round in which all the rules are in effect but there are no consequences just yet for getting the fewest points.

This is a transition period during which everything about the metrics—goals, reporting, and feedback on how each leader is doing—is fully operational yet no real money is involved. This way, leaders can experience what it will all look and feel like, and can in fact see real scores of how they are performing along the way. This will tell them how their pay that year would have been affected if the full accountabilities had been in play. It is also an opportunity for the players to discuss these rules and metrics and to ensure they feel they have the tools and structures in place to have a fair shot at winning.

After that practice year, everyone not only knows that pay will be at stake but also will have a better sense of how the process will work, and their strengths and vulnerabilities going into it, and will be better prepared to take the necessary steps to achieve their goals. A practice-run year also provides an opportunity to consider whether there will be unintended consequences and to address these prior to the larger rollout.

4. COMMUNICATE, MONITOR, AND REPORT

Nothing is more unfair than giving leaders targets to achieve, with pay at stake, and then not providing them with regular and accurate progress reports on how they are doing. Leaders will need to be provided with a dashboard so they can easily review their progress and make any adjustments, if needed.

Set expectations for how often they will get updated reports, whether monthly, quarterly, or on some other schedule, and make sure someone in HR is helping them interpret the trend lines and is partnering with them on a collaborative game plan to meet the goals. Make sure to keep all stakeholders up to speed so that everyone can play a part in making a difference according to the goals. CEOs as well as peer pressure are effective levers to keep everyone focused.

5. BE TRUE TO THE PROCESS

Authenticity and transparency are key. Highlight and celebrate success when progress happens, but do not try to hide or cover gaps and challenges whenever those appear. That only leads to frustration and a sense that leaders and managers within the organization are not taking the process seriously. Also, be faithful to the processes you have laid out. Deliver updates on time and make sure everyone is taking the respective steps to plan sessions to strategize and problem solve where progress is not being made.

So, we have nailed down the process, but what really should be at stake? How should leaders be held accountable for inclusive behaviors and equitable outcomes for all talent? Just as there is no one right metric, there also is not just one type of accountability upside or consequence. The meaningful reward or takeaway for achieving or not achieving DE&I goals should be congruent with the organization's development and advancement process as well as with its pay and rewards philosophy. It should not feel like something foreign and different.

Most importantly, the best metrics for your company—determined by using the methodology presented here—will be the ones that will help propel your organization toward even greater levels of diversity, equity, and inclusion as well as sustainable long-term business prosperity.

PREDICTING REPRESENTATION WHILE YOU STILL CAN DO SOMETHING ABOUT IT

One of the most frustrating metrics that leaders often receive with a great deal of dismay is the representation of women and racial and ethnic minorities in positions of leadership and influence. They experience this frustration not only because of low and embarrassing numbers, but also because it's a lagging indicator that no one can do anything about—it's the final score of a particular cycle.

This final score basically says how poorly the organization did, after time has run out and there is no room to take fast, corrective action. In fact, the representation metric sits staring at leadership, confronting them with the immutable fact that whatever they thought they were doing on behalf of advancing diversity did not work. Plus, it's a passive number that does not give insight into what went wrong or what to do to avoid the same metric fate again in the following talent cycle.

A leading indicator such as the strength of the pipeline can be much more actionable and can be delivered in the middle of a talent cycle, when there is still time on the clock to take corrective or enhanced action. A strong or weak percentage of underrepresented talent in the succession or high-potential pool can be an indicator of where things may end up, given that it's still in the middle of the talent cycle. Like any coach of a team that is losing or trying to keep and extend its lead, leadership can adjust strategies and tactics just in time to respond to what the scoreboard is indicating.

CASE STUDY: LARGE GLOBAL FINANCIAL SERVICES COMPANY

Here's the story of one predictive metric that was unearthed at a twenty-thousand-employee global financial services company through the methodology we have just described. Once the in-depth root cause analysis was complete, it led to an Aha! moment and a game-changing predictive metric.

Although this company did not have formal development processes, it was phenomenal at informal development. The diversity, equity, and inclusion diagnostic revealed that lateral moves in the form of short-term assignments, expat deployments, and high-visibility projects were culturally endemic throughout the organization. In fact, a deep quantitative diagnostic revealed that there was a strong predictive pattern in which four lateral moves consistently led to promotions to vice president level, and six lateral moves led to senior vice president level.

But when a structural inclusion equity analysis was performed, it revealed a good amount of opportunity disparity. In looking at the informal horizontal movements more closely, it became clear that white men were the ones who consistently and disproportionately got more of those assignments. In fact, women were two times less likely to get those moves, Latino and Latina employees were six times less likely, and Black/African American employees were fourteen times less likely.

As a result of this insight, the company changed the key accountability metric for managers, from representation or promotions (both examples of lagging indicators) to a key short-term metric of lateral movement of underrepresented talent (their predictive leading indicator).

This company did the necessary work of discovering the most telling metric of its organization and then followed up by a metrics and accountability approach that corresponded to the contours of its DE&I strategy.

Better yet is a predictive metric that both gives a sense of what may be and indicates the likely outcome. And the one outcome you want to be able to predict is representation at all levels. In fact, this should be prized as the ultimate outcome, because if, after all your inclusion and equity efforts, your organization still does not reflect the vast diversity of the qualified labor force in leadership and influence positions, then change is not taking place in ways that ultimately matter.

See the case study on how we helped a company do this.

How DE&I Enables Environmental, Social, and Governance (ESG)

Many make the case that DE&I lives within the *S* of ESG: social. But this is a limited understanding of the field. In our work, we believe DE&I is relevant in the *E* and the *G* as well. Here's how.

Environmental criteria consider how a company performs as a steward of nature. Factors include the contribution a company makes to reducing climate change by, for example, cutting greenhouse gas emissions, improving waste management, and conserving resources.

Diversity, equity, and inclusion implications: Reducing the negative impact on the environment, and in fact, reversing global warming, is going to require an unprecedented amount of innovation. The research is clear that diversity of all kinds of backgrounds, experiences, and thinking styles—activated inclusively and equitably—consistently generates more innovation.

Social criteria examine how a company manages relationships with employees, suppliers, customers, and the communities in which the company operates. Factors include human rights; labor standards in the supply chain; any exposure to illegal child labor; more routine issues such as adherence to workplace health, safety, and well-being; and larger economic development investments in underserved communities.

Diversity, equity, and inclusion implications: The fair and equitable treatment of all employees in terms of pay, professional development, and opportunities to get promoted, as well as whether their alternative perspectives are sought after, respected, and leveraged, are all measures that need to be addressed with regard to social impact. A social score also rises if a company is well integrated with its local community and therefore has a "social license" to operate with consent.

All forms of demographic diversity exist in the myriad communities in which companies operate. To be well-integrated with their local communities requires that companies grasp the diversity, equity, and inclusion dynamics that exist between the company and the community. For example, is the company investing in suppliers from the community, including those that are majority owned by women, ethnic minority or LGBTQ+ people, or people with disabilities? Are they investing in educational institutions in the community to foster a more educated labor force with the skills for the jobs of tomorrow? And does the company care in general for the holistic well-being of the community whose roads, water, police, fire, and refuse services the company is using?

Governance criteria deal with a company's decision-making structures and processes, executive pay, audits, internal controls, and shareholder rights. Factors include principles defining rights, responsibilities, and the expectations of different stakeholders. A well-defined corporate governance system can be used to balance and align interests between stakeholders and can work as a tool to support a company's long-term strategy.

Diversity, equity, and inclusion implications: Governance strategies and policies that do not ensure all voices are represented at the board, in the C-suite, and in other influential roles will not lead to sustainability. Are the different demographic groups who are stakeholders in what the company does represented equitably in the decision-making positions? Are their health, economic, and civil rights protected and advocated for by these companies?

Korn Ferry research has identified a wide gap between what organizations are doing with respect to business strategy, operational goals, and technology to achieve sustainability goals and what they are doing people-wise. For example, while many companies have been working tirelessly with environmental scientists to find their path to net zero emissions, they have not considered the behavioral science behind what their people will need to do differently, and how. In this instance, knowing how to address the differentiated worldviews of different demographic groups will be vital for an effective application of behavioral science that needs to be cross-culturally effective.

The role that DE&I plays in ESG is inclusive sustainability. This is about the cumulative effect that DE&I can have on all three aspects of ESG, on generating greater good beyond the common definition of profits. Profitability should also be about what benefits people, society, and the environment.

With 80% of the world's five thousand biggest companies reporting their sustainability performance,[1] the linkage between DE&I and ESG creates unprecedented synergistic opportunities for inclusive organizations to accelerate transformative change on various fronts, including in the four vital tasks.

Excerpted from Andrés T. Tapia, Alina Polonskaia, and Andrea Walsh, "Inclusive Sustainability: ESG Is the New Way of Action and Measuring What Is Mutually Good for Profits, People, and the Planet—and DE&I Lies at the Heart of It" (Korn Ferry, 2021).

Research Methodology of a Korn Ferry Root Cause DE&I Diagnostic

OUR RESEARCH METHODOLOGY—AS SUPPORTED BY MORE THAN fifty DE&I diagnostics performed for our clients over the past seven years—consists of both quantitative and qualitative organizational diagnostic components that shed light on the maturity of both behavioral and structural inclusion (see figure 6).

On the **quantitative** side, we use a *talent flow analysis*, which captures the dynamic nature of how talent of different demographic groups moves throughout—in, horizontally, diagonally, vertically, and out of—the organization in relation to one another. We also use our *employee DE&I survey*, which is a quantifiable capture of a series of qualitative experiences of people within the organization.

On the **qualitative** side, we use *one-on-one interviews* with executives and key stakeholders as well as *focus groups* with employees who are members of those demographic groups where our quantitative analysis showed perception gaps. The focus groups usually illuminate the *why* behind the *what*, bringing to light the reasons for what the numbers are telling us about what is happening between when the glass ceiling is beginning to crystalize and where it's rock solid.

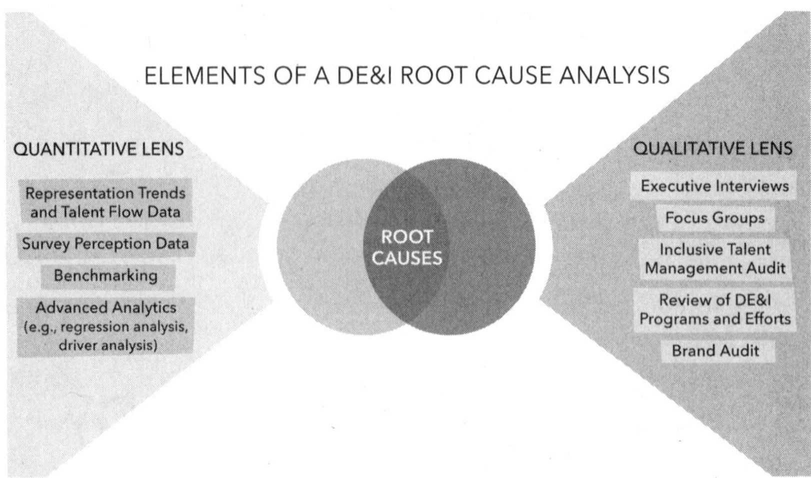

Figure 6: Elements of a Korn Ferry DE&I Root Cause Analysis.

We also use methods that combine the quantitative and the qualitative. Our inclusive talent management audit, for instance, looks at the practices, policies, structures, and employee experiences within the six major talent systems (talent acquisition, performance management, talent and succession, people development, engagement, and total rewards) to surface any potential biases within the process that could be leading to quantitative inequities in the outcomes (performance ratings, percentage of promotions, and diversity in the high-potential pools). At the same time, this audit deciphers the qualitative experiences of talent as they encounter these processes. We spend time with the process owners to determine their intent even before looking at the outcomes.

Where indicated, we also conduct a *brand audit,* which helps us understand an organization's external DE&I presence. We review the organization's DE&I representation within high-level marketing for key digital properties across a specific time period. Digital properties we include in our review are Facebook, Twitter, Instagram, LinkedIn, and Glassdoor, among others.

Other diagnostic components that are often applied are a *pay equity analysis, regretted loss interviews,* and *benchmarking.*

The outcomes of each research component are then analyzed and synthesized, and root causes are unearthed that identify the true levers for change behind the more obvious symptoms.

Summary: The Five Disciplines of Inclusive Organizations

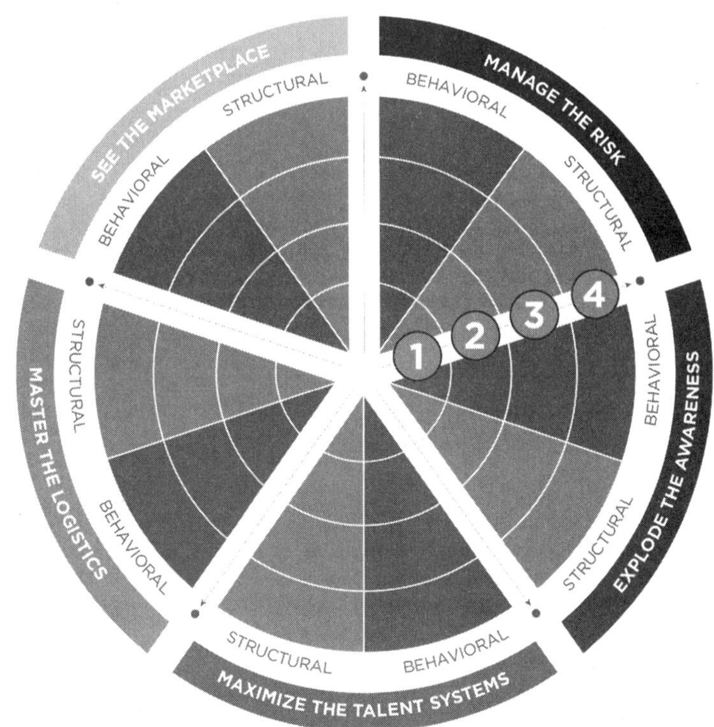

Figure 7: The 5 Disciplines of Inclusive Organizations, based on the Korn Ferry DE&I Maturity Model 2022.

DISCIPLINE 1: MANAGE THE RISK

The extent to which an organization effectively manages DE&I-related risk.

This essentially determines the extent to which an organization has the infrastructure, capabilities, and behaviors necessary to identify, quantify, mitigate, and prevent DE&I-related risks. Structural inclusion in Manage the Risk is achieved when DE&I is approached from a broader risk management perspective as opposed to just addressing bad behaviors when someone musters the courage to speak up. Human resources, leadership, and the board proactively monitor broader organizational risks, such as the need to have good reporting and whistle-blower systems in place, and where there are well-understood consequences and processes for those who violate company policies and values, regardless of their level and status. An organization that is fully mature in the behavioral inclusion aspect of Manage the Risk displays full awareness, by all stakeholders, of the risks and impacts associated with workplace harassment, bullying, and discrimination of its employees—and also, in some cases, of its clients by its employees.

DISCIPLINE 2: EXPLODE THE AWARENESS

The extent to which an organization's leaders and employees are aware of and committed to the value of DE&I.

Structural inclusion in Explode the Awareness is demonstrated through robust and integrated DE&I governance and accountability (such as councils, employee resource groups, or metrics), and by external recognition of the organization's DE&I efforts through awards and certifications related to the quality of these types of DE&I efforts, bestowed by an outside organization. The spectrum of efforts in behavioral inclusion covers awareness building, advocacy, and knowledge of DE&I, communicating its business value, and driving employee engagement. Leaders transition from having DE&I passion to DE&I competence, and from unconscious bias to conscious inclusion. The CEO and business leaders fiercely advocate for DE&I, authentically model inclusion, and are seen as "walking the talk."

DISCIPLINE 3: MAXIMIZE THE TALENT SYSTEMS

The extent to which an organization has integrated diversity, equity, and inclusion into its talent systems, and to which leaders and managers display inclusive behaviors in all aspects of talent management.

When structural inclusion is fully actualized in Maximize the Talent Systems, the organization's DE&I strategy is integrated into its talent strategy, talent processes are reviewed for unconscious biases, leaders and managers are held accountable for DE&I integration into talent management, and robust talent analytics are applied to monitor for equity and to inform talent decisions. When behavioral inclusion is fully actualized, inclusive behaviors become part of the entire talent management life cycle and show up in key talent decisions. Leaders and managers display inclusion skills and leverage the diversity of talent for better decision-making and team performance.

DISCIPLINE 4: MASTER THE LOGISTICS

The bottom-line impact of integrating DE&I into the organization's operations in ways that lead to improved efficiencies.

For structural inclusion, the spectrum of efforts includes DE&I being fully leveraged within the operational ecosystem, such as in the Lean philosophy and the Six Sigma and Kaizen processes, which require input from every team member, innovating new processes for greater safety, managing mergers and acquisitions work streams, and more. The spectrum of efforts in behavioral inclusion includes functional leaders and middle managers modeling inclusion and displaying inclusive leadership skills by deliberately putting together high-performing, diverse-by-design teams for operational tasks and projects.

DISCIPLINE 5: SEE THE MARKETPLACE

The top-line impact of integrating DE&I into marketplace efforts through expanding to markets of new consumers, enhanced customer service, and effective partnerships with communities.

From a structural inclusion perspective, well-understood processes affecting the marketplace, such as innovation, product testing, marketing focus groups, and campaigns, are enhanced by greater DE&I. From a behavioral inclusion perspective, organizations that are mature in See the Marketplace from a DE&I perspective are those where inclusion and cross-cultural competencies are applied in key decisions and market initiatives and where leaders and employees recognize their own need for cross-cultural competence and seek out further education.

DE&I metrics are also embedded in all lines of management in all markets and expected business outcomes, due to leveraging of the organization's DE&I, and are regularly evaluated to ensure sustainability. An organization will also maintain active communications with diverse community and professional organizations, and their employee resource groups may help generate innovative solutions for diverse markets and customers. This requires behavioral inclusion by leaders and others choosing to participate in these events, and the structural inclusion of establishing well-structured strategic partnerships.

NOTES

Introduction

1. Frances J. Milliken, "Diversity and Corporate Social Responsibility: Exploring the Potential Connections between Top Management Team/Board Diversity, CSR, and Workforce Diversity," in Abagail McWilliams, Deborah E. Rupp, Donald S. Siegel, Günter K. Stahl, and David A. Waldman (eds.), *The Oxford Handbook of Corporate Social Responsibility: Psychological and Organizational Perspectives* (Oxford University Press, 2019), 96–123.

2. Douglas Broom, "An Overwhelming Majority of People Want Real Change after COVID-19," *World Economic Forum*, September 18, 2020, https://www.weforum.org/agenda/2020/09/ sustainable-equitable-change-post-coronavirus-survey.

3. Chase Charaba, "Employee Retention: The Real Cost of Losing an Employee," PeopleKeep, June 28, 2022, https://www.peoplekeep.com/blog/employee-retention-the-real-cost-of -losing-an-employee.

4. Maya Kosoff, "What Is the Real Cost of the Great Resignation?," The Org, January 19, 2022, https://theorg.com/iterate/what-is-the-real-cost-of-the-great-resignation.

5. Erik Larson, "New Research: Diversity + Inclusion = Better Decision Making at Work," *Forbes*, September 21, 2017, https://www.forbes.com/sites/eriklarson/2017/09/21/ new-research-diversity-inclusion-better-decision-making-at-work/?sh=2cb53b8f4cbf.

6. Marta Chmielowicz, "Reaching New Heights," *HRO Today*, June 18, 2019, https://www .hrotoday.com/workforce-management/reaching-new-heights-2.

Chapter 1

1. Chanelle Leslie, "10 of the Biggest EEOC Settlements Ever," *Human Resources Director*, June 6, 2014, https://www.hcamag.com/us/news/general/10-of-the-biggest-eeoc-settlements -ever/156010.

2. This is compared to $1.58 billion in 2020 and $1.34 billion in 2019. The main reasons for this record (and the trend is expected to continue into 2022) are COVID-19 as well as the transition to the Biden administration, both of which resulted in greater workers' rights. Edward Segal, "Workplace Class Action Settlements Set New Record in 2021: Report," *Forbes*, January 4, 2022, https://www.forbes.com/sites/edwardsegal/2022/01/04/ workplace-class-action-settlements-set-new-record-in-2021-report/?sh=44edce3140b8.

3. *The Business Imperative for Social Justice Today*, Porter Novelli Purpose Tracker, June 2020, https://www.porternovelli.com/wp-content/uploads/2020/06/PN-Purpose-Tracker _Business-Imperative-for-Social-Justice-Today.pdf; "2020 Edelman Trust Barometer," Edelman, January 19, 2020, https://www.edelman.com/trust/2020-trust-barometer; Accenture, "Majority of Consumers Buying From Companies That Take a Stand on Issues They Care About and Ditching Those That Don't, Accenture Study Finds," *Newsroom*, December 5, 2018, https://newsroom.accenture.com/news/majority-of-consumers -buying-from-companies-that-take-a-stand-on-issues-they-care-about-and-ditching -those-that-dont-accenture-study-finds.htm.

4. Cited in Ruchika Tulshyan, "Do Your Diversity Efforts Reflect the Experiences of Women of Color?," *Harvard Business Review*, July 1, 2019, https://hbr.org/2019/07/do-your-diversity-efforts-reflect-the-experiences-of-women-of-color.

Chapter 2

1. Liz Sablich, "7 Things That Illustrate Racial Disparities in Education," *Brookings*, June 6, 2016, https://www.brookings.edu/blog/brown-center-chalkboard/2016/06/06/7-findings-that-illustrate-racial-disparities-in-education; Natalie Marchant, "Study: Almost All Black British Children Have Experienced Racism at School," *World Economic Forum*, November 18, 2020, https://www.weforum.org/agenda/2020/11/racism-united-kingdom-schools-black-children-inequality; Tiffany Yip, "Addressing Inequities in Education: Considerations for LGBTQ+ Children and Youth in the Era of COVID-19," Society for Research in Child Development, September 8, 2020, https://www.srcd.org/research/addressing-inequities-education-considerations-lgbtq-children-and-youth-era-covid-19; "Selected Findings on LGBTQ Student Achievement and Educational Attainment," American Educational Research Association, https://www.utep.edu/education/el3lab /_Files/docs/LGBTQ-Fact-Sheet---Student-Achievement-and-Educational-Attainment .pdf; Nhan Truong, Adrian Zongrone, and Joseph Kosciw, *Erasure and Resilience: The Experiences of LGBTQ Students of Color* (GLSEN, 2020), https://files.eric.ed.gov/fulltext/ED603844.pdf; Christiane Cordero and Grace Manthey, "Indigenous Students Can Face Large Gaps: Here's How One School Is Trying to Close Them," *KABC News*, November 23, 2021, https://abc7.com/native-american-education-indigenous-students-achievement -gaps-school/11263264; *Meeting the Needs of Colombia's Indigenous Children*, UNICEF, February 2013, https://www.unicefusa.org/sites/default/files/NextGen%20Colombia%20-%20Proposal.pdf; Miriam Jordan, "Children from Immigrant Families Are Increasingly the Face of Higher Education," *New York Times*, October 15, 2020, https://www.nytimes.com/2020/10/15/us/immigrant-families-students-college.html; David McKenzie and Hillel Rapoport, *Migration and Education Inequality in Rural Mexico*, Institute for the Integration of Latin America and the Caribbean, November 2006, https://publications.iadb.org/publications/english/document/Migration-and-Education-Inequality-in-Rural-Mexico.pdf; "Refugee Education in Crisis: More Than Half of the World's School-Age Refugee Children Do Not Get an Education," UN High Commissioner for Refugees, August 30, 2019, https://www.unhcr.org/en-us/news/press/2019/8/5d67b2f47/refugee-education -crisis-half-worlds-school-age-refugee-children -education.html; "Greece: Stop Denying Refugee Children an Education," *Human Rights Watch*, July 29, 2021, https://www.hrw .org/news/2021/07/29/greece-stop-denying-refugee -children-education; Katherine Schaeffer, "As Schools Shift to Online Learning Amid Pandemic, Here's What We Know About Disabled Students in the US," Pew Research Center, April 23, 2020, https://www.pewresearch.org/fact-tank/2020/04/23/as-schools-shift-to-online -learning-amid-pandemic-heres-what-we-know-about-disabled-students-in-the-u-s; Laura Mills, *Insisting on Inclusion: Institutionalization and Barriers to Education for Children with Disabilities in Kyrgyzstan* (Human Rights Watch, 2020), https://www.hrw.org/sites/default/files/media_2020/12/kyrgyzstan1220_web_0.pdf; Philip Tang, "9 Facts About Disability and Poverty in China," Borgen Project, July 1, 2021, https://borgenproject.org/disability-and-poverty.

2. Liz Mineo, "Racial Wealth Gap May Be a Key to Other Inequities," *Harvard Business Review*, June 3, 2021, https://news.harvard.edu/gazette/story/2021/06/racial-wealth-gap-may-be-a -key-to-other-inequities; Natalya Anderson, "The Black Wealth Gap in Canada," Canadian Family Offices, July 20, 2021, https://canadianfamilyoffices.com/wealth/the-black -wealth-gap-in-canada; "The Wage Gap Among LGBTQ+ Workers in the United States," Human Rights Campaign, https://www.hrc.org/resources/the-wage-gap-among-lgbtq -workers-in-the-united-states; Nicole Denier and Sean Waite, "Sexual Orientation Wage Gaps Across Local Labour Market Contexts: Evidence from Canada," *Relations industrielles/Industrial Relations* 72, no. 4 (January 11, 2018), https://www.erudit.org/en/journals/ri/1900 -v1-n1-ri03400/1043174ar/; "Native Households Make 8 Cents for Every Dollar a White Household Has," National Indian Council on Aging, April 5, 2021, https://www.nicoa.org/native-households-make-8-cents-for-every-dollar-a-white -household-has; Daniel Wilson and David Macdonald, *The Income Gap Between Aboriginal Peoples and the Rest of Canada* (Canadian Centre for Policy Alternatives, 2010), https://policyalternatives.ca/sites/default/files/uploads/publications/reports/docs/Aboriginal%20Income%20Gap.pdf; Gerrit Manthei, "The Effects of Refugee Immigration on Income

Inequality in Germany: A Case Study," *Diskussionsbeiträge* 72 (2020), https://www.econstor .eu/handle/10419/234743; Stacey Fitzsimmons, Jen Baggs, and Mary Yoko Brannen, "Research: The Immigrant Income Gap," *Harvard Business Review*, May 7, 2020, https://hbr .org/2020/05/research-the-immigrant-income-gap; Thomas Mathä, Alessandro Porpiglia, and Eva Sierminska, *The Immigrant/Native Wealth Gap in Germany, Italy, and Luxembourg* (European Central Bank, 2011), https://www.ecb.europa.eu/pub/pdf/scpwps/ecbwp1302.pdf; "Facts on People with Disabilities in China," International Labour Organization, https://www .ilo.org/wcmsp5/groups/public/---asia/---ro-bangkok/---ilo-beijing/documents/publication/ wcms_142315.pdf; Tang, "9 Facts About Disability and Poverty in China"; Ryan Golden, "Why Do Pay Gaps Persist for US Workers with Disabilities?," *HR Dive*, July 16, 2020, https:// www.hrdive.com/news/why-do-pay-gaps-persist-for-us-workers-with-disabilities/581533.

3. Drew Desilver, Michael Lipka, and Dalia Fahmy, "10 Things We Know About Race and Policing in the US, Pew Research Center," June 3, 2020, https://www.pewresearch.org/fact- tank/2020/06/03/10-things-we-know-about-race-and-policing-in-the-u-s/; Rokhaya Diallo, "France Is Still in Denial About Racism and Police Brutality," *Aljazeera*, June 17, 2020, https:// www.aljazeera.com/opinions/2020/6/11/france-is-still-in-denial-about-racism-and-police -brutality; Alexi Jones, "Visualizing the Unequal Treatment of LGBTQ People in the Criminal Justice System," *Prison Policy Initiative*, March 2, 2021, https://www.prisonpolicy. org/blog/2021/03/02/lgbtq; "Tunisia: Police Arrest, Use Violence Against LGBTI Activities," *Human Rights Watch*, February 23, 2021, https://www.hrw.org/news/2021/02/23/tunisia -police-arrest-use-violence-against-lgbti-activists; "Under Suspicion: Issues Raised By Indigenous People," Ontario Human Rights Commission, https://www.ohrc.on.ca/en/under- suspicion-issues-raised-indigenous-peoples; Frances Mao, "Why Aboriginal People Are Still Dying in Police Custody," *BBC News*, April 15, 2021, https://www.bbc.com/news/world -australia-56728328; Radley Balko, "There's Overwhelming Evidence That the Criminal Justice System Is Racist. Here's the Proof," *Washington Post*, June 10, 2020, https://www .washingtonpost.com/graphics/2020/opinions/systemic-racism-police-evidence-criminal -justice-system; Susan Kelley, "People with Disabilities More Likely to Be Arrested," *Cornell Chronicle*, November 30, 2017, https://news.cornell.edu/stories/2017/11/ people-disabilities-more-likely-be-arrested; "Police 'Fail' Disabled People Suffering Hate Crimes," *BBC News*, June 20, 2011, https://www.bbc.com/news/ uk-13836337; Mia Swart, "Anger in South Africa as Disabled Teen Dies After Police Shooting," *Aljazeera*, August 28, 2020, https://www.aljazeera.com/news/2020/8/28/ anger-in-south-africa-as-disabled-teen-dies-after-police-shooting.

4. Dima Williams, "A Look at Housing Inequality and Racism in the US," *Forbes*, June 3, 2020, https://www.forbes.com/sites/dimawilliams/2020/06/03/in-light-of-george-floyd-protests -a-look-at-housing-inequality; Pauline Turuban, "Is Racism a Problem in Switzerland? A Look at the Latest Numbers," *Swissinfo.ch*, June 9, 2020, https://www.swissinfo.ch/eng/ is-racism-a-problem-in-switzerland--a-look-at-the-2019-statistics/45824452; Maya Brennan, Ally Livingston, and Veronica Gaitán, "Five Facts About Housing Access for LGBT People," *Housing Matters*, June 13, 2018, https://housingmatters.urban.org/articles/five-facts-about -housing-access-lgbt-people; Kim Harrisberg, "'Stigma Follows Us': Cape Town's Homeless, Transgender Women Fight for Recognition," *Reuters*, November 6, 2019, https://www.reuters .com/article/us-safrica-lgbt-homelessness-trfn/stigma-follows-us-cape-towns-homeless -transgender-women-fight-for-recognition-idUSKBN1XG1ET; Greg Mercer, "'Beggars in Our Own Land': Canada's First Nation Housing Crisis," *Guardian*, March 8, 2019, https:// www.theguardian.com/cities/2019/mar/08/beggars-in-our-own-land-canadas-first -nation-housing-crisis; "To Be Indigenous and a Citizen of Latin America," World Bank, August 9, 2017, https://www.worldbank.org/en/news/feature/2017/08/09/ser-indigena -ciudadano-latinoamerica; Miriam Jordan, "A Refugee Crisis Runs Into a Housing Crisis," *New York Times*, December 16, 2021, https://www.nytimes.com/2021/12/15/us/afghan- refugees-housing.html; *The Effects of Discrimination on Refugee and Migrant Housing Needs* (Settlement Council of Australia, 2019), http://scoa.org.au/wp-content/uploads/2019/08/ The-Effects-of-Discrimination-of-Refugee-and-Migrant-Housing-Needs.pdf; "Housing," Latino Policy Forum, https://www.latinopolicyforum.org/issues/housing; Jaboa Lake, Valerie Novack, and Mia Ives-Rublee, "Recognizing and Addressing Housing Insecurity for Disabled Renters," Center for American Progress, May 27, 2021, https:// www.americanprogress.org/article/recognizing-addressing-housing-insecurity-disabled -renters; Patrick Butler, "Black, Asian and Disabled Tenants 'More Likely to Face Housing Discrimination,'" *Guardian*, May 25, 2021, https://www.theguardian.com/society/2021/ may/26/black-asian-disabled-tenants-more-likely-face-housing-discrimination.

5. Adriana Rezal, "The Racial Makeup of America's Prisons," *US News*, October 13, 2021, https://www.usnews.com/news/best-states/articles/2021-10-13/report-highlights -staggering-racial-disparities-in-us-incarceration-rates; Randeep Ramesh, "More Black People Jailed in England and Wales Proportionally Than in US," *Guardian*, October 10, 2010, https://www.theguardian.com/society/2010/oct/11/black-prison-population-increase -england; Jones, "Visualizing the Unequal Treatment of LGBTQ People"; Neela Ghoshal, "In Cameroon Transgender Women Given Five Years in Prison," *Human Rights Watch*, May 12, 2021, https://www.hrw.org/news/2021/05/12/cameroon-transgender-women-given -five-years-prison; "Under Suspicion: Issues Raised By Indigenous People"; Elias Visontay, "Indigenous Prison Population Continues to Increase, While Non-Indigenous Incarceration Rate Falls," *Guardian*, January 21, 2021, https://www.theguardian.com/ australia-news/2021/jan/22/indigenous-prison-population-continues-to-increase-while- non-indigenous-incarceration-rate-falls; Stephen Dinan, "Illegal Immigrants Make Up 13% of Federal Prison Population," *AP News*, April 17, 2019, https://apnews.com/ article/7a4db70b81879a9d71abf6ea34a6988c; "Canada: Stop Incarcerating Immigration Detainees in Provincial Jails," Amnesty International, October 15, 2021, https://www.amnesty .org/en/latest/news/2021/10/canada-stop-incarcerating-immigration-detainees-provincial-jails; "Australia: Deaths of Prisoners with Disabilities," *Human Rights Watch*, September 15, 2020, https://www.hrw.org/news/2020/09/15/australia-deaths-prisoners-disabilities; Cynthia Stadel, "Disability and Criminal Justice Reform," Learning Disabilities Association of America, https://ldaamerica.org/lda_today/disability-and-criminal-justice-reform.

6. Another example is Blooming Founders, a London-based organization that helps early -stage female entrepreneurs turn ideas into profitable businesses and provides an avenue for shared community engagement under banners such as "All for One and One for All."

Chapter 3

1. See "DE&I Post 2020: Real Progress or Just for Show?," Korn Ferry, on-demand webinar series, https://www.kornferry.com/about-us/events-webinars/d-e-i-real-progress-or-just -for-show.

2. Glenn Llopis, "Study on Hispanic Professionals Reveals Low Productivity and Engagement in the Workplace," *Forbes*, July 30, 2015, https://www.forbes.com/sites/glennllopis/2015/07/30/ study-on-hispanic-professionals-reveals-low-productivity-and-engagement-in-the-workplace/ ?sh=34c80e9b6acf.

3. "DE&I post 2020."

4. Alexis Krivkovich, Wei Wei Liu, Hilary Nguyen, Ishanaa Rambachan, Nicole Robinson, Monne Williams, and Lareina Yee, "Women in the Workplace 2022," McKinsey & Company, October 18, 2022, https://www.mckinsey.com/featured-insights/diversity-and-inclusion/ women-in-the-workplace.

5. "Persons with a Disability: Labor Force Characteristics–2021," Bureau of Labor Statistics, February 24, 2022, https://www.bls.gov/news.release/pdf/disabl.pdf.

6. "Nations with Anti-LGBT Laws: 49% Muslim, 44% Christian," *Erasing 76 Crimes*, April 2022, https://76crimes.com/nations-with-anti-lgbt-laws-49-muslim-44-christian.

7. "Coqual Unveils New In-Depth Research Study on Building Equity in the Corporate World," Coqual, October 6, 2021, https://coqual.org/wp-content/uploads/2021/10/Equity -1-Press-Release-FINAL.pdf.

8. Jessica Miley, "Autonomous Cars Can't Recognize Pedestrians with Darker Skin Tones," *Interesting Engineering*, April 21, 2021, https://interestingengineering.com/autonomous -cars-cant-recognise-pedestrians-with-darker-skin-tones; "Automated Vehicles," Law Commission, https://www.lawcom.gov.uk/project/automated-vehicles.

9. *Report of the Task Group on Reference Man*, International Commission on Radiological Protection Publication 23 (Pergamon Press, 1975).

10. Kieran Snyder and Aileen Lee, "No More 'Abrasive,' 'Opinionated,' or 'Nice': Why Managers Need to Stop Giving Women and People of Color Feedback on Their Personality," *Fortune*, June 15, 2022, https://fortune-com.cdn.ampproject.org/c/s/fortune.com/2022/06/15/ performance-reviews-bias-gender-race-language-textio-kieran-snyder-aileen-lee/amp.

11. "The Rooney Rule," NFL Football Operations, https://operations.nfl.com/inside-football
-ops/diversity-inclusion/the-rooney-rule; Zac Al-Khateeb, "What Is the Rooney Rule?
Explaining NFL Mandate to Interview Minority Candidates, Its Effectiveness and Criticisms,"
Sporting News, March 28, 2022, https://www.sportingnews.com/us/nfl/news/what-is-rooney
-rule-nfl-minority-candidates-effectiveness-criticisms/1k4m7oilxr8nv1xjs9f9bw2k7d.

12. Scott Neuman, "Why a 20-Year Effort by the NFL Hasn't Led to More Minorities in Top
Coaching Jobs," National Public Radio, February 3, 2022, https://www.npr.org/2022/02
/03/1075520411/rooney-rule-nfl.

13. Stefanie K. Johnson, David R. Hekman, and Elsa T. Chan, "If There's Only One Woman in
Your Candidate Pool, There's Statistically No Chance She'll Be Hired," *Harvard Business
Review*, April 26, 2016, https://hbr.org/2016/04/if-theres-only-one-woman-in
-your-candidate-pool-theres-statistically-no-chance-shell-be-hired.

Chapter 4

1. Rocío Lorenzo, Nicole Voigt, Miki Tsusaka, Matt Krentz, and Katie Abouzahr, "How Diverse
Leadership Teams Boost Innovation," Boston Consulting Group, January 23, 2018, https://
www.bcg.com/en-us/publications/2018/how-diverse-leadership-teams-boost-innovation.

2. Elisabeth Bumiller, "Letting Women Reach Women in Afghan War," *New York Times*, March
6, 2010, https://www.nytimes.com/2010/03/07/world/asia/07women.html.

3. "Introducing Our First Community Service & Wellness Dog," City of Highland Park, Illinois,
February 8, 2022, https://cityhpil.com/news_detail_T21_R857.php.

4. Larry Huston and Nabil Sakkab, "P&G's New Innovation Model," *Harvard Business School*,
March 20, 2006, https://hbswk.hbs.edu/archive/pg-s-new-innovation-model.

5. "Lean Thinking and Methods–Kaizen," United States Environmental Protection Agency,
https://www.epa.gov/sustainability/lean-thinking-and-methods-kaizen; Aytekin Tank, "The
Secret to Trader Joe's Success? Embracing This Japanese Business Strategy," *Entrepreneur*,
April 18, 2022, https://www.entrepreneur.com/article/422951; "Trader Joe's and Kaizen:
A Marriage Made in Heaven," Six Sigma, July 30, 2017, https://www.6sigma.us/kaizen/
trader-joes-kaizen-marriage-made-heaven; Eric Pfanner, "Subaru Employs 'Kaizen' to Meet
Booming US Demand," *Wall Street Journal*, October 5, 2015, https://www.wsj.com/articles/
BL-JRTB-20888.

6. Kaitlin Dunn, "Marriott CEO Arne Sorenson on Diversity, Coronavirus, and Personal
Challenges," Hospitality Sales & Marketing Association International, https://global
.hsmai.org/insight/marriott-ceo-arne-sorenson-on-diversity-coronavirus-and-personal
-challenges.

7. Larson, "New Research."

Chapter 5

1. Tony Maglio, "Nike Loses $3.75 Billion in Market Cap After Colin Kaepernick Named Face
of 'Just Do It' Ads," *The Wrap*, September 4, 2018, https://www.thewrap.com/colin
-kaepernick-nike-stock-loses-4-billion-market-cap.

2. Simran Kaleka, "Nike Celebrates Title IX 50th Anniversary," *Made for the W*, June 23, 2022,
https://madeforthew.com/stories/nike-celebrates-title-ix-50th-anniversary%EF%BF%BC.

3. Lillian Martinez, "The Horrors of Cross-Cultural Advertising Translations," Nativa blog,
March 10, 2016, https://thenativa.com/blog/cross-cultural-advertising-translations.

4. Jonathan Edwards, "Children's Museum Apologizes for Selling Juneteenth Watermelon
Salad," *Washington Post*, June 6, 2022, https://www.washingtonpost.com/nation/2022/06/06/
museum-juneteenth-watermelon-salad.

5. Jenny Strasburg, "Abercrombie & Glitch: Asian Americans Rip Retailer for Stereotypes on
T-shirts," *SFGate*, April 18, 2002, https://www.sfgate.com/news/article/ABERCROMBIE-
GLITCH-Asian-Americans-rip-2850702.php.

6. Samantha Masunaga and Jackeline Luna, "Big Banks Want Communities of Color to Trust Them. But It's Not So Simple," *Los Angeles Times*, June 19, 2021, https://www
.latimes.com/business/story/2021-06-19/big-banks-banks-community-people-of
-color-trust.

7. "Ethno-Marketing–Ausländer, die unterschätzte Zielgruppe" [in German], *Genios*, https://
www.genios.de/wirtschaft/ethno_marketing_ausl_nder__die_untersch/c_marketing
_20070806.html.

8. Jamie Feldman, "Sephora's Genius Basket System Is An Introvert's Dream Come True," *HuffPost*, November 5, 2019, https://www.huffpost.com/entry/sephora-basket
-system_l_5dc19326e4b0615b8a9a00e4.

9. "Ethno-Marketing–Ausländer, die unterschätzte Zielgruppe" [in German], *Genios*, https://
www.genios.de/wirtschaft/ethno_marketing_ausl_nder__die_untersch/c_marketing
_20070806.html.

10. "Behind the Design X The Gap Collective," Gap Inc., February 26, 2021, https://www
.gapinc.com/en-us/articles/2021/02/behind-the-design-x-the-gap-collective.

11. "Old Navy Imagines a More Inclusive World with Project WE Artist Tee Series," Gap Inc.,
January 28, 2021, https://www.gapinc.com/en-gb/articles/2021/01/old-navy
-imagines-a-more-inclusive-world-with-proj.

12. Katie Richards, "How Gap Inc.'s Company-Wide Diversity and Inclusion Council
Is Driving Sales," *Glossy*, October 29, 2019, https://www.glossy.co/fashion/
how-gap-inc-s-company-wide-diversity-and-inclusion-council-is-driving-sales.

13. Daphne Howland, "Athleta Extends Sizing Across Its Collection," *Retail Dive*,
January 22, 2021, https://www.retaildive.com/news/athleta-extends-sizing-across-its
-collection/593826.

14. Richards, "How Gap Inc.'s Company-Wide Diversity and Inclusion Council Is Driving Sales."

15. Dominique Fluker, "Meet the Woman Changing the Diversity and Inclusion
Status Quo at Gap Inc.," *Forbes*, November 30, 2019, https://www.forbes.com/sites/
dominiquefluker/2019/11/30/bahja-johnson/?sh=4ba62b3e78f5.

16. Quoted in "Racial Profiling By Retailers Creates an Unwelcome Climate for Black
Shoppers, Study Shows," *The Daily*, November 16, 2017, https://thedaily.case.edu/
racial-profiling-retailers-creates-unwelcome-climate-black-shoppers-study-shows.

17. Matthew Murphy, "'Laughing My Head Off': Branson on That Complaint Letter," *Traveller*,
April 3, 2017, https://www.traveller.com.au/laughing-my-head-off-branson-on-that
-complaint-letter-84eg.

18. "6 Examples of Brands Who Got Multicultural Marketing Right," Refuel Agency, https://
www.refuelagency.com/blog/multicultural/examples-of-brands-who-got-multicultural
-marketing-right.

19. Crystal Harrell and Liv Lewis, "P&G Addresses Racial Bias with New Film 'The Look,'"
P&G news release, June 27, 2019, https://news.pg.com/news-releases/news-details/2019/
PG-Addresses-Racial-Bias-With-New-Film-The-Look/default.aspx.

Chapter 7

1. Suyin Haynes, "The Global Gender Gap Will Take an Extra 36 Years to Close After the
COVID-19 Pandemic, Report Finds," *Time*, March 30, 2021, https://time.com/5951101/
global-gender-gap-135-years.

2. Emma Hinchliffe, "The Female CEOs on This Year's Fortune 500 Just Broke Three
All-Time Records," *Fortune*, June 2, 2021, https://fortune.com/2021/06/02/female
-ceos-fortune-500-2021-women-ceo-list-roz-brewer-walgreens-karen-lynch
-cvs-thasunda-brown-duckett-tiaa.

3. *Women in the Workplace 2019*, McKinsey & Company, https://wiw-report.s3.amazonaws
.com/Women_in_the_Workplace_2019_mobile.pdf.

4. Paige McGlauflin, "The Number of Black Fortune 500 CEOs Returns to Record High–Meet the 6 Chief Executives," *Fortune*, May 23, 2022, https://fortune.com/2022/05/23/meet-6-black-ceos-fortune-500-first-black-founder-to-ever-make-list; Jeff Green, "'Sea of White': Latino Leaders Fight to Reshape US Boardrooms," *Bloomberg*, March 22, 2022, https://www.bloomberg.com/news/articles/2022-03-22/-sea-of-white-latino-leaders-fight-to-reshape-u-s-boardrooms.

5. Andy Kiersz, "Asian Americans Still Aren't Reaching the C-suite—and it All Comes Down to Promotions. These 4 Charts Put the Problem in Perspective," *Insider*, May 26, 2021, https://www.businessinsider.com/asian-american-ceos-rare-lack-of-promotions-2021-5.

6. Richard L. Zweigenhaft, "Diversity Among Fortune 500 CEOs from 2000 to 2020: White Women, Hi-Tech South Asians, and Economically Privileged Multilingual Immigrants from Around the World," *Who Rules America?*, January 2021, https://whorulesamerica.ucsc.edu/power/diversity_update_2020.html.

7. "Women on Corporate Boards (Quick Take)," Catalyst, November 5, 2021, https://www.catalyst.org/research/women-on-corporate-boards.

8. "Facts and Figures: Women's Leadership and Political Participation," UN Women, September 19, 2022, https://www.unwomen.org/en/what-we-do/leadership-and-political-participation/facts-and-figures.

9. Katherine Schaeffer, "Racial, Ethnic Diversity Increases Yet Again with the 117th Congress," Pew Research Center, January 28, 2021, https://www.pewresearch.org/fact-tank/2021/01/28/racial-ethnic-diversity-increases-yet-again-with-the-117th-congress.

10. Vanessa Rubio, "Today's Latin America Has No Female Presidents. It's Not Going Well," *Americas Quarterly*, April 7, 2021, https://www.americasquarterly.org/article/todays-latin-america-has-no-female-presidents-its-not-going-well.

11. This conclusion is based on consistent patterns that emerged in dozens of DE&I Root Causes Analyses Korn Ferry has conducted over the last decade.

12. Gender Statistics Database, European Institute for Gender Equality, https://eige.europa.eu/gender-statistics/dgs. Accessed October 20, 2022.

13. Ana Cléssia Pereira Lima de Araújo, Maria Analice D. Santos Sampaio, Edward Martins Costa, Ahmad Saeed Khan, Guilherme Irffi, and Rayssa Alexandre Costa, "The Quotas Law for People with Disabilities in Brazil: Is It a Guarantee of Employment?," *International Review of Applied Economics* 36, no. 4, 496–525, https://repositorio.ufc.br/bitstream/riufc/60695/1/2021_art_acplaraujo.pdf.

14. "Revisiting Rwanda Five Years After Record-Breaking Parliamentary Elections," UN Women, August 13, 2018, https://www.unwomen.org/en/news/stories/2018/8/feature-rwanda-women-in-parliament.

15. Netina Tan, "Are Gender Quotas Helping Female Politicians in Asia?," *East Asia Forum*, June 24, 2016, https://www.eastasiaforum.org/2016/06/24/are-gender-quotas-helping-female-politicians-in-asia.

16. Adrienne Woltersdorf, "Are Timor Leste's Quotas for Women in Government a Good Thing? 'Of Course!' Say Female MPs," *Friedrich Ebert Stiftung*, September 20, 2018, https://asia.fes.de/news/are-timor-lestes-quotas-for-women-in-government-a-good-thing-of-course-say-female-mps.

17. Krivkovich et al., "Women in the Workplace 2022."

18. Susanne Gabrielsen and Jan Thibodeau, "Proof Point: Diversity and Inclusion Program Doubles Representation of Women of Color Executives in 4 Years," Korn Ferry Institute, https://www.kornferry.com/content/dam/kornferry/docs/article-migration/Diversity-Women-of-Color-Proof-Point.pdf.

19. Saadia Zahidi, "We Need a Global Reskilling Revolution—Here's Why," *World Economic Forum*, January 22, 2020, https://www.weforum.org/agenda/2020/01/reskilling-revolution-jobs-future-skills.

Chapter 8

1 . Daron Acemoglu, Suresh Naidu, Pascual Restrepo, and James A. Robinson, "Democracy Does Cause Growth," *Journal of Political Economy* 127, no. 1 (February 2019). See also Daron Acemoglu, "Does Democracy Boost Economic Growth?," World Economic Forum, May 20, 2014, https://www.weforum.org/agenda/2014/05/democracy-boost-economic-growth.

2. "1 in 4 Employees Negatively Affected by Political Talk at Work This Election Season, Finds New Survey," American Psychological Association, 2016, https://www.apa.org/news/press/releases/2016/09/employees-political-talk.

3. Martin Reeves, Leesa Quinlan, Mathieu Lefèvre, and Georg Kell, "How Business Leaders Can Reduce Polarization," *Harvard Business Review*, October 8, 2021, https://hbr.org/2021/10/how-business-leaders-can-reduce-polarization.

4. Martin Reeves, Mathieu Lefèvre, and Leesa Quinlan, "Growing Apart: Understanding and Addressing the Business Ramifications of Social Polarization," Boston Consulting Group, April 12, 2021, https://www.bcg.com/publications/2021/understanding-business-ramifications-of-social-polarization.

5. Elizabeth Hopper, "What Is the Contact Hypothesis in Psychology?," *ThoughtCo*, October 26, 2019, https://www.thoughtco.com/contact-hypothesis-4772161.

6. Thomas F. Pettigrew, Linda R. Tropp, Ulrich Wagner, and Oliver Christ, "Recent Advances in Intergroup Contact Theory," *International Journal of Intercultural Relations* 35, no. 3 (May 2011), 271–280.

7. As described in Dr. Milton Bennett's long-standing and deeply researched work. See Bennett, "Developmental Model of Intercultural Sensitivity," Intercultural Development Research Institute, 2017, https://www.idrinstitute.org/wp-content/uploads/2019/02/DMIS-IDRI.pdf.

8. TV2 Denmark, "All That We Share," NoA Agency video, 3:00, 2017, https://www.thenorthalliance.com/our-work/all-that-we-share.

9. Sahana Udupa, Iginio Gagliardone, Alexandra Deem, and Laura Csuka, "Hate Speech, Information Disorder, and Conflict," *MediaWell*, April 7, 2020, https://mediawell.ssrc.org/literature-reviews/hate-speech-information-disorder-and-conflict/versions/1-0.

10. Adrian Mulligan, "The Rise of Corporate Research Funding," *Training Journal*, January 19, 2022, https://www.trainingjournal.com/articles/features/rise-corporate-research-funding.

11. Reeves et al., "How Business Leaders Can Reduce Polarization."

12. Aubri Juhasz, "Instagram Now Lets You Control Your Bully's Comments," National Public Radio, October 3, 2019, https://www.npr.org/2019/10/03/766507832/instagram-now-lets-you-control-your-bullys-comments.

Chapter 9

1. Lauren Zumbach, "Discover to Bring Nearly 1,000 Jobs to South Side As It Opens Call Center in Former Chatham Target Store," *Chicago Tribune*, March 4, 2021, https://www.chicagotribune.com/business/ct-biz-discover-chatham-call-center-jobs-20210304-fb7g2puam5fslbposisgpwhwgu-story.html.

2. Paul A. Argenti, "When Should Your Company Speak Up About a Social Issue?," *Harvard Business Review*, October 16, 2020, https://hbr.org/2020/10/when-should-your-company-speak-up-about-a-social-issue.

3. "Respect Human Rights," Unilever, https://www.unilever.com/planet-and-society/respect-human-rights.

4. Brakkton Booker, "Uncle Ben's Changing Name to Ben's Original after Criticism of Racial Stereotyping," National Public Radio, September 23, 2020, https://www.npr.org/sections/live-updates-protests-for-racial-justice/2020/09/23/916012582/uncle-bens-changing-name-to-ben-s-original-after-criticism-of-racial-stereotypin.

5. Guardian Sports, "Nike Releases Full Ad Featuring Colin Kaepernick," YouTube video, 1:01, September 7, 2018, https://www.youtube.com/watch?v=-grjIUWKoBA.

6. Konrad Putzier, "Marriott CEO: Trump's Travel Ban Is Hurting Hotels," *Insider*, April 15, 2017 https://www.businessinsider.com/marriott-ceo-trumps-travel-ban-is-hurting -hotels-2017-4.

7. Melissa Repko, "Ulta Beauty to Double Black-Owned Brands in Its Stores, Feature More Black Women in Ads," CNBC, February 2, 2021, https://www.cnbc.com/2021/02/02/ ulta-beauty-to-double-black-owned-brands-feature-black-women-in-ads.html.

8. Patagonia Action Works, "Demand Environmental Justice," https://www.patagonia.com/ actionworks/campaigns/environmental-justice-is-racial-justice.

9. Joe Hernandez, "Disney Workers Walk Out Over the Company's Response to So-Called 'Don't Say Gay' Bill," National Public Radio, March 22, 2022, https://www.npr.org/2022 /03/22/1088048998/disney-walkout-dont-say-gay-bill.

10. Max Zahn, "Amazon, Starbucks among Corporations Bolstering Abortion Coverage," *ABC News*, May 20, 2022, https://abcnews.go.com/Business/amazon-starbucks-corporations -bolstering-abortion-coverage/story?id=84846669.

11. "Global Garment and Textile Industries: Workers, Rights and Working Conditions," Solidarity Center, https://www.solidaritycenter.org/wp-content/uploads/2019/08/Garment -Textile-Industry-Fact-Sheet.8.2019.pdf.

12. Kathy Calvin, "Making the Workplace Work for Women: How to Stand Up for Women's Rights and Health," *Forbes*, June 6, 2019, https://www.forbes.com/sites/ forbesnonprofitcouncil/2019/06/06/making-the-workplace-work-for-women-how-to -stand-up-for-womens-rights-and-health.

13. "Growing Economies Through Gender Parity," Council on Foreign Relations, https://www .cfr.org/womens-participation-in-global-economy; Kweilin Ellingrud, Anu Madgavkar, James Manyika, Jonathan Woetzel, Vivian Riefberg, Mekala Krishnan, and Mili Seoni, "The Power of Parity: Advancing Women's Equality in the United States," McKinsey & Company, April 7, 2016, https://www.mckinsey.com/featured-insights/employment-and-growth/ the-power-of-parity-advancing-womens-equality-in-the-united-states.

14. Frederick E. Allen, "Howard Schultz to Anti-Gay-Marriage Starbucks Shareholder: 'You Can Sell Your Shares,'" *Forbes*, March 22, 2013, https://www.forbes.com/sites/frederickallen /2013/03/22/howard-schultz-to-anti-gay-marriage-starbucks-shareholder-you-can-sell -your-shares.

15. Matt Gonzalez, "Effects of LGBTQ Wage Gap Linger," Society for Human Resource Management, February 16, 2022, https://www.shrm.org/resourcesandtools/hr-topics/ behavioral-competencies/global-and-cultural-effectiveness/pages/effects-of-lgbtq-wage -gap-linger.aspx.

16. "Facts About LGBTQ Youth Suicide," The Trevor Project, https://www.thetrevorproject .org/resources/article/facts-about-lgbtq-youth-suicide.

17. Tori B. Powell, "45% of LGBTQ Youth Seriously Considered Suicide in the Past Year, Trevor Project Survey Finds," *CBS News*, May 4, 2022, https://www.cbsnews.com/news/lgbtq-youth -suicide-the-trevor-project-mental-health-2022. For the nonprofit Trevor Project's fourth edition of its National Survey on LGBTQ Youth Mental Health, researchers surveyed nearly 34,000 LGBTQ people between the ages of thirteen and twenty-four in the United States, between September 20 and December 31, 2021. With 45% of respondents being people of color and 48% being transgender or nonbinary, the annual survey is "one of the most diverse surveys of LGBTQ youth ever conducted," according to the Trevor Project.

18. "The Wage Gap Among LGBTQ+ Workers in the United States," Human Rights Campaign Foundation, https://www.hrc.org/resources/the-wage-gap-among-lgbtq-workers-in -the-united-states.

19. "The Global Context for LGBT People," Stonewall, https://www.stonewall.org.uk/global- context-lgbt-people; Dan Avery, "Half of LGBTQ Workers Have Faced Job Discrimination, Report Finds," *NBC News*, September 8, 2021, https://www.nbcnews.com/nbc-out/out-news/ half-lgbtq-workers-faced-job-discrimination-report-finds-rcna1935.

20. "Report Details Workplace Discrimination Faced by LGBTI People in China, the Philippines and Thailand," United Nations Development Programme, June 27, 2018, https://www.cn .undp.org/content/china/en/home/presscenter/pressreleases/2018/report-details-workplace -discrimination-faced-by-lgbti-people-in.html.

21. Rachel Ranosa, "Asia 'at a Crossroads' in Fight for LGBTQ+ Rights," *HRD Asia*, December 8, 2020, https://www.hcamag.com/asia/specialisation/diversity-inclusion/asia-at-a-crossroads-in-fight-for-lgbtq-rights/241414.

22. Antonio Zappulla, "The Simple Reason Why So Many Businesses Support LGBT Rights," *World Economic Forum*, January 14, 2017, https://www.weforum.org/agenda/2017/01/why-so-many-businesses-support-lgbt-rights.

23. Jake Hall, "Can the Russian World Cup Sponsors Call Themselves LGBTQ-Friendly?," *Vice*, June 22, 2018, https://www.vice.com/en/article/nekg7b/can-the-russian-world-cup-sponsors-call-themselves-lgbtq-friendly.

24. Rachel Savage, "Victoria's Secret Hires First Transgender Model after Criticism," *Reuters*, August 6, 2019, https://www.reuters.com/article/usa-lgbt-fashion-idLTAL8N2522PH.

25. "Report Details Workplace Discrimination."

26. Andreea Danielescu, "Building Tech That Reflects Our Diversity," Accenture, December 16, 2020, https://www.accenture.com/us-en/blogs/technology-innovation/danielescu-building-tech-that-reflects-our-diversity.

27. Tim Fitzsimons, "Over 200 Major Companies Sign Supreme Court Brief in Favor of LGBTQ Workers," *NBC News*, July 2, 2019, https://www.nbcnews.com/feature/nbc-out/over-200-major-companies-sign-supreme-court-brief-favor-lgbtq-n1025826.

28. "How Coca-Cola Supports Inclusion and Equality for the LGBTQ+ Community," Coca-Cola Company, March 26, 2019, https://www.coca-colacompany.com/news/coca-cola-fosters-inclusive-lgbtq-community.

29. "Chhattisgarh: BALCO Inducts Transgender Employees into Its Workforce," *Times of India*, April 24, 2022, https://timesofindia.indiatimes.com/city/raipur/chhattisgarh-balco-inducts-transgender-employees-into-its-workforce/articleshow/91044567.cms.

30. "Disability Inclusion," World Bank, April 14, 2022, https://www.worldbank.org/en/topic/disability#1.

31. Andrés T. Tapia, *The Inclusion Paradox: The Post-Obama Era and the Transformation of Global Diversity* (CreateSpace, 2016).

32. Tapia, *Inclusion Paradox*, 244.

33. Tapia, *Inclusion Paradox*, 245.

34. Kendra Mayfield, "Raising the Accessibility Bar," *Wired*, July 22, 2002, https://www.wired.com/2002/07/raising-the-accessibility-bar.

35. Marc Hagen, "Accessibility for Fire and Kindle," Closing the Gap, October 9, 2018, https://www.closingthegap.com/amazon-accessibility-for-fire-and-kindle.

36. Shelly Brisbin, "A Timeline of iOS Accessibility: It Started with 36 Seconds," *MacStories*, July 11, 2019, https://www.macstories.net/stories/a-timeline-of-ios-accessibility-it-started-with-36-seconds.

37. Arturo Ardila-Gomez, "How a Ramp for People with Disabilities Can Make a Difference for a Big City," *World Bank Blogs*, August 1, 2013, https://blogs.worldbank.org/latinamerica/how-ramp-people-disabilities-can-make-difference-big-city.

38. "Figures at a Glance," UN High Commissioner for Refugees, June 16, 2022, https://www.unhcr.org/en-us/figures-at-a-glance.html.

39. Kristina Stoewe, *Education Levels of Refugees: Training and Education in the Main Countries of Origin*, IW-Report 37/2017 (Köln: Institut der Deutschen Wirtschaft), https://www.iwkoeln.de/fileadmin/user_upload/Studien/Report/PDF/2017/IW-Report_2017_37_Education_Levels_of_Refugees.pdf.

40. David Gelles, "Hamdi Ulukaya of Chobani Talks Greek Yogurt and the American Dream," *New York Times*, August 24, 2018, https://www.nytimes.com/2018/08/24/business/hamdi-ulukaya-chobani-corner-office.html.

41. Paola Peralta, "Amazon, Facebook, Pfizer Join Efforts to Create Jobs for Afghan Refugees," *Employee Benefit News*, October 1, 2021, https://www.benefitnews.com/news/amazon-facebook-pfizer-pledge-are-finding-jobs-for-afghanistan-refugees.

42. "Our Refugees Program," Barilla, https://www.barillagroup.com/en/purpose/
diversity-inclusion/refugees.

43. "Industry-First Refugee Employment Program Graduates First Cohort," Sodexo, press
release, March 13, 2022, https://au.sodexo.com/media/news-room/sodexo-graduate-refugee
-employment-program.html.

44. Leslie P. Norton, "The Number of Black Board Members Surged after George Floyd's Death,"
Barrons, October 27, 2020, https://www.barrons.com/articles/after-george-floyds
-death-the-number-of-black-board-members-surges-51603809011; Jena McGregor, "A Third
of Newly Added Corporate Directors Were Black Last Year, Up from 11%," *Forbes*, October
19, 2021, https://www.forbes.com/sites/jenamcgregor/2021/10/19/a-third-of-newly-added
-corporate-directors-were-black-last-year-up-from-11.

45. "Diversity: 2021 UK Spencer Stuart Board Index," SpencerStuart, https://www
.spencerstuart.com/research-and-insight/uk-board-index/diversity; "Most Say Police More
Likely to Use Excessive Force on Black Individuals," Monmouth University, June 2, 2020,
https://www.monmouth.edu/polling-institute/reports/monmouthpoll_us_060220.

46. "The Future of Work Trends in 2022: The New Era of Humanity," Korn Ferry, https://www
.kornferry.com/insights/featured-topics/future-of-work/2022-future-of-work-trends.

47. "Equilar Report: Roughly 15% of Russell 3000 Directors Were Ethnically Diverse in 2021,"
Business Wire, May 11, 2022, https://www.businesswire.com/news/home
/20220511005337/en/Equilar-Report-Roughly-15-of-Russell-3000-Directors-Were
-Ethnically-Diverse-in-2021.

48. Michael Volpe, "Meet the 16 Hispanic CEOs of Top S&P 500 Companies," *Al Día*, February 3,
2021, https://aldianews.com/leadership/advocacy/hispanics-sp-500.

49. TelevisaUnivision, "The Power of the US Hispanic Consumer," *Adweek*, https://www
.adweek.com/sponsored/the-power-of-the-u-s-hispanic-consumer.

50. Rosa Escandon, "Asian American Consumer Market Is Now $1.2 Trillion and What
That Means for Digital Brands," *Forbes*, May 22, 2020, https://www.forbes.com/sites/
rosaescandon/2020/05/22/asian-american-consumer-market-is-now-12-trillion-and
-what-that-means-for-digital-brands.

Chapter 10

1. Laur Hesse Fisher, interview with oceanographer Sylvia Earle, on "E1 & 2: TIL About the
Changing Ocean," *TILclimate (Today I Learned: Climate)*, season 4, episodes 1 and 2, podcast
audio, April 27, 2022, https://climate.mit.edu/podcasts/til-about-the-changing-ocean.

2. World Economic Forum, "Here's What to Expect from Our Planet in the Next 100 Years
If We Take No Action on Climate Change," video, 2:36, July 2, 2021, https://www
.weforum.org/videos/20257-2021-what-to-expect-from-our-planet-in-the-next-100
-years-if-we-take-no-action-on-climate-change-uplinkmp4-a6c42fe4ce.

3. Joe Phelan, "What Countries and Cities Will Disappear Due to Rising Sea Levels?," *Live
Science*, March 27, 2022, https://www.livescience.com/what-places-disappear-rising
-sea-levels.

4. "Climate Change Could Force 216 Million People to Migrate Within Their Own Countries
by 2050," World Bank, September 13, 2021, https://www.worldbank.org/en/news/press
-release/2021/09/13/climate-change-could-force-216-million-people-to-migrate-within
-their-own-countries-by-2050.

5. John Podesta, "The Climate Crisis, Migration, and Refugees," *Brookings*, July 25, 2019, https://
www.brookings.edu/research/the-climate-crisis-migration-and-refugees.

6. Deepa Shivaram, "Extreme Heat Is Worse for Low-Income, Nonwhite Americans, a New
Study Shows," National Public Radio, July 14, 2021, https://www.npr.org/2021/07/14/
1015983700/extreme-heat-is-getting-worse-for-low-income-non-white-americans
-a-new-study-sho.

7. "Climate Change Will Affect Developing Countries More Than Rich Ones,"
Economist, May 9, 2018, https://www.economist.com/graphic-detail/2018/05/09/
climate-change-will-affect-developing-countries-more-than-rich-ones.

8. For more information on the Youth4Climate summit, visit https://youth4climate.live.

9. "Exposure to Smoke from Fires," New York State Department of Health, January 2020, https://health.ny.gov/environmental/outdoors/air/smoke_from_fire.htm.

10. Stephen C. Bondy and Arezoo Campbell, "Water Quality and Brain Function," *International Journal of Environmental Research and Public Health* 15, no. 1 (2018), https://www.ncbi.nlm.nih.gov/pmc/articles/PMC5800103.

11. Damian Carrington, "Air Pollution Significantly Raises Risk of Infertility, Study Finds," *Guardian*, February 17, 2021, https://www.theguardian.com/environment/2021/feb/17/air-pollution-significantly-raises-risk-of-infertility-study-finds.

12. John A. Romley, Andrew Hackbarth, and Dana P. Goldman, "Cost and Health Consequences of Air Pollution in California," Rand Corporation, https://www.rand.org/pubs/research_briefs/RB9501.html.

13. "Climate Change and Health," World Health Organization, October 30, 2021, https://www.who.int/news-room/fact-sheets/detail/climate-change-and-health.

14. Elena Grinza and François Rycx, *The Impact of Sickness Absenteeism on Productivity: New Evidence from Belgian Matched Panel Data*, IZA Discussion Paper no. 11543 (Bonn: IZA Institute of Labor Economics, 2018), https://docs.iza.org/dp11543.pdf.

15. Allie Willison, "What Is Planned Obsolescence and Does It Impact Sustainability?," Blueland, May 18, 2021, https://www.blueland.com/articles/what-is-planned-obsolescence.

16. Samantha Putt del Pino, Eliot Metzger, Deborah Drew, and Kevin Moss, *Elephant in the Boardroom: Why Unchecked Consumption Is Not an Option in Tomorrow's Markets*, working paper, World Resources Institute, March 24, 2017, https://www.wri.org/research/elephant-boardroom-why-unchecked-consumption-not-option-tomorrows-markets.

17. Jane Thier, "Here Are the Youngest CEOs on the Fortune 500," *Fortune*, May 24, 2022, https://fortune.com/2022/05/24/youngest-ceos-fortune-500-zuckerberg-coinbase-compass-meta.

18. Veronica Magan, "How Old Is the 117th Congress?," FiscalNote, February 2, 2021, https://fiscalnote.com/blog/how-old-is-the-117th-congress.

19. David Gelles, "Billionaire No More: Patagonia Founder Gives Away the Company," *New York Times*, September 14, 2022, https://www.nytimes.com/2022/09/14/climate/patagonia-climate-philanthropy-chouinard.html.

20. Valentina Ruiz Leotaud, "Researchers Link Cobalt Mining in the DRC to Violence, Substance Abuse, Food-Water Insecurity," Right Energy Partnership, January 12, 2022, https://www.rightenergypartnership-indigenous.org/news/2022/1/12/researchers-link-cobalt-mining-in-the-drc-to-violence-substance-abuse-food-water-insecurity.

21. XiaoZhi Lim, "Millions of Electric Car Batteries Will Retire in the Next Decade. What Happens to Them?," *Guardian*, August 20, 2021, https://www.theguardian.com/environment/2021/aug/20/electric-car-batteries-what-happens-to-them.

22. Radhika Viswanathan, "Why Starbucks, Disney, and the EU Are All Shunning Plastic Straws," *Vox*, December 21, 2018, https://www.vox.com/2018/6/25/17488336/plastic-straw-ban-ocean-pollution.

23. Stella Nyambura Mbau, "Misplaced Positivity on Climate Is Harmful. Preparing for Breakdown Could Help," *Resilience*, July 26, 2022, https://www.resilience.org/stories/2022-07-26/misplaced-positivity-on-climate-is-harmful-preparing-for-breakdown-could-help.

24. Laura Millan Lombrana, "Climate Change Linked to 5 Million Deaths a Year, New Study Shows," *Bloomberg*, July 7, 2021, https://www.bloomberg.com/news/articles/2021-07-07/climate-change-linked-to-5-million-deaths-a-year-new-study-shows.

25. Ellen MacArthur Foundation, "What Is a Circular Economy?," https://ellenmacarthurfoundation.org/topics/circular-economy-introduction/overview; and "Regenerate Nature," https://ellenmacarthurfoundation.org/regenerate-nature.

26. Ellen MacArthur Foundation, "Eliminate Waste and Pollution," https://ellenmacarthurfoundation.org/eliminate-waste-and-pollution.

27. Ellen MacArthur Foundation, "Circulate Products and Materials," https://ellenmacarthurfoundation.org/circulate-products-and-materials.

28. "Regenerative Agriculture 101," Natural Resources Defense Council, November 29, 2021, https://www.nrdc.org/stories/regenerative-agriculture-101.

29. Gina-Marie Cheeseman, "Puma x First Mile Collection Embraces Circularity and Social Impact," *Triple Pundit*, March 2, 2020, https://www.triplepundit.com/story/2020/puma-x-first-mile-collection-embraces-circularity-and-social-impact/86736.

30. "Circular Economy Route Map for Glasgow 2020–2030," Glasgow City Council, https://www.glasgow.gov.uk/councillorsandcommittees/viewSelectedDocument.asp?c=P62AFQDNDX2UT1NTNT.

31. Jonathan Weisman and Jazmine Ulloa, "As the Planet Cooks, Climate Stalls as a Political Issue," *New York Times*, July 17, 2022, https://www.nytimes.com/2022/07/17/us/politics/climate-change-manchin-biden.html.

32. Alan Murray and Ellen McGirt, "Doug McMillon on Walmart's Regenerative Future," Leadership Next, podcast audio, June 7, 2022, https://podcasts.apple.com/us/podcast/doug-mcmillon-on-walmarts-regenerative-future/id1501891506?i=1000565484401.

33. Walmart, *Standards for Suppliers (Product Suppliers)*, https://corporate.walmart.com/media-library/document/standards-for-suppliers-english/_proxyDocument?id=0000015c-e70f-d3b4-a57e-ff4f3f510000; Dominick Reuter, "Meet the Typical Walmart Shopper, a 59-Year-Old White Suburban Woman Earning $80,000 a Year," *Insider*, January 17, 2022, https://www.businessinsider.com/typical-walmart-shopper-demographic-white-woman-earning-middle-income-2021-7.

34. Olivia Rosane, "US Has Cost the World More Than $1.9 Trillion in Climate Damages Since 1990, Study Finds," *Nation of Change*, July 14, 2022, https://www.nationofchange.org/2022/07/14/u-s-has-cost-the-world-more-than-1-9-trillion-in-climate-damages-since-1990-study-finds.

35. "10 Facts About Single-Use Plastic Bags," Center for Biological Diversity, https://www.biologicaldiversity.org/programs/population_and_sustainability/sustainability/plastic_bag_facts.html; Laura Parker, "Fast Facts About Plastic Pollution," *National Geographic*, December 20, 2018, https://www.nationalgeographic.com/science/article/plastics-facts-infographics-ocean-pollution.

36. "Unearthing the Truth About Reusable Grocery Bags," MaCorr Research Blog, https://www.macorr.com/blog/?p=142

37. John Hite, "The Truth About Plastic Bag Bans," Conservation Law Foundation, June 16, 2020, https://www.clf.org/blog/the-truth-about-plastic-bag-bans.

38. Kaitlin Grable, "Success! Trader Joe's Will Cut 1 Million Pounds of Plastic From Its Stores!," Greenpeace, https://www.greenpeace.org/usa/victories/trader-joes-will-cut-1-million-pounds-of-plastic-from-stores.

39. City of Highland Park, City Council Meeting Minutes, March 14, 2022.

40. Margaret Osborn, "The United States Will Phase Out Incandescent Light Bulbs," *Smithsonian Magazine*, April 28, 2022, https://www.smithsonianmag.com/smart-news/the-us-is-phasing-out-incandescent-light-bulbs-180979992.

41. "Plant-Based Meat for a Growing World," Good Food Institute, 2019, https://gfi.org/resource/environmental-impact-of-meat-vs-plant-based-meat.

42. Charlie Campbell, "How China Could Change the World by Taking Meat Off the Menu," *Time*, January 22, 2021, https://time.com/5930095/china-plant-based-meat.

43. "Zeroing in on Healthy Air: A National Assessment of Health and Climate Benefits of Zero-Emission Transportation and Electricity," American Lung Association, https://www.lung.org/clean-air/electric-vehicle-report.

Conclusion

1. Sundiatu Dixon-Fyle, Kevin Dolan, Dame Vivian Hunt, and Sara Prince, "Diversity Wins: How Inclusion Matters," McKinsey & Company, May 19, 2020, https://www.mckinsey.com/ featured-insights/diversity-and-inclusion/diversity-wins-how-inclusion-matters.

2. "Mental Health Disorder Statistics," Johns Hopkins Medicine, https://www .hopkinsmedicine.org/health/wellness-and-prevention/mental-health-disorder-statistics.

3. Rialda Kovacevic, "Mental Health: Lessons Learned in 2020 for 2021 and Forward," *World Bank Blogs*, February 11, 2021, https://blogs.worldbank.org/health/ mental-health-lessons-learned-2020-2021-and-forward.

Appendix B

1. Richard Threlfall, "ESG Reporting: Sustainability in Both Words and Deeds," *KPMG Blog*, April 8, 2021, https://home.kpmg/xx/en/blogs/home/posts/2021/04/esg-reporting -sustainability-in-both-words-and-deeds.html.

BIBLIOGRAPHY

Nonfiction

A Call to Conscience: The Landmark Speeches of Dr. Martin Luther King, Jr., edited by Clayborne Carson and Kris Shepard. Grand Central Publishing, 2002.

Between the World and Me, Ta-Nehisi Coates. One World Publications, 2015.

Caste: The Origins of Our Discontents, Isabel Wilkerson. Penguin Random House, 2020.

Designing Organizations: Strategy Structure and Process at the Business Unit and Enterprise Levels, Jay R. Galbraith. Jossey-Bass, 2014.

The 5 Disciplines of Inclusive Leaders: Unleashing the Power of All of Us, Andrés T. Tapia and Alina Polonskaia. Berrett-Koehler Publishers, 2020.

Hot, Flat and Crowded: Why We Need a Green Revolution, Thomas Friedman. Farrar, Straus and Giroux, 2008.

How to Become an Antiracist, Ibram X. Kendi. One World Publications, 2019.

The Inclusion Paradox: The Post-Obama Era and the Transformation of Global Diversity, Andrés T. Tapia. CreateSpace, 2016.

Long Walk to Freedom: The Autobiography of Nelson Mandela. Back Bay Books, 1995.

Nudge: The Final Edition, Richard H. Thaler and Cass R. Sunstein. Penguin Books, 2021.

Post Growth: Life After Capitalism, Tim Jackson. Polity, 2021.

Sustaining Democracy: What We Owe to the Other Side, Robert B. Talisse. Oxford University Press, 2021.

Think Again, Adam Grant. Viking Press, 2021.

The Uninhabitable Earth: Life After Warming, David Wallace-Wells. Tim Duggan Books, 2019.

Why We're Polarized, Ezra Klein. Avid Reader Press, 2020.

Novels

The *Foundation* series, Isaac Asimov. Bantam Spectra Books, 1991. An epic exploration of predicting the future via math.

Passing, Nella Larsen. Martino Fine Books, 2011. A novel about race, identity, and friendship in the 1920s.

Korn Ferry White Papers

"Asleep at the Wheel: Why a Singular Focus on Unconscious Bias Is Driving DE&I Off the Road"

"The DE&I Metrics That Really Matter"

"The Diversity, Equity, and Inclusion Maturity Model"

"Five Classic DE&I Mistakes"

"The 5 Disciplines of Inclusive Leaders"

"Head and Heart Inclusive Leaders for an Equitable Future"

"Inclusive Sustainability"
"Owning Success: Six Choices That Empower Underrepresented Talent to Own Their Success"
"The 'Reference Man' Rules: Why One Size Fits All Leaves Most of Us Out"

Korn Ferry Webinars

Eliminating Unconscious Bias in Talent Systems
How to Create a DE&I Strategy That Works

Films

An Inconvenient Truth. Documentary by Al Gore. Directed by Davis Guggenheim (Lawrence Bender Productions, 2006)
Don't Look Up. Directed by Adam McKay (Netflix, 2021)
Inception. Directed by Christopher Nolan (Warner Brothers Pictures, 2010)
The *Matrix* series. Directed by Lana Wachowski and Lilly Wachowski, (Joel Silver 1999, 2003)
White Hot: The Rise & Fall of Abercrombie & Fitch. Documentary. Directed by Alison Klayman (Alison Klayman, Emmet McDermott, Hayley Pappas, 2022)

ACKNOWLEDGMENTS

Gracias! Danke! Thank You!

FIRST TO OUR FAMILIES.

Andrés: To Lori, who truly sees, loves, and supports the writer in me—which I realize is not without consequences. I will always be grateful for this perennial selfless gift. And to Marisela, for whom my quest for a better world is always personalized to a better world for you.

Fayruz: Thank you to my husband, Jesse, and my daughters for your support always and for cheering me on from the sidelines as I embarked on this project. Camila and Tessa—you are the Tomorrow that inspires my work every day.

* * *

At Korn Ferry every day we seek to be an exemplary inclusive organization, pressing on in our own maturity journey. It took an inclusive organization to be able to pull this book together.

And within it, here are the individuals we want to thank, since without you we don't get this done!

SUPER CONTRIBUTORS

THE PRODUCTION TEAM

Stephanie Collins, Associate Consultant: Wow. You are that type of young professional that shows up unassumingly, simply ready to do the work. And then you dazzle. The research! The attention to detail! The persistence! You were an editorial matador ready to grab the full content charge by the horns and lead it to gentle book pages pastures.

Karlrenz Rusit, Unit Coordinator: While Stephanie took the front stage of the editorial process, you quietly took the backstage, sweeping up a thousand loose ends. You were that reassuring, I've-got-this presence. In the end, it's the unaddressed loose ends that can sink the integrity of a book project. You helped keep us buoyant and sailing along.

Trisha Messina, Executive Assistant: What is a road without guardrails, and lane dividers, and stoplights, and speed limits? It's chaos. You are the master time-traffic manager of our working lives that made sure we did not descend into that.

THE PEER REVIEWER TEAM

Barry Callender, MBA, Associate Client Partner: You're a practitioner's practitioner. Here, we so benefited from your deep social consciousness, your intellectual rigor, your vast practitioner experience—all of which you brought to bear in stress testing our findings and ideas.

Karen Huang, PhD, Senior Director of Search Assessment: You're a writer's writer. You have such an elegance to your wording of suggestions in the context of your vast intellectual repertoire and very wide spectrum of current event and academic research knowledge.

Sarah Hezlett, PhD, VP Assessment Science, Korn Ferry Institute: You're a researcher's researcher. You give going down a rabbit hole a good name. Your ability to discern the implications of our assertions based on our interpretation of the research to ensure we did not have blind spots leading to flawed thinking or inferences was invaluable.

CONTRIBUTORS

You offered your reflections on best and next practices of diversity, equity, and inclusion. You shared concrete examples of, as well as your musings on, the five disciplines and the vital tasks. You inspired our thinking.

FOUNDATIONAL WHITE PAPER COLLABORATORS

There were several Korn Ferry colleagues with whom we collaborated on previously published white papers that we drew from for this book and with whom we conferred as we refined and updated ideas to fit the narrative of the book.

Alina Polonskaia, MBA, Senior Client Partner, Global DE&I Practice Leader, Toronto

Andrea Walsh, Senior Client Partner, Global ESG Solutions Leader, Chicago

David Herrera Delgado, MSc, Associate Client Partner, Toronto

Gustavo Gisbert, PhD, Senior Principal, Chicago

THOUGHT PARTNERS

A special thanks to the Korn Ferry colleagues who sent us items, ideas, encouragements, and stories for us to consider: Brandon Farrugia, MA; Caitlyn Dipierro, MA; Cheryl D'Cruz Young, MA; Jamie Small, MA; Izabel Loinaz, MBA; Lina Khatib, MPA; Marji Marcus; Mark Royal, PhD; Taly Zinger; Tony Malinauskas, MBA; Victoria Baxter, MA; and Yuki Kawashima, MA.

ADDITIONAL SIDEBAR AUTHORS

"The Encore Legacy Track: Disrupting Assumptions of the Older Worker," Annamarya Scaccia, MJ, Director, Communications, Korn Ferry Institute, with Andrés Tapia

"Should Pay Be Linked to Diversity, Equity, and Inclusion?," Tom McMullen, MBA, Senior Client Partner

"Sodexo: From Risk Management Meltdown to Exemplar Company," Stephanie Collins, MS, Associate Consultant

"What if the Reference Man Were an Asian American Woman?," Karen Huang, PhD, Senior Director, Search Assessment Services

PRODUCTION

It also takes partners inside and outside Korn Ferry to get things done.

EDITING

Danielle Goodman, MBA, Developmental Editor

Neal Maillet, Commissioning Editor, Berrett-Koehler Publishers

PRODUCTION

Stephanie Collins, MS, and Karlrenz Rusit, Editorial and Project Management

Lizzie Cave, Photos and Images

Sonia Yousuf, Fact-Checking

Daniel Tesser, Cover Designer

Richard Whitaker, Seventeenth Street Studios, Book Producer

Katelyn Keating, Production Coordinator

Ashley Ingram, Art Director

MARKETING

Michael Crowley, Berrett-Koehler Publishers

Lizzie Cave, Korn Ferry

Tracy Kurschner, Korn Ferry

INDEX

Note: Information in figures and tables is indicated by f and t.

A

Abercrombie and Fitch, 94
aboriginal peoples, 102–103
Accenture, 160
accountability, 73–74
activity metrics, 206
Adidas, 154
Adobe, 100–101
Advanced Maturity Level, 10
    in awareness, 41–42, 44–45
    in market integration, 96,
      100–101
    in operations integration,
      79–80, 84–85
    in risk management, 25–26,
      27–28
    in talent integration, 62–63, 67
adverse impact analysis, 24–25
Affinity Groups, 41
AI. *See* artificial intelligence (AI)
Allport, Gordon, 141
Amazon, 57
Anand, Rohini, 35
Apple, 2, 155
artificial intelligence (AI), 57

AstraZeneca, 2
Australia, 102–103
autism, 157
awareness, 195
    actionable, 50
    backlash and, 49–50
    behavioral, 43–46
    case study, 46–48
    as discipline of inclusive
      organization, 11–12, 12f,
      37–51, 224
    easy fix in, 48–49
    indicators, 205t
    performative aspect of, 50–54
    questions in, 39
    responsibility for, 11t
    structural, 40–43
    training and, 49
    trip ups in, 48–51
Axtell, Roger E., 93

B

backlash, awareness and,
    49–50
Barilla, ix–x, 163

Basic Maturity Level, 10
    in awareness, 40–41, 43
    in market integration, 93–94,
        98–100
    in operations integration,
        78–79, 82–84
    in risk management, 24, 26–27
    in talent integration, 59–62,
        64–66
Beam Suntory, 84
behavioral awareness, 43–46
behavioral market integration,
    98–103
behavioral operations
    integration, 82–87
behavioral risk management,
    26–29
behavioral talent integration,
    64–68
Berner, Joerg, 76
bias, organizational
    unconscious, 123–124
Boston Scientific, 161
bottom line, 87–89
Branson, Richard, 99–100
Brennan, Molly, 6
BRGs. *See* business resource
    groups (BRGs)
Bristo, Marca, 157
British Columbia Golf, 50–51
Brown, Brené, 133
business resource groups
    (BRGs), 42–43

C

cars, electric, 187–188
change, pace of, 203
Cheeseman, Gina-Marie, 182
Children's Museum of
    Indianapolis, 94
China, 158–159
Chobani, 162–163
Chouinard, Yvon, 177–178
circular economy, 179–182
Cisco, 160

climate change, x
    2030, 170
    2040, 170
    2050, 170
    2100, 170
    2150, 170
    circular economy and, 179–182
    corporations and, 171–172
    delusions with, 175–179
    downstream implications of, 173
    empowerment and, 182–184
    environmental mitigation and,
        174
    future generations and, 177
    "green" technology and, 178
    "growth" focus and, 176–177
    health issues in, 173
    organizational issues with,
        173–174
    virtuous actions and, 179
    as vital task, 169–188
Coca-Cola, 155
Collins, Stephanie, 35–36
commonality, 142–143
compliance, ridicule of, 33
composting, 186–187
Conscious Inclusion, 47
contact hypothesis, 141
costs, of employee turnover, 4
COVID-19 pandemic, 3, 75–76,
    145, 184
cross-cultural agility, 124–125
culture, diversification and,
    121–125
CVS Health, 161

D

Dagit, Deb, 159
DEI. *See* diversity, equity,
    inclusion (DEI)
Dell, 160
delusions, with climate change,
    175–179
democracy, 134–135

Detroit Energy (DTE), 1–2,
    180–181
Deutsche Bank, 95
Dipierro, Caitlyn, 146
disability justice, 156–157
Discover (company), 149–150
disinformation, 144–146
Disney, 151
diversification
    commitment required for,
        125–130
    culture and, 121–125
    development and, 128–129
    of leadership, 117–131
    quotas, 125–127
    talent supply and, 119–121
diversity, equity, inclusion
    (DEI), ix, x, xi, 1–2, 3, 5–10,
    9f, 13–14
    bottom line and, 87–89
    ESG and, 113, 217–219
    external message vs. internal
        work in, 103–104
    pay and, 122–123
    polarization and, 136
    promising the impossible in,
        104–105
    risk and, 22
    root cause of, as DEI issue,
        69–73
    scorecard, 205–219
    societal background in, 38
    teams and, 89–90
Drew, Deborah, 176
DTE. *See* Detroit Energy (DTE)

E

Earle, Sylvia, 169
Eastabrook, Diane, 72
economy, circular, 179–182
education, early childhood,
    129
electric cars, 187–188
empathy, 193–194

employee resource groups
    (ERGs), 41–42
employee turnover, 4
empowerment, climate change
    and, 182–184
environmental, social, and
    governance (ESG), ix, x, xi–
    xii, 3, 113, 217–219
equality, 58
equity, 3–4, 32, 151
erasure, 142
ERGs. *See* employee resource
    groups (ERGs)
Explode the Awareness. *See*
    awareness

F

Floyd, George, 137, 164
focus groups, 221
football, 68, 91–92

G

Galetti, Beth, 163
Gap Inc., 97
gender equity, 32
gender justice, 152–153
Goethe, Johann Wolfgang von,
    189
Google, 2
governments, inclusive,
    194–197
Great Resignation, 4–5
"green" technology, 178

H

HAVI, 85–86
Hearst, 46–48
Hedley, Darren, 163
Hela, 153
Herman Miller, 72
Highland Park, Illinois, 186–187,
    196–197
Hochschild, Roger, 149–150

Hopper, Grace, 107
Huang, Karen, 60–61
Hurricane Katrina, 183–184

I

IKEA, 2
impossible, promising the,
    104–105
inclusive design, 157–159
Inclusive Leader model, xiv
indicators
    awareness, 207t
    lagging, 206
    leading, 206
    market integration, 208t
    operations integration, 208t
    risk management, 207t
    talent integration, 207t
indigenous peoples, 102–103
inequities, 59
Intel, 161
intersectionality, 105–106
interviews, one-on-one, 221

J

Jogmen, Lou, 80
joint projects, polarization and,
    140–142
Jonasson, Kris, 50–51
Juneteenth, 94
justice
    achieving, 149–168
    disability, 156–157
    gender, 152–153
    inclusive design and, 157–159
    LGBTQ+, 153–156
    "people first" philosophy and,
        162–163
    profits and, 150–152
    publicity and, 167
    racial, 164–168
    refugee, 159–162
    universal design and, 157–159

K

Kaepernick, Colin, 91–92
kaizen, 81, 83
Kendi, Ibram X., 149
Khera, Shiv, 1
King, Jordan, 95
Kitchener, Roy, 88

L

lagging indicators, 204
Landel, Michel, 35
Latinos, 54, 55, 105, 166
leadership
    bias and, 123–124
    commitment and, 125–130
    development and, 128–129
    diversification of, 117–131
    inclusive, limited focus on, 121
    quotas and, 125–127
    talent supply and, 119–121
    women in, 118
Leading Edge Maturity Level, 11
    in awareness, 42–43
    in market integration, 96–98,
        101
    in operations integration,
        80–82, 86–87
    in risk management, 26, 28–29
    in talent integration, 63–64,
        67–68
leading indicators, 206
legacy track, 70–72
Le Pen, Marine, 32
Lewnes, Anne, 100–101
LGBTQ+ justice, 153–156
light bulbs, 187
listening sessions, 137–139
logistics. See operations
    integration
Loinaz, Izabel, 175, 179, 186
L'Oreal, 160

M

MacArthur, Ellen, 179
Malinauskas, Tony, 140–141
Manage the Risk. *See* risk
    management
Mandela, Nelson, 149
Marine Corps, 79–80
market integration, 195
    behavioral, 98–103
    as discipline of inclusive
      organization, 11–12, 12f,
      227–228
    indicators, 208t
    intersectionality and, 105–106
    responsibility for, 11t
    structural, 93–98
    trip ups in, 103–105
Marriott, 84–86
Mars (company), 185
Maturity Models, 8–11, 9f, 209
Maximize the Talent Systems.
    See talent integration
McLane, Brendan, 88
McMullen, Tom, 122–123
meat, plant-based, 187
Mercedes Benz, 96
Merck, 159
metrics
    activity, 206
    predictive, 209
    process, 206
Metzger, Eliot, 176
Microsoft, 2, 160
minimization, 142
Moody, Greg, 51
Moss, Kevin, 176
Murakawa, Naomi, 37

N

Nakate, Vanessa, 171
National Football League, 68,
    91–92

National Gallery of Art,
    190–191
Navy, 88–89
neurodiversity, 157
Nike, 91–92
Norcia, Jerry, 1
norms polarization and,
    139–140

O

Ogun, Toyin, 84
older workers, 70–72
Old Navy, 97–98
"one job away" excuse,
    120–121
operations integration, 195
    behavioral, 82–87
    as discipline of inclusive
      organization, 11–12, 12f,
      75–90, 227
    indicators, 208t
    responsibility for, 11t
    structural, 78–82
    trip ups in, 87–90
organizational structure,
    polarization and, 134
organizational unconscious
    bias, 123–124

P

pace of change, 205
pandemic, 3, 75–76, 145, 184
Parker Pen Company, 93
Patagonia (company), 177–178
pay, DEI and, 122–123
"people first" philosophy,
    162–163
performative aspect, of
    awareness, 50–54
Pink, 154
Pittman, Cassi, 99
Pizza2Go, 97
plant-based meat, 187

plastic social, 182
polarization
    business case against, 146–147
    commonality and, 142–143
    contact hypothesis and, 141
    disinformation and, 144–146
    eradication of, 133–147
    increase in, 133
    joint projects and, 140–142
    listening sessions and, 137–139
    norms and, 139–140
    organizational structure and,
      134
    pragmatic takedown of,
      136–142
    social media and, 156
    sociopolitical stability vs.,
      134–136
    strategic takedown of, 142–146
Pottinger, Matt, 80
poverty, 3
predictive metrics, 209
Pritchard, Marc, 101
process metrics, 206
Procter & Gamble, 81, 101, 160
Progressing Maturity Level, 10
    in awareness, 41, 43–44
    in market integration, 94–95,
      99–100
    in operations integration, 79, 84
    in risk management, 24–25, 27
    in talent integration, 62, 66–67
Puma (company), 182
Putt del Pino, Samantha, 176

Q

quotas, 125–127

R

race, 29–31, 32–33, 44–45,
    54–56, 94, 97, 118, 127,
    137–138, 165–168
racial justice, 164–165
Real Talk, 137, 139, 146

Reference Man, 57–58, 60–61
refugee justice, 159–162
Regents of the University of
    California v. Bakke, 126
Reid, Grant F., 185
Rent the Runway, 176–177
responsibility, 11–13, 11t,
    189–198
résumés, 65–66
retirement, 70–72
Reys, Shelley, 102–103
risk management, 194
    behavioral, 26–29
    case study, 29–31
    competition and, 23
    compliance ridicule and, 33
    as discipline of inclusive
      organization, 11–12, 12f,
      21–36, 226
    employees and, 23–24
    indicators, 207t
    lawyers ruling, as problem, 34
    need for, 22
    overindexing in, 32–33
    responsibility for, 11t
    structural, 24–26
    trip ups in, 32–34
Rooney Rule, 68
root cause analysis, 202, 214,
    221–223, 222f
Russell, Victoria, 84
Russell Investments, 146

S

Scaccia, Annamarya, 70–71
Schultz, Howard, 153
scorecard, DEI, 201–215
Scott, Lee, 183
self-awareness, 39
Sephora, 96
Serasa Experian, 25–26
Siemens Healthineers, 76–78
Six Sigma, 83
social media, 156
social plastic, 182

sociopolitical stability, 134–136
Sodexo, 35–36, 163
Sorenson, Arne, 86
Specialisterne, 157
Starbucks, 153
structural awareness, 40–43
structural market integration, 93–98
structural operations integration,
    78–82
structural risk management, 24–26
structural talent integration, 59–64
support systems, 211
sustainability, 3–4

T

talent flow analysis, 221
talent integration, 195
    accountability and, 73–74
    behavioral, 64–68
    as discipline of inclusive
      organization, 11–12, 12f,
      53–74, 227
    inclusive design for, 58–59
    indicators, 207t
    Reference Man and, 57–58
    representation vs pipeline in,
      68–69
    responsibility for, 11t
    structural, 59–64
    trip ups in, 68–74
talent supply, 119–121
Tapia, Andrés, 70–71, 196–197
teams, power of inclusive,
    89–90, 192–193
technology, "green," 178
Timor Leste, 127
tokenism, 126–127
Tomasetti, Daniel, 85, 86
Torres Strait Islander people,
    102–103

Trader Joe's, 82
training, awareness and, 49
trip ups
    in awareness, 48–51
    in market integration, 103–105
    in operations integration, 87–90
    in risk management, 32–34
    in talent integration, 68–74
Tsai Ing-wen, 127
Tung, Suen Yiu, 155
turnover, 4
TV2 (Denmark), 143

U

Ukraine, 88–89
Ulukaya, Hamdi, 162–163
Unamuno, Miguel de, 169
unconscious bias,
    organizational, 123–124
Unilever, 2
universal design, 157–159
US Soccer, 21–22

V

Virgin Atlantic, 99–100
visual impairment, 85–86

W

Wallace-Wells, David, 171
Walmart, 183–184
Waters, Dave, 75
women, 118, 152–153
Women's National Soccer
    Team, 21–22

Z

Zhu, Pearl, 53

ABOUT THE AUTHORS

Andrés Tapia

Korn Ferry Senior Partner, Global DE&I and ESG
Strategist and R&D Leader

Andrés Tapia is a well-known diversity and inclusion authority, often sought as a public speaker and role model for building global diversity and inclusion strategies. A prominent thought leader who guides Korn Ferry clients toward higher performance by increasing innovation and new ways of working, he has been one of the leading voices in shaping a contemporary, next-generation approach to diversity and inclusion. His approach is global, deeply integrated into talent systems, and focused on enabling marketplace success. He leverages more than twenty-five years of experience as a C-suite management consultant, diversity executive, organizational development and training professional, and journalist to transform organizations. Throughout Europe, Asia, North America, and his native Latin America, Andrés has served clients in shaping their enterprise-wide diversity and inclusion business cases and strategies across industries—including financial, technology, health care, retail, manufacturing, government, nonprofits, and education—with dozens of Global 500 organizations as well as non-US multinationals in Brazil, South Korea, and India.

An experienced author, Andrés published a groundbreaking book, *The Inclusion Paradox: The Obama Era and the Transformation of Global Diversity* as well as coauthoring *Auténtico: The Definitive Guide to Latino Career Success* and *The 5 Disciplines of Inclusive Leaders: Unleashing the Power of All of Us*. A global speaker on the topic of diversity and inclusion, he is published in major dailies throughout the United States and Latin America through his writing for the New America Media wire service as well as on the *Huffington Post*. He is the recipient of numerous leadership and diversity awards and has contributed value through his current service on the national board of Jobs for the Future, the boards of Leadership Greater Chicago and Ravinia Festival, and previously the editorial board of *Diversity Executive* magazine, the corporate advisory board for the Bentley University Center for Women and Business, the Hispanic Alliance for Career Enhancement (HACE), and Luna Negra Dance Theater.

Andrés received a bachelor's degree in modern history from Northwestern University with an emphasis in journalism and political science. He grew up in a bilingual/bicultural home in Lima, Perú.

Fayruz Kirtzman

Korn Ferry Senior Partner, Global DE&I Diagnostics Solutions Leader

Fayruz Kirtzman is an innovator and a thought leader in Korn Ferry's Diversity, Equity, and Inclusion practice. She oversees Korn Ferry's Global DE&I Diagnostics solution, a synergistic quantitative and qualitative data analysis and synthesis methodology that unearths the root causes preventing organizations from being as inclusive and diverse as they aspire to be. Fayruz then leads teams that develop optimized DE&I strategic road maps, including actionable steps to activate both behavioral and structural inclusion, with the ultimate goal of diversifying the workplace and leadership, unleashing innovation, and increasing performance.

For more than twenty years, Fayruz has served as a trusted advisor to clients in a variety of industries, such as consumer goods, financial services, technology, manufacturing, and professional services. She was part of the founding facilitation team at Cornell University's "Advanced Diversity Strategies" workshop for experienced diversity practitioners and has presented on diversity, equity, and inclusion at conferences such as The Conference Board and Linkage. Fayruz has authored numerous white papers and articles, has participated in national and global panels, and has led webinars. She applies her professional and personal experiences—spanning three cultures, three countries, and three religions—to provide insights into leveraging the power of diversity for increased team and organizational effectiveness.

Fayruz was born and raised in Germany and holds a BA in Translation from the Fachhochschule Köln, Germany. She is fluent in German and English, is conversant in French, and is currently learning Arabic. Fayruz lives in New York City with her husband; they have two grown daughters.

ABOUT KORN FERRY

Korn Ferry is a global organizational consulting firm. We work with our clients to design optimal organization structures, roles, and responsibilities. We help them hire the right people and advise them on how to reward and motivate their workforce while developing professionals as they navigate and advance their careers.

Dear reader,

Thank you for picking up this book and welcome to the worldwide BK community! You're joining a special group of people who have come together to create positive change in their lives, organizations, and communities.

What's BK all about?

Our mission is to connect people and ideas to create a world that works for all.

Why? Our communities, organizations, and lives get bogged down by old paradigms of self-interest, exclusion, hierarchy, and privilege. But we believe that can change. That's why we seek the leading experts on these challenges—and share their actionable ideas with you.

A welcome gift

To help you get started, we'd like to offer you a **free copy** of one of our bestselling ebooks:

www.bkconnection.com/welcome

When you claim your **free ebook**, you'll also be subscribed to our blog.

Our freshest insights

Access the best new tools and ideas for leaders at all levels on our blog at ideas.bkconnection.com.

Sincerely,

Your friends at Berrett-Koehler

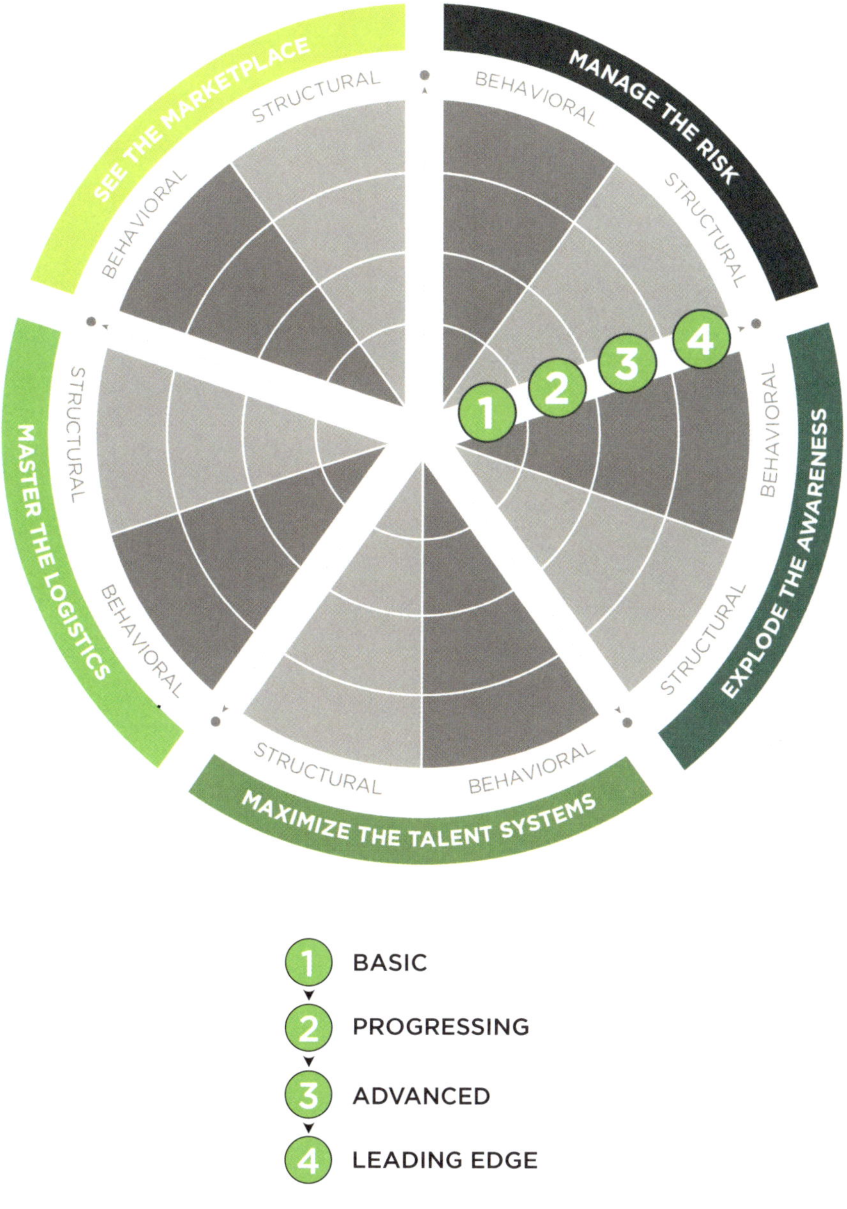

The 5 Disciplines of Inclusive Organizations,
based on the Korn Ferry DE&I Maturity Model 2022.

Source: Korn Ferry, 2022.